Evaluation of Damages in International Arbitration

Edited by Yves Derains
and
Richard H. Kreindler

INTERNATIONAL CHAMBER OF COMMERCE
The world business organization

DOSSIERS
ICC Institute of World Business Law

Published in June 2006 by

ICC SERVICES
Publications Department
33-43 avenue du Président Wilson,
75116 Paris – France

www.storeiccwbo.org

ICC Publication No. 668
ISBN-10: 92-842-1363-0
ISBN-13: 978-92-842-1363-4

Contents

Foreword

By ***Serge Lazareff***
Member of the Paris Bar, France;
Chairman, ICC Institute of World Business Law

Once again, welcome to a new Dossier of the Institute.

In most cases, before state courts or arbitral tribunals, the bottom line is *damages.*

How to assess them? Practice shows that often, too often, damages are globally assessed simply because, in most cases, it is quite difficult to arrive at a fully justified estimate. This is not only true in very complex construction cases, but also in the simplest procedures. Whether or not their origin is contractual, damages are supposed to compensate the victim. What a delicate task!

Even though, from a strictly legal point of view, damages should be calculated in a cold and abstract way, the judge, be he state or arbitrator, will take human and behavioural aspects into consideration. How to measure good and bad faith? In the majority of situations, the assessment is based on a personal approach. This is good, because the true purpose of arbitration is to introduce into the law, not only the stipulations of the contract and the trade usages, as required by Article 17.2 of the ICC Rules, but also the expectations of the parties.

In addition to the recurring topics, it is interesting to see the importance that arbitrators give to the mitigation of damages, which shows that the burden not only rests on the author of the damage, but also on the victim.

In recent times, the notion of direct damage has been extended and, as discussed in this Dossier, now includes punitive damages and the delicate question of the recovery of the costs involved in arbitral proceedings. But which costs? What should they include? Should the winner take all? Should the winner not lose on the costs?

In fact, modern arbitration evolves. It is the duty of the ICC Institute to stay ahead of this evolution, every year, to focus on the combination of classical problems and new questions, and to give the unique answers that arbitration provides.

All questions linked to this very topical issue are discussed by eminent specialists in this Dossier.

Welcome to this fascinating issue. Now, you have to wait for next year's Dossier!

My kind regards to each of you.

Introduction

By ***Richard H. Kreindler***
Co-Editor
Partner, Shearman & Sterling LLP, Germany;
Council Member of the ICC Institute of World Business Law

It is often said that an arbitral award is worth only as much as the ability to secure its enforceability. To the extent the vast majority of prayers for relief in arbitration are for money damages, an arbitral award granting damages is worth only as much as the ability to obtain payment, voluntary or compulsory, of such damages.

In international commercial, construction and investment arbitration, the prospect of cross-border enforcement of damage awards makes this test of "worth" all the more important, and often precarious. It also serves to focus the arbitrator, the counsel and the merchant alike on the practical need for certainty and clarity in achieving monetary satisfaction, and in properly pleading claims for damages in the first place.

Of all of the practical, legal and scientific issues which befall the arbitrator or the counsel, that of pleading, proving and calculating money damages is perhaps the most elemental and most commercially significant. Notwithstanding all other highly significant and thorny issues of procedure, choice of law, taking of evidence, compatibility with public policy under the *lex arbitri* and *lex causae*, etc. – it is the bottom-line quest for damages that informs the entire arbitration and the assessment of victory and failure by the parties. Agreements and disagreements on the procedural framework, the applicable substantive law, the means of presenting and proving allegations and enforceability of any award at the seat or elsewhere are all, ultimately, sideshows in comparison with the end result – did the claim for damages prevail and if so, in what amount? Of course, the fact that the end result is so unforgivingly transparent does not make these procedural, substantive and tactical stepping stones along the way any less significant, but it does show them to be means to an end.

The following papers are based upon presentations given at the 25th annual meeting of the ICC Institute of World Business Law in Paris on 28 November 2005. The presenters are well-known and highly experienced practitioners, counsel, arbitrators and academicians from various corners of the world, various legal cultures and thus various overlapping international perspectives. The common mission of the presenters and of these papers was to focus, more than has been the case in perhaps any other comparable symposium in the recent past, on damages *per se*. Presented here are analyses of the nature of damages, their legal, factual and forensic underpinnings, the problems of contractual and *de lege* constraints on damages recovery, the differing means of proving money damage claims, and newly developing areas such as damages in investment arbitration.

The range of analysis in the papers which follow is impressive and comprehensive, both from a legal and a commercial perspective. As an appropriate introduction to the subject, the general characteristics of recoverable damages in international arbitration are addressed, including foreseeability as treated in recent awards, treaties, model laws and such supranational instruments as the UNIDROIT Principles and the Vienna Sales Convention/CISG. Following hard upon the question of foreseeability is that of mitigation and the sources in national law and jurisprudence for a duty to seek to limit one's own damages as a precondition to a right to full compensation.

Perhaps no issue of damages has caused such challenges and controversy as that of loss of profit and loss of opportunity, *lucrum cessans*. Both commercial and investment arbitrations in recent years have had to contend with complex issues of lost profit recovery. Is a party entitled to them? Can they be excluded or limited? How are they to be reliably calculated? Which substantive law or laws should apply to the question of their recoverability and calculation? In particular, the issue of the discounted cash flow method has proven to be a special challenge for arbitrators and practitioners alike, in addition to the ever-present question of just how foreseeable lost profits must be in order to be recoverable. In turn, party attempts to contractually limit or exclude certain kinds of indirect or consequential damages are examined, as well as public policy constraints on such damages and other kinds of indirect damages, including punitive and exemplary damages.

When discussing damage claims, questions of burden of presentation and burden of proof are also never far removed. The following papers include expert approaches, from various perspectives, of burden of proof as a procedural versus a substantive law issue, and possible conflicts in assigning the appropriate burden depending on which substantive law is applied. In this connection, perceived tensions in the requirements for substantiation of damages are also addressed in the comparison between civil law and common law approaches and the stereotypes associated with these approaches.

The final areas of analysis in the papers include interest as a sub-species of damages and acceptable kinds of damages recovery in international investment arbitration. Moratory and compensatory interest continue to be inevitable questions in most international commercial arbitrations, but alas they attract vastly different and not always reconcilable approaches. With regard to investment, the last three to four years have seen unique legal challenges to damages claims in investment disputes related to claims for wasted costs as opposed to those for loss of profit. In addition, the approach to damages for unlawful expropriation has evolved in recent years, complicated by the fact that certain damage claims may be characterized as contract claims, others as treaty claims and still others as mixed. Finally, the papers approach the perenially thorny issues of delay and disruption damages in construction arbitration and costs of arbitration as damages.

With this compendium of intellectually and culturally stimulating legal analysis, a gap in the recent treatment of commercial, construction and investment arbitration proceedings and awards has been addressed and filled. Damages remain not only the most elemental aspect of arbitration, both for the parties and the tribunal, but also, in many respects, the most problematic. They are rooted in fact as well as in specific legal concepts. At the same time, they are also open to variable and shifting trends in forensic accounting, in transnational public policy and in the art of advocacy. Against this background, the papers in this volume provide a welcome and insightful roadmap to the challenges awaiting international arbitration in the area of damages for several years to come.

1

General characteristics of recoverable damages in international arbitration

By **Paul-A. Gélinas**
Member of the Montreal and Paris Bars;
Council Member of the ICC Institute of World Business Law

Much has been written, both in terms of their scope and desirability, concerning the application of transnational rules to international contracts and possible ensuing disputes. This paper will examine the impact or role of the general principles of international law in relation to the notions of certainty and of foreseeability with respect to compensatory damages. Others will focus on specific areas of the recovery of damages, such as the principles of mitigation of damages, compensatory interest, quantification of the loss of profit, exclusion of consequential damages, punitive damages, etc. In the light of their contributions, it will be interesting to see if an answer will emerge to the following question: "Can a set of transnational general principles of damages recovery be identified?"

1. CERTAINTY AND FORESEEABILITY: TWO PILLARS OF RECOVERY

The breach of a contractual obligation normally calls for making good the consequences. The repair can take the form of specific performance, cancellation or a condemnation in damages. In the area of international commercial trade, thus of international contracts, the most frequently sought remedy is a condemnation consisting of an award of damages.

International arbitrators are bound to apply the national law provided for in the contract from which the dispute derives. In the absence of an express or clear provision, arbitrators are nonetheless obliged to apply the rules of law they will have determined in order to arrive at a proper compensation or remedy for the breach. In either case, are or should the arbitrators be influenced by, or apply transnational legal principles and rules?

Overall, it can be said at the outset that many aspects of the recovery of damages in international arbitration have given rise to principles that are widely accepted today, as will be illustrated by the other commentators. We will examine here two basic characteristics of recoverable damages, namely certainty and foreseeability, and explore some of the limits of these concepts. As a general rule, it can be said that whether the arbitrators are called upon to decide under a specific national law or not, they will, in almost all cases, pay attention to the principles of certainty and foreseeability.

2. CERTAINTY

There are not many examples of express reference to this element in arbitral case law, but arbitrators will, in most cases, carefully examine the evidence in order to quantify, with an acceptable degree of certainty, the damages for which entitlement has been found. However, since they enjoy practically unrestricted freedom in appreciating the evidence, arbitrators will assess the damages, whenever possible, in such a way as to arrive at a fair figure.

Leaving aside liquidated damages and those claims which do not leave any room for interpretation, arbitral tribunals will find juridical ways and means to arrive at a figure which, given all the circumstances of the case, will lead to an equitable finding. That being said, when it comes to assessment, the notion of what constitutes certainty raises its head. Ignoring "nominal" damages and, at the other end of the spectrum, "exemplary" or "punitive" damages, the award will seek to compensate actual or real loss.

The measure of damages is "that sum of money which will put the party who has been injured, or who has suffered, in the same position as he would have been in if he had not sustained the wrong for which he is now getting his compensation or reparation". This statement by Lord Blackburn dates back to 1880[1] but has been reaffirmed consistently by the English courts and still holds true.[2] It also prevails under other common law systems.[3] The principle of *restitutio in integrum* is also applied by arbitrators deciding pursuant to provisions of civil law.[4]

The measurement of damages is predicated upon the possibility of identifying, with precision and accuracy, the prejudice sustained.

In practice, one can hardly find a single instance where all the heads of claims correspond to an exact and precise loss. While some items can be easily quantified (e.g. replacement or residual costs of physical assets), a number of monetary condemnations do not result from straightforward mathematical operations involving uncontested numbers.

In the ancient tradition of English law, which is still in fashion, the claimant must do his best to ascertain his damages precisely. There is a clear principle that as much certainty and particularity as is reasonably possible must be insisted upon, having regard to the circumstances and nature of the acts themselves causing the damage.[5] In their appreciation of the efforts deployed by the successful party in establishing with as much certainty as possible the reality of the damages claimed, arbitral tribunals will, in all likelihood, dismiss a claim lacking sufficient concrete economic support or detailed cost-related elements.

Many arbitrations may not have materialized or could have been settled if the litigants had a clear and realistic awareness of the difficulties to establish quantum with a degree of certainty. The parties' insensibility to this aspect is often compounded by the frequent lack of understanding of their legal advisers. French lawyers, for instance, tend to be relaxed about the legal requirement of assessing damages with certainty; arbitrators with a continental background could be tempted to follow the lead of judges in their jurisdiction, who, when confronted with problems of quantification, will simply make *une souveraine appréciation* to fix the damages by awarding a lump sum, even though they should have expended some effort at quantification.

Fortunately, most international arbitrators will devote the necessary time to assess the evidence in order to establish, with a satisfactory degree of certainty, the amount of damages claimed. For several years, training has been available to enable contract negotiators and advisers, as well as parties in litigation and arbitrations, to deal more effectively with damages-related issues. In arbitrations involving more or less substantial amounts, costs and damages analysis has been developed and presented by accounting and financial professionals. Major accounting and consultancy firms have departments specifically versed in the quantification of damages to ensure they are as certain as they can be.

The ICSID award in the *Ancoven/Venezuela* case[6] recognized that indemnification for lost profits, to the extent that the amount claimed is in line with the damages actually suffered, as provided for under Venezuelan law, was consistent with the practice of international tribunals. This is a well-entrenched principle in the jurisprudence of ICSID tribunals and of the Iran-US Claims Tribunals. The panel stressed that claims for lost profit would have been dismissed if "the claimant had not proven with a sufficient degree of certainty that the project would not have resulted in a profit".

The inescapable relevance of the standard of reasonable certainty can sometimes become a mere formality when it is decided at the outset that liquidated damages – the damages to be paid by the defaulting party are agreed upon in advance – will be owed in case of a proven contractual violation. Liquidated damages clauses are meant to prevent unnecessary litigation. When such stipulations are carefully crafted to obtain a genuine pre-estimate of the anticipated damages that can result from the breach of one or more terms of the contract, an exact measure of compensation will be readily available to the arbitrator and the requirement of certainty will be satisfied.[7]

3. FORESEEABILTY

In principle, parties are free to prove their case and discharge their burden of proof by any means. One of the hurdles in doing so with respect to the foreseeability test is first to establish causation (entitlement) by showing that the breach and the damages are linked, the latter being the necessary consequence of the former or a direct and immediate result. In practice, causation often becomes blurred with the notion of foreseeability.

When deciding under common law rules, arbitrators will not hesitate to quote the famous 1854 *Hadley* v. *Baxendale* decision.[8] The test as to whether the damages can be deemed to be arising naturally became known as "direct" loss or damages. The second test is whether the party found responsible for the breach reasonably contemplated or ought to have reasonably contemplated the damages; this latter became known as "indirect or consequential" loss or damages. In any event, it is generally accepted that a loss to be claimant must have been susceptible of being envisaged at the time the parties contracted.

Over the years, the principles laid down in *Hadley* v. *Baxendale* became somewhat clouded, and loss of profit, even when intended to be excluded pursuant to an "indirect, special or consequential loss" clause, would no longer necessarily exclude all liability for the loss of profit that was the normal loss of profit.[9]

Section 2-715 of the UCC, a rare piece of legislation dealing expressly with the notion, provides that the consequential damages resulting from the seller's breach include any loss resulting from the general or particular requirements and needs of which the seller at the time of contracting had reason to know, and which could not reasonably be prevented by cover or otherwise. Consequential damages can be equated with losses that result indirectly from an injurious act or from a breach of contract, i.e. they do not flow directly and immediately from the act or the breach. The word "indirect", however, results in different consequences under various national legislations.

The trouble with the notion of "foreseeability" is that it is not readily reconcilable with the definition encountered in individual national legislations.

Article 1151 of the French Civil Code provides that only those damages which are *une suite immédiate et directe de l'inexécution de la convention* are compensable. Wording to the same effect is found in the laws of most countries that belong to a continental or civil system of law. Put differently, the breaching party can only be held responsible for those damages which were foreseen or which ought to have been foreseen at the time the contract was made, absent gross fault (Art. 1150 French Civil Code). While the criteria set in the two articles of the French Civil Code are, in theory, different, they are not, in practice, very well distinguished. The words "direct" and "foreseeable" appear to be interchangeable in many awards.

In theory, the term "direct" in Article 1151 of the French Civil Code is associated with causation whereas foreseeability connotes a test which must be appreciated *in abstracto,* that is, in the case of someone who is normally prudent and reasonable. Of course, specific circumstances that can be deduced from the type of contract or the professional expertise of the parties must be taken into account.

Foreseeability is understood as of the time that the contract is entered into. Indeed, at the time they make their contractual arrangements, it is natural for the parties to envisage, consciously or not, that certain damages, i.e. those foreseeable, could arise in the event of a breach. In that sense, those foreseeable damages enter the ambit of the contract, because they are generally agreed upon. It should be noted that what must be foreseen is the *scope* of the damages and not the *cause* of the damages.

It is not our purpose to examine here the concepts of "certainty" and "foreseeability" in any further detail, nor to consider the law of specific countries (this is dealt with by many authors and case law), but rather to consider how these concepts have been applied in an international legal environment, in particular in the context of arbitral awards, transnational rules (UNIDROIT, CSIG, treaties and model law). It is also to determine whether transnational general principles applicable to the recovery of damages in arbitration have emerged.

4. POSSIBLE LIMITATIONS TO THE PRINCIPLES OF CERTAINTY AND FORESEEABILITY

Contractual limitation

The most classical approach to limit the amount of the damages resulting from a breach is to negotiate contract clauses to cap the damages that would otherwise be allowed, or to exclude certain types of liability or damages.

As an example, the General Conditions of Contract for Construction, FIDIC 1998, provides, in Clause 17.6, a limitation of liability: "Neither Party shall be liable to the other Party for loss of use of any Works, loss of profit, loss of any contract or for any indirect or consequential loss or damage which may be suffered by the other Party in connection with the Contract, other than under Sub-Clause 17.1 [Indemnities] or in the event of termination under Clause 16 [Default of Employer]."

The second paragraph of the clause also provides that the total liability of the contractor to the employer, under reserve of certain exceptions, shall not exceed the sum stated in the particular conditions or (if a sum is not so stated) the accepted contract amount. It is further stated that this sub-clause shall not limit liability in any case of fraud, wilful misconduct or gross negligence by the defaulting party.

Such limiting provisions, even if drafted with care, will nonetheless, in many instances, require interpretation by arbitral tribunals as to their exact scope. This is particularly true in an international context where a definition of a given term (consequential damages, for example) will not be understood in the same manner by the other party who originates from another jurisdiction, let alone from another system of law.

In this context, the following clause is particularly instructive:

"18.1. Where either Party is liable in damages to the other under this Contract, those shall not exceed the damages which the Party in default could reasonably have foreseen at the time of conclusion of this contract.

18.2. However, neither party shall be liable for indirect or consequential damages under this Contract except in case of gross negligence or fraud … ."

In one case, the tribunal did enter into a discussion as to the meaning of the expression "consequential damages" borrowed from the common law tradition but embodied in a contract governed by the Egyptian Civil Code.[10] The respondent argued that this expression prohibited any claim for loss of profit and that it had no defined meaning under Egyptian law; accordingly, the respondent said that its interpretation should be consistent with the practice prevailing in international commercial contracts, which favours an interpretation excluding, as in the instant case, any liability for loss of profit. For its part, the claimant argued that Egyptian law provided, in any event, compensation for loss of profit, because this was a repairable direct and normal loss deriving from a breach of contract. The tribunal did not embark on any exercise to define the expression "consequential damages"; it merely stated that loss of profit was a direct and foreseeable consequence of the delay in completing the plant and of breaching the performance and deliveries guarantees. Compensation for loss of profit was awarded.

Liquidated damages

Instead of leaving it up to the arbitrators to decide what damages can be awarded, the parties themselves can provide, in order to be certain, what the amount of the damages will be in the event of a violation of the contractual provisions. In other words, the parties can by agreement "liquidate" the damages likely to be attributed to a breach. Whereas in the French tradition, this will be referred to as a *clause pénale*, the common law steers away from the word "penalties" in this context, preferring the expressions "lump sum damage" or "liquidated damages".

Such a contractual provision has the advantage for the parties, as well as for the arbitrators, of fixing the amount of damages that will be awarded in the event of a given breach ahead of the dispute. However, difficulties could surface at the time of negotiating the amount of possible future damages. Even in the case of a daily, weekly or monthly penalty for the late delivery of merchandise or a project, it is often hazardous to predict what the real damages will be at the time the prejudice arises.

Of course, to avoid becoming voidable under many legislations, a liquidated damages provision must not be tantamount to a penalty. In France, Art. 1226 of the Civil Code recognizes that the parties can agree ahead of time to fix the amount of damages by providing for a compensatory lump sum payment. Although called a *clause pénale*, such a provision aims at making certain the quantum independent of the actual loss suffered, which can prove to be less or more than what the parties had fixed as liquidated damages. However, the judge may, even *ex officio*, reduce or increase the agreed-upon "penalty" (*peine*), should it be patently excessive or ridiculously low. Any stipulation to the contrary would be considered to be non-existent (Art. 1152 Civil Code).

There is nothing unusual in arbitration awarding "liquidated damages", especially in relation to international construction contracts, as long as the damages are not characterized as penalties. This distinction is found in the common law as well as in the civil law tradition. In ICC Case No. 3267, 1979, the tribunal clearly expressed that since the parties had agreed on an arrangement that resulted in liquidated damages, it became irrelevant to examine evidence as to how the arrangement was arrived at, nor as to what were the "real damages". No specific national law applied, and the tribunal decided in accordance with the general principles of law largely admitted to be the governing rules in international trade.[11]

The principle of *pacta sunt servanda* may not always prevent the application of other rules. For instance, Art. 7.4.13 of the UNIDROIT Principles says that where a party who does not perform is to pay a specified sum, the aggrieved party is entitled to that sum irrespective of its actual harm, but further that such sum can be reduced to a reasonable amount where it is grossly excessive in relation to the harm resulting from the non-performance and other circumstances. Of course, the arbitrators will have to give the word "excessive" a concrete meaning. This is likely to be done by placing in civil law systems, at least in France, the bar higher than in the United States. If the amount of the liquidated damages is tantamount to a penalty, then it might be set aside altogether as being in the nature of a penal clause; the amount fixed by the parties to facilitate the recovery of damages could, therefore, thwart their intent.

Equity in the assessment of damages

Equity is relatively often referred to by arbitrators when assessing damages. A review of awards in this connection is provided by Bernard Hanotiau.[12] The principle of equity can be used to interpret a contractual clause and allow the parties to round off figures on the basis of the objective elements produced in evidence. This can occur, for instance, if an important devaluation takes place between the time of the contract and the time of the delivery of the merchandise, especially if there is a long delay in paying the invoices. At other times – and this is largely recognized – the arbitrators can evaluate the damages by an *appreciation souveraine* or by invoking equity in order to make an overall judgment of various damages when they are not precisely identified, but when it is proven that damages have been suffered. The arbitrators can also order the payment of a lump sum.

Deciding in equity can be more delicate if there is an applicable national law, although various techniques exist (interpretation) to arrive at the equitable solution desired by the arbitrator, even if he does not so state.

In deciding what was a fair interpretation, the arbitrator, sitting in the *Liamco* v. *Libya* case cited by Mr Hanotiau, referred to the general principles of law as they have been applied by international tribunals, the general principles of which form a compendium of legal precepts and maxims universally accepted in theory and in practice.[13]

Using amiable composition can achieve similar results.

Mitigation of damages

Even in the presence of damages that were foreseeable and of which the amount can be ascertained, the award may not allow for their full recovery to the extent that the damages could have been mitigated or were contributed in part through the fault of the other party.

Other limits

Damages will not be awarded, even when their amount can be ascertained and even if they had been foreseeable, when it is clear that the defendant has committed no fault, when a force majeure has intervened to relieve the debtor of the obligation, when the cause of the damages lies entirely with a third party or when the breach can be attributed to the creditor of the obligation himself.

The doctrine of abuse of right, albeit still controversial, can be applied by arbitral tribunals to keep claims, otherwise legitimate, within tolerable norms "on the grounds that it would be intolerable in the present case to uphold claims for lost profits from investment not yet incurred", as this doctrine was applied in the *Himpurna* v. *PLN* award and fully discussed in Jan Paulson's presentation.[14]

A further limitation on the amount of damages claimed, which may or may not be applied by arbitral tribunals, concerns punitive and exemplary damages. These all depend on the applicable law and perhaps, to a certain extent, on the sensitivity of arbitrators to this issue. Jacques Werner's presentation is very enlightening in this connection.[15]

There can also be limits on recoverable damages imposed by some applicable national or international regulations, such as in the case of international transport.

Conversely, arbitral tribunals can be called upon to set aside or curtail the application of clauses limiting or excluding liability for certain kinds of damages. National laws differ in this area. For instance, Art. 1150 of the French Civil Code obliges the debtor to repair unforeseen damages when they result from his gross fault or negligence (*faute lourde*) in performing the contract, even if this was not intentional. A similar provision is not found, for instance, in Art. 74 CISG.

5. RESORT TO TRANSNATIONAL LAW GENERALLY

In his review of the book published by Professor Peter Klaus Berger, the late Philippe Fouchard recalls that the enquiry conducted by a Research Team of the Center for Transnational Law (CENTRAL), directed by Professor Berger, provides the following statistics (based on 808 responses from 78 different countries): 42 percent of the practitioners have come across the use of transnational rules in the context of international arbitrations, such rules being understood as general principles of law (between 21 and 28 percent), the *lex mercatoria* (between 12 and 18 percent) and the UNIDROIT Principles (between eight and 13 percent). The survey results also indicate that transnational rules were most often applied to supplement or interpret the applicable municipal law rather than to replace it.[16]

In the *Aucoven* v. *Venezuela* ICSID case, the tribunal, applying Venezuelan law, examined whether Aucoven's claim for lost profit met the test of certainty. In line with a jurisprudence of the Venezuelan Supreme Court, the tribunal reiterated that it could not award loss of profit on the basis of speculative assessments and added that this was consistent with the practice of international tribunals. The tribunal noted that "Decisions issued by ICSID tribunals and by the Iran-US Claims Tribunal have often dismissed claims for lost profits in cases of breach of contract on the ground that they were speculative and that the claimant had not proven with a sufficient degree of certainty that the project would have resulted in a profit." In this connection, the tribunal referred to certain authorities.[17]

In the same matter, the tribunal reviewed four cases put forth by Venezuela corroborating the proposition that lost profits cannot be awarded where they are not justified by economic evidence.[18] The tribunal went on to observe that the four decisions cited by Venezuela showed that ICSID tribunals are reluctant to award lost profits to a beginning industry and unperformed work, and noted that the same reluctance of ICSID tribunals is confirmed by the practice of the Iran-US Claims Tribunal. This enabled the panel to consider that Aucoven's claim for future profits did not rest on sufficiently certain economic projections and thus appeared to be speculative: Aucoven had no record of profit, since it never built the viaduct required by the Concession Agreement.

This relatively recent international award in the *Aucoven* v. *Venezuela* case can be seen as a natural *penchant* of international arbitrators to work toward the building up of an *autonomous corpus* of rules susceptible of being applied in international trade. This can be best illustrated by the tribunal's following *obiter dictum*: "Hence, it [the Venezuela claim] does not meet the standards for an award of lost profits under Venezuelan law, nor would it meet these standards under international law, if the latter were applicable."

6. RESORT TO UNIDROIT PRINCIPLES

According to Alexander Komarov, President of the Court of International Arbitration of the Chamber of Commerce & Industry of the Russian Federation, the UNIDROIT Principles found their way into six arbitral proceedings pursuant to the rules of this institution.[19]

In one case, the arbitral tribunal applied the Principles on its own as reflecting international trade usages required to be applied pursuant to the rules. In another case, the Principles were used to support the application of a rule of domestic law to show the appropriateness of the latter to international contracts. Among the examples given by Mr Komarov, it is interesting to note that for many years, tribunals and courts often reduced the sum stipulated by the parties as liquidated damages, basically to safeguard a state interest. Since the UNIDROIT Principles enunciate that the rule of good faith must be taken into account in matters of compensation, arbitrators therefore refer to the Principles in order to show that the rules of domestic origin are also applicable to international situations, and the amount of liquidated damages is less likely to be reduced.

Award 229/1996 of 5 June 1997 of the Russian Chamber dealt with the validity of a contractual clause providing for an amount to be paid by the buyer as a penalty in the event of late payment. In response to the buyer's argument that the stipulated amount was excessive and in the absence of any relevant provision in the CISG, the arbitral tribunal applied Art. 7.4.13 (2) of the UNIDROIT Principles and reduced the penalty to a reasonable amount. The arbitral tribunal further pointed out that the Principles were applicable pursuant to Art. 9 (2) CISG since "they reflect usages of which the parties knew or ought to have known and which are widely known in international trade".[20]

During the May 1994 to December 1998 period, 23 ICC awards made reference to the UNIDROIT Principles.[21] For the period 1999–2000, 14 ICC awards mentioning the UNIDROIT Principles have been reviewed by Professor Fabrizio Marrella.[22] According to this survey, four awards only applied the Principles as the proper law of the contract, while nine show the use of the Principles as a means of interpreting/supplementing the applicable national law and one the former Uniform Law on the International Sale of Corporate Property. Emmanuel Jolivet, General Counsel, ICC International Court of Arbitration, reviewed 10 awards made in 2001 and 2002 referring to the UNIDROIT Principles.[23]

We will examine here some of those awards which deal with the issue of damages and in particular with the elements of "certainty" and "foreseeability".

In line with the classical notion of foreseeability, the 1985 Chinese law on foreign economic contracts provides that damages must not exceed the loss that was foreseeable by the breaching party at the time the contact was made. A claimant had sought compensatory as well as punitive damages. Although both parties agreed that Chinese law governed the merits of the dispute, they requested the arbitral tribunal to apply the UNIDROIT Principles as an expression of international practices.[24] The tribunal was therefore able to shore up its decision to reject the claimed punitive damages – after having found that they exceeded normal foreseeable compensatory damages as provided under Chinese law – by concluding it was obvious that there was no international trade practice favouring punitive damages.

In a 1996 award under the Rules of the Camera Arbitrale Nazionale ed Internazionale di Milano, the parties agreed, in the absence of a choice of law clause, to have their dispute settled in conformity with the UNIDROIT Principles tempered by recourse to equity. By reference to Articles 7.4.1 and 7.4.2 of the Principles, the tribunal affirmed the right to full compensation for the harm suffered by the aggrieved party due to the other party's non-performance, but excluded compensation for emotional suffering and distress on the ground that the aggrieved party was a corporate entity. Likewise, the tribunal excluded compensation for the purchase of a house in the place where the contract was to be performed.[25]

In ICC Case No. 8264, the arbitral tribunal was authorized, in addition to the applicable Algerian law, to consider "the general principles of law and the usages of trade".[26] The tribunal found that the UNIDROIT Principles reflected the practice of international contracts and, referring to Article 7.4.3 (2) of the Principles, that it was authorized to compensate the "loss of a chance", since the licensor (claimant) had not kept the licensee (respondent) regularly informed that it had not made any improvements to the equipment, and therefore that it had no technical advancements to communicate. Since the licensee could not integrate this information into its plant expansion programme, it therefore necessarily lost business opportunities by having been prevented thereby from timely reorganization of the industrial plant that it had built to manufacture the equipment pursuant to the license agreement. While the tribunal recognized that the loss of a chance could be compensated when sufficiently proven, it nonetheless tempered its decision by taking into account that the non-communication by the claimant of the information that no improvement had been made to its technology was only a contributory factor to the loss of a large part of the respondent's investment:

> "En d'autres termes, en raison de l'attitude de la partie demanderesse, la partie défenderesse a perdu une chance de rentabiliser convenablement des installations industrielles fort onéreuses. Certes, l'échec actuel de la partie défenderesse, qui se traduit par l'arrêt presque complet de la fabrication des compresseurs et compacteurs visés par le contrat de licence, est dû à des causes diverses, mais le comportement de la partie demanderesse a sûrement contribué, dans une certaine mesure, à ce fiasco industriel."

An ICC award rendered in December 2000 in Case No. 10346 clearly sets out the general principles applying to damage recovery, in particular under Colombian law, applicable to the contract.[27] The tribunal refers to civil law commentators as well as to Anglo-Saxon sources. Having recalled the two categories into which recoverable damages can be classified, *damnum emergens* and *lucrum cessans*, the tribunal proceeded to define the parameters that must be applied in evaluating the prejudice once, of course, the figures have been proven. The tribunal lists the following conditions :

> "i. Fullness of the compensation, referable to the need to place the aggrieved party in the position it would have been in absent [sic] the loss;

ii. Certainty of the loss, material in the case of consequential loss (crystallized situation) and legal in the case of loss of profit (contingent situation);

iii. Direct character, that is to say resulting exclusively from the cause-effect relationship; and

iv. Foreseeability, referring to the harmful consequences of their actions being within the reasonable contemplation of the Parties".

In this December 2000 award, the arbitral tribunal was obviously largely influenced by the UNIDROIT Principles, although it had to apply Colombian law. In relation to the "certainty" of the loss, the tribunal made it clear that it would not order compensation of a loss that would merely be "contingent". To illustrate this point, the tribunal referred to Article 7.4.3 of the UNIDROIT Principles and recalled the illustration given in the commentary on this article, where the owner of a horse that arrives too late to run in a race as a result of a delay in transport cannot recover the whole of the prize money, even though the horse was the favourite.

The tribunal stressed that the exercise of classifying damages as certain or as contingent constitutes a necessary filter for the determination of the reasonableness of losses. If the losses are 100 percent certain, then they can be awarded in total, provided, of course, that the other criteria for damage recovery are met. The tribunal then turned to an examination of the inevitability of the damage and underlined that this had to be found in order to award damages. It differentiated this notion from the intermediate or immediate character of a loss.

The tribunal went on to examine the condition of foreseeability and, in line with the 1854 English case of *Hadley* v. *Baxendale*, concluded that the foreseeability rule requires the tribunal to determine whether the type of losses had been ordinarily and reasonably within the contemplation of the breaching party as being associated with its breach, in order to decide whether or not compensation should be ordered and, if so, the amount of such compensation. This requirement is clearly met, as specified under Article 7.4.4 of the UNIDROIT Principles, when the loss of profit could have been reasonably expected by the party that breached the contract at the time of entering into it, as the probable consequence of its breach. In the instant case, the tribunal had no hesitation in concluding that it must have been obvious to the breaching party that the essential objective of the aggrieved party in taking part in the public tender and, naturally, in entering into the contract, was to obtain a return on its investment. The tribunal therefore allocated damages on this basis.

The reasoning of the arbitral tribunal in this ICC case is illustrative of the influence that the international principles of law, and in particular the UNIDROIT Principles, will have on the application of a given national provision of law when applied by an arbitrator sitting in a case involving parties from different jurisdictions. The reference to, and sometimes reliance on, transnational rules provide the desired flexibility in applying domestic rules to an international relationship.

When legislators adopt laws in their respective countries, and in particular rules applying to contracts, they primarily, if not exclusively, have in mind a national application, i.e. the use of these laws by citizens of their country. This is why the publication, albeit in sanitized form, of international awards becomes essential if national laws are to continue to be applied in world trade. These constitute precedents concerning how national norms can be successfully transposed into the transnational arena. International awards and principles of law restated (UNIDROIT Principles, CSIG, UCC, model laws) largely contribute to resolve many difficulties that the application of a national rule may entail when tested in an international context.

ICC Case No. 8817, decided in 1997, offers an interesting solution for identifying international rules to be applied in the absence of a governing law.[28] The tribunal noted that both Spain and Denmark had adopted the CISG sometime before the litigious contract had been entered into, thereby allowing time for the CISG to have been studied and commented on in these jurisdictions. Accordingly, the CISG represented a *tronc commun* of the principles that would apply in each country. The arbitral tribunal then proceeded to resolve the main issues by applying the relevant principles found in the CISG. The tribunal further noted that the provisions of the CISG and its general principles were also contained in the UNIDROIT Principles, so that the CISG rules were perfectly suited for resolving the dispute.

The arbitral tribunal then proceeded to analyze the facts of the case in the light of Article 77 of CISG and Art. 7.4.8 of the UNIDROIT Principles in so far as mitigation of damages was concerned. Although this case did not deal directly with the notion of certainty and foreseeability, the interest resides in the reasoning of the tribunal in arriving at the rules of law to be applied in an international dispute where no domestic law has been provided. The tribunal considered that the CISG and the UNIDROIT Principles provided an adequate *tronc commun* of principles to resolve the dispute.[29]

It is worth noting that when the contract is silent as to the applicable law, tribunals will often determine the case by reference, first, to the provisions of the contract itself and then to the *lex mercatoria* or the international principles of law which, in many instances, mean reference to the UNIDROIT Principles to the extent that they are largely viewed and accepted as a codification or restatement of those transnational rules.

In ICC Case No. 5835 (1996) opposing Kuwaiti and Italian parties, the arbitrator was not convinced that the parties had expressly decided upon a national applicable law.[30] The tribunal did not accept the respondent's argument that the parties had made a "negative choice" in that the national law of neither party was intended to be applied. The respondent derived from this negative choice that the law to be applied should be the *tronc commun* principles containing that part of the Kuwaiti and Italian legislations which were common to them at the time the agreement was entered into. The tribunal finally decided that Kuwaiti law, which presented the closest link with the contract, should be applied. However, the tribunal went on to state that "in accordance with the well-established practice in International Commercial Arbitration, the arbitrators shall take account also of the principles generally applicable in international commerce...". This statement was "particularly justified in view of the fact that the Parties refrained from choosing explicitly Kuwaiti law as the law on the merits ... ".

Having reached this conclusion, the tribunal was able to interpret Art. 300 Sect. 1 of the Kuwaiti Civil Law No. 67 of 1980, which provides that compensation shall be "estimated" by the court. The tribunal equated the meaning of the Kuwaiti legal provision to mean what Art. 7.4.3, para. 3 of the UNIDROIT Principles states: "Where the amount of damages cannot be established with a sufficient degree of certainty the assessment is at the discretion of the court."

This is a remarkable illustration of how a municipal law meant to regulate contractual relations between residents of the same country can be interpreted by an international tribunal to suit the decision-making process in disputes involving international elements.

Comfort was sought from international norms by another arbitral tribunal in 1999, when it could have resolved the dispute on the basis of the English law chosen by the parties.[31] After having reviewed the leading English cases, the tribunal found it appropriate to add that "a similar standard has been established internationally, primarily in the UNIDROIT Principles of International Commercial Contracts (1994) which enunciates in sub-section (1) of Article 7.4.8", that in essence the aggrieved party has an obligation to mitigate its damages. In connection with the "foreseeability" test, the tribunal cited the *Hadley* v. *Baxendale* 1884 case and the Sale of Goods Act, 1979, but did not find it necessary nor useful to refer to Article 7.4.4 of the UNIDROIT Principles embodying the principle of limitation of the recoverable harm to that which is foreseeable, this rule also corresponding to the language found in Article 74 CISG.

Although the unpublished *ad hoc* arbitration award rendered in 1997 between Argentinean and Chilean parties does not deal with an issue of damages,[32] this case offers an example where reference is made to the Model Law. The arbitral tribunal took the argument in Section 4 of Art. 28 of the Model Law to state that the UNIDROIT Principles constituted "usages of international trade reflecting the solutions of different legal systems and of international contract practice" and as such, the tribunal determined that these Principles should prevail over any domestic law.[33] Despite the fact that the arbitrators acted as *amiables compositeurs*, they nonetheless sought comfort in the Model Law and the UNIDROIT Principles.

Another *ad hoc* arbitration cited in Bonell shows that even if the tribunal were able to reach its decision purely on the applicable domestic law (reduction of an excessively high penalty or liquidated damages), it nonetheless found it worthwhile to corroborate its finding by referring to Article 7.4.13 (2) of the UNIDROIT Principles, which provides for a penalty to be reduced to a reasonable amount where it appears grossly excessive under the given circumstances.[34]

The final award rendered in Case No. 9950 in June 2001,[35] where the arbitral tribunal faced with the complexities of quantification and given the judicial discretion that it enjoyed in the allocation of damages as foreseen under the Egyptian Civil Code, looked to Article 42 of the applicable substantive law, the Swiss Code of Obligations (Geneva being the site of the arbitration).[36] The tribunal sought further support in the exercise of its discretion to assess damages in the UNIDROIT Principles, in particular from Article 7.4.3. The tribunal was careful to state that such discretion must not be tantamount to deciding in *amiable composition* and insisted that it continued to operate within the legal framework relevant in this matter.

Another recent award rendered in July 2001 in ICC Case No. 11051 gives an example of an arbitral tribunal referring to the UNIDROIT Principles (Art. 7.4.9), this time in relation to the question of interest, even though Italian law had been chosen by the parties.[37] This solution, as stated by the tribunal, is consistent with the relevant customs of international trade, of which the UNIDROIT Principles are an expression.

The final award rendered in ICC Case No. 10422 in 2001 held, failing a stipulation by the parties as to a clear choice of applicable law, that the parties had intended their contractual relationships to be governed by a neutral solution.[38] Accordingly, relying on Article 17(1) of the ICC Rules of Arbitration, the arbitral tribunal considered that the most appropriate solution to meet the parties' intent for a neutral set of rules was to resort to the UNIDROIT Principles as representing a restatement of the rules governing business relationships in international trade, those rules conforming to the interest and expectations of the parties.[39] The tribunal referred to previous awards where this reasoning was recognized. In any event, this decision acknowledges that the Principles can be directly applied as a material rule in relation to the quantification of damages.[40]

The sole arbitrator in this ICC Case No. 10422 noted that the UNIDROIT Principles were a component part of the *lex mercatoria*. This award confirms that the UNIDROIT Principles are now part of the international rules used by negotiators and drafters of international commercial contracts. It also supports the proposition that the Principles constitute a substantive set of rules that can be directly applied by arbitral tribunals, at least when the parties have not provided expressly for an applicable law. Emmanuel Jolivet, the General Counsel to the ICC Court of Arbitration, concluded that this award provides a very instructive example of the application of the UNIDROIT Principles.[41] Mr Jolivet recalled that constant arbitral jurisprudence has now established for a number of years that in applying the notion of *lucrum cessans*, the loss of profit is not calculated on the basis of the gross margin on the sale price, but on the net profit after deduction of all expenses. In applying the UNIDROIT Principles, the arbitral tribunal had the necessary discretion to determine what the reasonable net margin was.

Another ICC award in Case No. 10578, also rendered in 2001, furnishes an example where the claimant, the parties not having relied in their contract on general principles of international trade law, invited the tribunal to refer to the UNIDROIT Principles and equity even though the contract was governed by Swedish law.[42] The tribunal had to examine several claims in damages, including loss of profit, costs incurred, lost goodwill and compensation for damaged trading image and interest.

The final award in ICC Case No. 6829, rendered in 1992, although more ancient, is noteworthy, since it illustrates how a tribunal limited a condemnation in damages to compensate lost profit. After having determined the total loss of profit sustained by the claimant over a period of 9.33 years, the tribunal subjected that sum to a discount rate to take account of the fact that the sum awarded would be paid to the claimant years in advance of the dates on which claimant would have otherwise received its profits had the respondent performed the contract for the whole of the term. The tribunal applied a discount rate of 6.5 percent, which it considered to be appropriate according to the practice prevailing in Luxembourg, the place of arbitration.[43]

CONCLUSION

For some time now, a considerable body of scholarly work has been devoted to the issue of whether there exists a body of transnational rules susceptible of being applied, particularly by international business operators and arbitrators, as the substantive law or *lex contractus*. Today, this is a generally accepted proposition as reflected in Art. 17 (1) of the ICC Rules of Arbitration in force as from 1 January 1998, which provides that "The party shall be free to agree upon the rules of law to be applied by the Arbitral Tribunal to the merits of the dispute." National courts have also validated the position that the *lex mercatoria*, as restated in the UNIDROIT Principles and other international instruments such as the CISG, can serve as a genuine law equivalent in their application to a specific municipal law.

However, is this proposition acceptable in relation to the recovery of damages? At the end of the day, once specific issues (mitigation of damages, interest, etc.) have been examined, the answer will likely be "yes" for certain rules and "no" for others.

In general, international arbitrators enjoy greater flexibility in assessing damages between parties coming from different jurisdictions than local judges who are bound by their own domestic legal rules. Arbitrators are often called upon to accommodate the perception of parties to an international dispute, as they do not always share the same understanding of the national rule of law retained in their contract. International arbitrators will naturally turn to arbitral precedents and to sets of transnational rules to arrive at the most appropriate solution in the precise circumstances of a given case. In order to support their determination, they can refer, for instance, to Art. 7.4.2 of the UNIDROIT Principles providing that the aggrieved party is entitled to full compensation, which will include lost profit (sometimes called "consequential damages"); Art. 7.4.3 which provides that the harm, including future harm, must be established with a reasonable degree of certainty, albeit leaving to the arbitrators – when such a sufficient degree of certainty cannot be proven – a discretion to assess the damages; and to Art. 7.4.4, which limits the recoverable harm to what was foreseeable at the time the contract was made.

Overall, the application of these principles does not cause any problems, quite the contrary. The relevance and particular interest of arbitral case law in this context is that awards offer concrete examples of the application of such principles, thereby creating a base of precedents more adapted to international disputes. On the other hand, there are still some contradictions in the application of transnational rules, including the UNIDROIT Principles, except in relation to specific topics such as the mitigation of damages. Some arbitrators exclude certain of the UNIDROIT Principles, such as hardship, as not reflecting international trade usages, but others will accept them.

There is a need to establish a compendium of arbitral awards, rendered pursuant to the rules of the various institutions, as well as pursuant to *ad hoc* procedures, to determine whether universally, if not generally, recognized transnational rules are emerging in the field of damage recovery as a whole (e.g. is there a common approach in applying Art. 7.4.9 (2) of the UNIDROIT Principles in determining "the average bank short-term lending rate to prime borrowers" when the arbitrator wants to award full compensation?).

Most international practitioners undoubtedly favour the development of uniform rules of law, even though resort to such rules is not always warranted. Hopefully, international practitioners in the field of damage recovery will make greater use of transnational rules of damage recovery. There are cases where arbitrators would have liked to use international rules to support their decision, but were reluctant to do so in the presence of an applicable national law. Other awards will borrow from transnational rules to interpret and fill gaps in the applicable domestic law whenever it is not adapted to an international context.

Some awards purely and simply retain transnational rules, in particular those embodied in the UNIDROIT Principles and the CISG, as the *lex contractus*. The adoption of a set of general principles of law as the substantive law applicable to the contract sometimes comes from an agreement of the parties either before or at the time the dispute comes to be arbitrated, or from a determination by the arbitral tribunal in the absence of an applicable national law.

As the globalization of trade develops, individuals and companies will increasingly encounter rules of a transnational nature, to use a generic expression, and will become more familiar with them over time. This will lead more and more to the adoption, at the time of negotiation, of such principles. Arbitral tribunals will more frequently invite the parties to refer to international principles of law at the time the arbitration is initiated, in particular when discussing the terms of reference as well as in the course of the proceedings. This will be the case even when a specific domestic law governs, in order to support a tribunal's decision to apply a national rule in an international context.

Should such steps – supported by activities sponsored by international organizations, institutions, universities and groups – ultimately bring about sets of readily applicable international rules, other issues could arise, namely, will there be more advocacy in favour of inserting transnational rules instead of national laws in international contracts and will *amiable composition* become obsolete in view of the accrued flexibility flowing from international rules that are more adapted to international situations? Will we witness a growing trend to add, in the governing law clause, some general principles of law in addition to a given national law?

END NOTES

1 *Livingstone* v. *Rawyards Coal Co* (1880) 5 App. Cas. 25 at 39, cited in *Mc Gregor on Damages*, London, Sweet and Maxwell Limited, 16th ed., 1997, p. 9.

2 See the cases cited in *Mc Gregor on Damages*, ibid, p. 9.

3 Cam Quyen Corinne Truong, *Les différends liés à la rupture des contrats internationaux de distribution dans les sentences arbitrales CCI*, Litec, 2002, 290-291, referring to ICC Case No. 5631 decided pursuant to British Columbia law.

4 See Cam Quyen Corinne Truong, ibid, 291, referring to ICC Case No. 7905 decided pursuant to French law.

5 *Ratcliffe* v. *Evans* (1892) 2 Q.B. 524 CA cited in *McGregor on Damages*, op. cit.,p. 358.

6 *Ancoven* v. *Venezuelan* ICSID Case No. ARB/00/05, 23 September 2003.

7 See Robert Ribeiro, *Damages and other remedies for breach of commercial contracts*, London, 2002, published by Thorogood, p. 48.

8 *Hadley* v. *Baxendale* (1854) 9 Exch. 341, 354; see, for instance, ICC Case No. 2404 in 1975, Sigvard Jarvin, Yves Derains, Jean-Jacques Arnaldez, *Collection of ICC Arbitral Awards 1974-1985*, ICC Publishing S.A., Paris/Kluwer Law and Taxation Publishers, Deventer, The Netherlands, 1990, pp. 280-282.

9 Robert Ribeiro, *Damages and other remedies for beach of commercial contracts*, London, 2002 published by Thorogood, pp. 19-21.

10 ICC Case No. 9950, Final Award rendered in 2001 in Geneva, *The UNIDROIT Principles: New Developments and Applications*, 2005 Special Supplement – ICC International Court of Arbitration Bulletin, pp. 77-79.

11 Published in *Journal de droit international,* Clunet, 1980, No. 4, 961-970; see also the *ICC Guide pour les clauses pénales et les clauses de dommages-intérêts libératoires,* ICC Publishing 1990; see for a general discussion of liquidated damages and penalty clauses in common law countries: the chapter on Delay under Australian law contributed by T. M. Burke, in *Selected Problems of Construction Law: International Approach*, Peter Gauch and Justin Sweet (ed.), University Press, Fribourg, Switzerland, Sweet and Maxwell, London, 1983.

12 Bernard Hanotiau, La détermination et l'évalutation du dommage réparable : principes généraux et principes en émergence, in Gaillard (ed.), *Transational Rules in International Commercial Arbitration* (ICC Publication No. 480, 4), ICC Publishing SA, Paris 1993, p. 209 *et seq.*

13 Bernard Hanotiau, see supra note 12.

14 See infra, Jan Paulsson, The expectation model.

15 See infra, Jacques Werner, *Punitive and exemplary damages in international arbitration.*

16 P. K. Berger (ed). *The Practice of Transnational Law*, Kluwer Law International, The Hague, 2001 reviewed by Philippe Fouchard in *Revue de l'Arbitrage*, 2002, No. 4, pp. 1077-1080.

17 *Metalclad Corp.* v. *The United Mexican States*, ICSID Case No. ARB(AF)/97/1, 30 August 2000; *Asian Agricultural Products* v. *Sri Lanka*, Award of 27 June 1990, in 4 ICSID Reports, pp. 245, 292-293; *American Manufacturing & Trading* v. *Republic of Zaire*, ICSID Case No. ARB 793/1, 7.14. G.H. Aldrich, *The Jurisprudence of the Iran-United States Tribunal*, Clarendon Press, Oxford 1996, p. 294. See in particular *Levitt* v. *Islamic Republic of Iran*, 14 Iran-US C.T.R. 191, 209; *Dadras International* v. *Islamic Republic of Iran*, Award No. 567-213/215-3 (Nov. 7, 1995), in G. Aldrich, op. cit., p. 296.

18 See S.P.P. (Middle East) Limited, *Southern Pacific Properties, Ltd* v. *The Arab Republic of Egypt*, ICC Arbitration No. YD/AS No. 3493, Award (Mar. 11, 1983), 22 I.L.M. 752 (1983), Resp. Auth. 21; *Asian Agricultural Products Limited* v. *Republic of Sri Lanka*, ICSID Case No. ARB/87/3, Award of 27 June 1990, 4 ICSID Rep. 245, Resp. Auth 17. *Metalclad Corp.* v. *United Mexican States*, ICSID Case No. ARB(AF)/97/1, Award (30 August 2000), 16 ICSID Rev. – FILJ 168, Cl. Auth. 5, pp. 197-199, § 119-122; *Wena Hotels Ltd* v. *Arab Republic of Egypt*, ICSID Case No. ARB/98/4, Award (8 December 2000), Resp. Auth. 23, pp. 64-70, § 118-130.

19 *The UNIDROIT Principles of International Commercial Contracts*, 2002 Special Supplement, ICC International Court of Arbitration Bulletin, pp. 144-145.

20 Cited by M. J. Bonell, *The UNIDROIT Principles of International Commercial Contracts*, 2002 Special Supplement, ICC International Court of Arbitration Bulletin, p. 36.

21 Fabrizio Marrella & Fabien Gélinas, *The UNIDROIT Principles of International Commercial Contracts in ICC Arbitration*, ICC International Court of Arbitration Bulletin, Vol. 10 No. 2, Fall 1999, pp. 26-32.

22 Fabrizio Marrella, ICC International Court of Arbitration Bulletin, Vol. 12 No. 2, Fall 2001, pp. 49-55.

23 *UNIDROIT Principles: New Developments and Applications,* 2005 Special Supplement, ICC International Court of Arbitration Bulletin, pp. 65-72.

24 ICC Case No. 10114, cited in Bonell, *The UNIDROIT Principles in Practice,* Transnational Publishers, Inc., Ardsley, New York, 2002, pp. 637-638.

25 Cited in Bonell, above n. 1, pp. 409-410. This case provides an illustration of the limits of foreseeability and, as an "international" precedent, is likely to find its way in decisions of international tribunals more easily than domestic standards, even where a national law applies.

26 See excerpts of the original text in French in ICC International Court of Arbitration Bulletin, Vol. 10 No. 2, Fall 1999, pp. 62-65.

27 ICC International Court of Arbitration Bulletin, Vol. 12 No. 2, Fall 2001, pp. 106-115 also cited in Bonell, *The UNIDROIT Principles in Practice*, Transnational Publishers, Inc., Ardsley, New York, 2002, 677-688.

28 ICC International Court of Arbitration Bulletin, Vol. 10 No. 2, Fall 1999, pp. 75-78.

29 See in connection with the *tronc commun* doctrine and other applicable transnational rules to the substance including those chosen by the arbitrators and the *lex mercatoria*, the developments in Rubino-Sammartano, *International Arbitration Law and Practice*, 2nd ed., Kluwer Law International, The Hague, 2001, pp. 417-456.

30 ICC International Court of Arbitration Bulletin, Vol. 10 No. 2, Fall 2001, pp. 73-76, also cited in Bonell, *The UNIDROIT Principles in Practice*, Transnational Publishers, Inc., Ardsley, New York, 2002, pp. 437-440.

31 Final Award in Case 9594, place of arbitration: London, UK, ICC International Court of Arbitration Bulletin, Vol. 12 No. 2, Fall 2001, pp. 73-76, p. 75.

32 Bonell, *The UNIDROIT Principles in Practice*, Transnational Publishers, Inc., Ardsley, New York, 2002, pp. 463-464, at least at the abstract cited.

33 Art. 28(4) of the Model Law reads as follows: "4. In all cases, the arbitral tribunal shall decide in accordance with the terms of the contract and shall take into account the usages of the trade applicable to the transaction."

34 Bonell, *The UNIDROIT Principles in Practice*, Transnational Publishers, Inc., Ardsley, New York, 2002, p. 515.

35 *UNIDROIT Principles: New Developments and Applications,* 2005 Special Supplement, ICC International Court of Arbitration Bulletin, pp. 77-79.

36 Article 42 of the Swiss Code of Obligations is to the effect that the judge must determine with fairness the amount of damages when it cannot be established with certainty, by taking in consideration the ordinary course of things and the efforts made by the aggrieved party to reduce the damages.

37 *UNIDROIT Principles: New Developments and Applications,* 2005 Special Supplement, ICC International Court of Arbitration Bulletin, pp. 86-87; Art. 7.4.9 of the UNIDROIT Principles provides that: " ... if a party does not pay a sum of money when it falls due the aggrieved party is entitled to interest upon that sum from the time when payment is due".

38 Note Emmanuel Jolivet, *Journal de Droit International,* Clunet, Vol. 4, 2003, at 1142-1156.

39 Art. 17(1) reads: "The parties shall be free to agree upon the rules of law to be applied by the Arbitral Tribunal to the merits of the dispute. In the absence of any such agreement, the Arbitral Tribunal shall apply the rules of law which it determines to be appropriate."

40 See in this connection, Pierre Lalive, The UNIDROIT Principles as *Lex Contractio*, With or Without an Explicit or Tacit Choice of Law: An Arbitrator's Perspective, *The UNIDROIT Principles of International Commercial Contracts,* 2002 Special Supplement, ICC International Court of Arbitration Bulletin, pp. 77-83.

41 Note Emmanuel Jolivet, *Journal de Droit International,* Clunet, Vol. 4, 2003, at 1156.

42 Final award in Case 10578, *UNIDROIT Principles: New Developments and Applications,* 2005 Special Supplement, ICC International Court of Arbitration Bulletin, pp. 65-72.

43 ICC Case No. 6829, 1991, Jean-Jacques Arnaldez, Yves Derains, Dominique Hascher, *Collection of ICC Arbitral Awards*, Kluwer Law International, The Hague, ICC Publishing SA, Paris, 1997, pp. 282-298; see also in this connection the Award in *Aucoven* v. *Venezuela*, ICSID Case No ARB/00/05 where the tribunal laid down the rules that lost profits, when a project never comes into operation, would be too speculative to be awarded [supra] and the *Himpurna* v. *PLN* case discussed by Jan Paulsson [infra].

2

Mitigation of damages

By ***Alexander S. Komarov***
President International Commercial Arbitration Court at the Russian Federation Chamber of Commerce and Industry; Council Member of the ICC Institute of World Business Law

It would not be a great exaggeration to say that the concept of mitigation of damages represents one of the basic notions of the law on contract damages well known to almost every lawyer practicing in the field of contract law, especially in international settings. That notwithstanding, it is one of the legal principles that are, in many instances, difficult to understand and to apply in particular cases.

In an authoritative comparative law treaty published about thirty years ago and devoted to the legal consequences of breach of contracts, the problem of mitigating damages was presented in a nutshell that revealed the universality of this concept in substance, although it exists in different forms.[1] In spite of the decades that have passed since that time, the approach to this classical problem of contract law in theory and practice has not changed in principle, and the same approach may be used at present when dealing with the topic.

1. THEORETICAL AND FORMAL SOURCES OF THE CONCEPT

In the context of the notion of mitigating damages, reference is often made to a "duty" to mitigate damages, but at the same time this mode of expression is often and justly criticized. The main reason, of course, is that this "duty" is not matched by any corresponding right of the defendant ensuring that mitigation takes place. As a consequence, there is no sanction for "breach" of this "duty"; the only possible result of the plaintiff's failure to mitigate is to reduce the amount of his recovery. Strictly speaking, he does not incur any legal liability in consequence of the breach of "duty".

Reference to mitigation of damages may imply at least three related ideas. The first is that the plaintiff cannot recover damages in respect of a loss that he ought to have avoided. The second is that if the plaintiff actually gains some benefit in consequence of the defendant's breach, he may have to take that benefit into account. Thus, damages may be reduced because the plaintiff is, as a result of the defendant's breach, discharged from his obligations to perform and so saves the expense of performing; or because he is enabled in consequence of the breach to obtain some profit or advantage that he would not otherwise have obtained. Under this second notion, the question is whether in fact his loss was reduced or "mitigated". Sometimes it is called "mitigation in fact". In some legal systems such as in common law countries, the expression "mitigation" is used in relation to both of the above ideas. In the civil law tradition, the distinction between them is sharper. Namely, the first situation is considered under the heading of the fault of both parties, and the second takes into account the compensating advantages.

The third related idea is what in common law jurisdictions is called contributory negligence. In civil law jurisdictions, this is treated as the situation in which loss is caused partly by the fault of the defendant and partly by that of the injured party. For the purposes of legal certainty, especially in the field of contractual relationships, it seems more plausible that this notion should be separated from that of the "duty" to mitigate since, unlike contributory negligence in mitigation, the plaintiff can only be charged with failing to take positive steps to avoid the harmful effects of an event brought about solely by the defendant's default. Another point that deserves to be taken into account from this perspective is that the notion of contributory negligence is predominantly associated with tort liability. But it should not be disregarded, since in borderline cases it might become necessary to consider this approach as well.

Mitigation as a legal concept directed to the limitation of damages has been developed in common law more extensively than in the civil law tradition, although considerable legal materials relating to the subject are to be found in national jurisdictions belonging to the former legal circle as well.

It would not be incorrect to state that it is universally accepted that the "duty" to mitigate loss may be said to have two aspects. First, the plaintiff may be bound to take positive steps to minimize the loss which would otherwise flow from the defendant's default. Second, he may be bound to refrain from taking steps which but for the default would have been properly taken under the contract, but which in view of the default may unjustifiably augment the loss.

The principle that the victim of a breach of contract cannot recover damages in respect of a loss that he ought to have avoided by taking reasonable steps is clearly recognized in practically all legal systems. In countries of the continental legal tradition, it is either expressly stated in the positive law, as in German law,[2] or established in case law as, for example, in France where codified law does not recognize the concept of mitigation as such, but some similar results may be obtained by application of the general rule about fault.[3] With regard to the law in France, the matter is considered, if at all, as an aspect of the need for a causal link.[4]

Following the continental legal tradition in its German version, the Russian Civil Code, similar to new civil codes in other CIS countries, includes a provision that reflects the idea of mitigation of damages, although under the heading "fault of the creditor". Article 404 of the Russian Federation Civil Code stipulates that the court shall also have the right to reduce the amount of liability of the debtor if the creditor intentionally or by negligence facilitated an increase in the amount of damages caused by non-performance or improper performance, or did not take reasonable measures to reduce it. The last part of the provision clearly points to the concept of mitigation of damages as it has evolved in modern practice. It should be mentioned that in the practice of the International Commercial Arbitration Court of the Russian Federation Chamber of Commerce and Industry, the court that at present occupies the dominant position in dealing with international commercial disputes in the post-Soviet area, reference to the rule relating to mitigation of damages is among the most frequently used rules when Russian law is applied to the merits of the dispute.

The common law doctrine of mitigation usually starts by stating that the principle breaks down into three basic rules. First, a party injured upon the occurrence of a breach of contract may not hold the contract breaker responsible in respect of losses that he could reasonably have avoided. Second, expenses reasonably incurred in avoiding or minimizing a loss resulting from breach of contract may be charged to the contract breaker.

Third, regardless of whether an injured party in the circumstances had to mitigate, any action he takes after the breach of contract, which in fact avoids or minimizes the loss, will serve correspondingly to diminish the contract breaker's liability in damages.[5]

In common law jurisdictions, the source of the rule is relevant case law.[6] But at the same time, even with regard to English law, according to authoritative opinions, the expression "mitigation of damage" is an umbrella term applied in books and cases to a number of matters, some of which are related and some of which are completely unconnected.[7] To a suprising degree, the subject is liable to hardly any critical examination in the leading texts.[8]

In the early sixties, an authority in the field of international commercial law submitted in English legal literature[9] the view that the establishment of the modern doctrine of mitigation used by the contract breaker as a frequent defence to reduce the damages he was liable to pay had undergone two stages. The first was the recognition that the loss reduced by an aggrieved party should be taken into account when calculating his damages against the contract breaker. In the second stage, the aggrieved party did not actually reduce his loss, but a reasonable person would have done so, and the question was whether the plaintiff's negative attitude, his failure to act, should be taken into account in the calculation of damages. Describing the true basis of the doctrine of mitigation in the same analysis, the author pointed to the rule governing the measure of damages, as laid down in, and derived from *Hadley* v. *Baxendale*.

Nowdays there are many factors pointing to the tendency to recognize the mitigation rule, not only in national laws but also in international arbitration practice.[10] It has also been submitted that the obligation to mitigate damages belongs to usage, reflected in mercantile practice, which seems regularly to guide merchants in their transactions and arbitrators in their decisions.[11]

Now it is not very difficult to find international arbitration cases where the rule on mitigation of damages has been considered to be a part of general principles of law and applied in international cases. For example, in an ICSID case the tribunal stating that the duty to mitigate damages was not expressly mentioned in the BIT, ruled, however, that this duty could be considered to be part of the General Principles of Law which, in turn, were a part of the rules of international law applicable in the dispute, according to Article 42 of the ICSID Convention.[12]

In the practice of the Iran-US Tribunal, the mitigation rule was applied in a number of instances. In one case, the rule was applied notwithstanding the tribunal stating that it was unable to discern a conflict between Iranian and United States law on the issue of mitigation.[13]

According to one observation,[14] in frequent cases of major international arbitral disputes on large construction cases or long-term contracts – where an arbitral tribunal had to resort to some denationalized rules as a primary, supplementary or corrective source of law to come to a justified and justifiable decision – the award was essentially based on not more than a handful of key notions. These may be said to form part of the general principles of law common to civilized nations or *lex mercatoria*, or of a transnational law. One of the most important of these notions is the duty to mitigate damages.

Another evidence of a fundamental character concerning the idea of mitigating damages in international relations is the Governing Council of the UN Compensation Commission's inclusion, in guidelines for awarding compensation for business losses caused by Iraq's unlawful invasion and occupation of Kuwait, a provision to the effect that the total amount of compensable losses would be reduced to the extent these losses could reasonably had been avoided.[15]

2. CONTENT OF THE CONCEPT IN PRACTICE

The principle of mitigation can be applied in a great variety of situations. But all of these can be summarized in a simple formula: an aggrieved party must take steps to minimize his loss, on the one hand, and he must abstain from doing anything to increase his loss on the other.

Along with this general idea, the following observation should be also taken into account: the party who ought to mitigate will not be held to an extraordinary standard of behaviour. The extent to which there should have been mitigation is a question of fact, and the plaintiff must take steps consistent with demands for reasonable and prudent action. The plaintiff will not have to embark on a difficult and hazardous course of action, nor to act in such a way as to impair his commercial reputation. Also it is worth noting that, as suggested, one should not make a fetish of the doctrine of mitigation.[16]

With regard to that part of the concept directed to minimizing loss, the most common approach to avoiding the loss is that an aggrieved party makes a substitute contract. For example, when a seller of goods fails to deliver, the buyer must go into the market at a relevant time to buy substitute goods. If he fails to do so, he cannot recover any further loss he may suffer because the market continues to rise or because he is deprived of the opportunity of making a profit out of the use or resale of the goods.[17] This means that the amount of loss he could have avoided by making a substitute contract is subtracted in calculating his damages. In the case of sale of goods, it has been suggested that this principle inspired the standard formulas under which the buyer's or seller's damages are based on the difference between the contract price and the market price in that market where the injured party could have arranged a substitute transaction for the purchase or sale of similar goods.[18]

Nevertheless, speaking of substitute transaction as a means of avoiding loss, it should be remembered that mitigation of damages will be adequate only if a new deal is a true substitute for the old one.

On the other hand, a tribunal could find that an adequate substitution deal would not be feasible as a means of avoiding the loss. So, while considering whether during a relevant period the claimant could have procured replacement supplies of similar goods and thereby mitigated the loss, one tribunal found, on the basis of witnesses' statements, that such possibilities did not exist. Due to production costs, environmental constraints, competitive factors and other reasons, no existing factory was prepared to supply necessary items to the claimant at prices making profitable a resale to the claimant's purchasers, who all manufactured or marketed the end product. The only alternative, therefore, was to wait for a new factory to be established similar to the factory figuring in the agreement between the parties.[19]

Sometimes, in order to meet the requirement to avoid unnecessary loss related to the breach of the contract, instead of entering into a cover deal the aggrieved party has to inform the other party of his intention to undertake other measures to mitigate damages in order to give the other party the opportunity to cooperate in order to reach optimal results. An illustration of this approach in a particular case can be found in the following situation based on an international arbitral award.[20] In this case, the buyer received a shipment of coffee from the seller that did not correspond with the quality description in the contract. According to Hamburg coffee trade usage, the buyer should then have determined the price of the agreed goods at the time of the incorrect performance by making a "coverage deal", that is, by buying a certain quantity of coffee of the contractually agreed quality. However, due to a temporary lack of suitable coffee on the market, the buyer bought coffee of a higher quality. The buyer also sold the coffee supplied by the seller to a third party and claimed damages in arbitration for the lower price he obtained for it. The arbitrators found that, while it was acceptable for the buyer to buy higher quality coffee for a coverage deal if there was a shortage of suitable coffee on the market, the buyer breached his obligations under the Hamburg usage by failing to mitigate damages and to inform the seller of his intention to re-sell the coffee to a third party, as the seller was thus incapable of "influencing the sale and the sale's timing".

The idea of necessary cooperation between the parties in cases where the problem of mitigating damages might arise finds its application in modem arbitration practice. In one case, an arbitral tribunal considering the claimant's request for a refund of the purchase price observed that although the defendant was obligated to perform according to the contract, the claimant had been forewarned by the defendant concerning its problems in providing for an essential part of the goods to be delivered, and could have limited the damages it suffered by terminating the contract at an earlier stage.[21]

In another award, the tribunal ruled that it appeared, at a minimum, that the claimant's offer to renew the contract for a certain period of time presented the defendant with an appropriate opportunity to mitigate its damages. The tribunal believed that it would be unfair for one of the parties to deny the other the opportunity to correct a situation created by its improper conduct.[22]

There is an example of the case where the tribunal found it would not be appropriate to reduce the compensation for damages suffered by reason of a failure of the claimant to observe its obligation to mitigate damages, taking into account the conduct of defaulting party. The circumstances, which led the tribunal to this decision, are as follows: the seller (respondent) argued that the buyer claiming damages for the delay and improper delivery of the goods could have, in sufficient time, offered its clients merchandise equivalent to the subject matter of the contract between the parties, in conformity with its obligation to take all appropriate steps to limit its damage and reduce its losses.

In this case, the boots, which were the subject matter of the contract, had a seasonal character and could not have been sold and delivered to the buyer's clients except at the beginning of the season at the latest. The seller, on the basis of promises made by its own supplier, had, up to a certain time and for a major part of the order, led the buyer to believe that it would be in a position to deliver the goods, admittedly late, but prior to the last moment. Its failure to fulfill these promises only became apparent after it was too late to obtain the merchandise elsewhere. In effect, having regard to the changing demand to which this kind of product was subject, suppliers kept very little in stock. The seller failed to identify the sources the buyer could have turned to in order to obtain merchandise equivalent to that described in the contract.

It is worth keeping in mind that it would be not very wise to claim that a substitute transaction should be always treated as a universal means to avoid the loss. In some cases, a substitute deal might not be adequate to serve as a measure. The authoritative restatement of the contract law in the US stressed that the mere fact that an injured party can make arrangements for the disposition of the goods or services he was to supply under the contract does not necessarily mean that by doing so he will avoid loss. If he entered into both transactions but for the breach, he would have "lost volume" as a result of the breach.[23]

The rule that an aggrieved party must act reasonably to avoid loss is widely recognized and understood to be an integral part of the concept of mitigating damages. That is why it would be useful to refer to its implication in the context of mitigation. In a case frequently cited in this connection, the English decision *Banco de Portugal v. Waterlow and Sons, Limited*, (1932) A.C. 452, 506, stated the rule as follows:

> "Where the sufferer from a breach of contract finds himself in consequence of that breach placed in a position of embarrassment the measures which he may be driven to adopt in order to extricate himself ought not to be weighed in nice scales at the instance of the party whose breach of contract has occasioned the difficulty. It is often easy after an emergency has passed to criticize the steps which have been taken to meet it, but such criticism does not come well from those who have themselves created the emergency. The law is satisfied if the party placed in a difficult situation by reason of the breach of a duty owed to him has acted reasonably in the adoption of remedial measures and he will not be held disentitled to recover the cost of such measures merely because the party in breach can suggest that other measures less burdensome to him might have been taken."

In practice, there are various examples of the application of the rule of reasonable behaviour in mitigating damages. In particular, a party is not bound to take steps to mitigate loss if such steps would be very expensive in relation to the loss to be avoided; he is not bound to engage in complicated litigation with third parties, even though its outcome might have been to reduce the loss; and he is not bound to take steps that are contrary to business ethics and that would tend to lower or ruin his commercial reputation.[24] Thus, in general he should not, for example, spend more on curing a defect in performance than the subject matter without the defect would be worth; nor should he continue to incur expenses for the purpose of tendering performance after the other party clearly indicates that he will refuse to accept it.[25] Whether an available alternative transaction is a suitable substitute depends on all of the circumstances, including the similarity of the performance and the times and places that they would be rendered. If the aggrieved party acts reasonably in an effort to minimize the loss, but in fact thereby increases it, he may be entitled to recover the increased loss.

The current practice of applying the rule on mitigation provides evidence that this concept could and should be used flexibly. This seems to be crucial to its correct application in the great variety of practical situations where damages are awarded for breach of contract.

Commercial practice provides a number of examples of particular actions or inactions that have been taken as reasonable to avoid loss when the breach of contract has taken place. Undertaking active behaviour seems to be more the rule than the opposite. But constructive arrangements need not only mean making a substitute deal or something similar.

Also, it seems logical that once a party has reason to know that performance by the other party will not be forthcoming, he is ordinarily expected to stop his own performance to avoid further expenditure and to take such affirmative steps as are appropriate to avoid loss by making substitute arrangements or otherwise.[26]

It is necessary to note that that difficult questions concerning application of the rules on mitigation of damages may arise in cases of anticipatory breach of the contract.

As to what could be accepted as an adequate response to comply with the "duty" to mitigate damages, the following example may be useful. In this case, the tribunal found that the conduct of a party amounted to acting under the general principle *exeptio non adimpleti contractus* when the other party turned out to be in default, and this was entirely consistent with the generally accepted principle of mitigation of harm.[27] In the decisions of the Iran-US Tribunal, quite often the claimant's timely disposition of goods or cancelling subcontracts or orders relating to agreements in the wake of the events that took place in Iran was accepted as a reasonable way to mitigate damages.

The following case gives an example of reasonable action of an aggrieved party to mitigate damages in not quite a standard fashion.[28] A Hungarian export company granted an English importer the sole and exclusive rights for the import and sale of certain Hungarian wines in the territory of the United Kingdom, including in particular a wine called X, for a quite substantial time period. After the exporter terminated the agreement to supply wine X, the importer resorted to arbitration against the exporter, claiming damages for wrongful repudiation of the agreement, consisting, in essence, of a loss of profits together with interest and costs. Among other things, the tribunal considered the problem of whether the claimants had breached their duty to mitigate loss, namely, whether the claimants had taken measures that would have been reasonable to avoid the loss they sustained as the result of the breach of the contract committed by the exporter.

The tribunal came to the conclusion that the claimants were not acting unreasonably in declining to attempt to expand their sales of Hungarian generic wines. If they had thought it was reasonably possible to sell larger volumes profitably, they could easily have obtained supplies from the defendants and would no doubt have done so. The tribunal accepted the evidence that they could not substantially increase sales of generic wines, and that to have any chance of increasing such sales would have required the launching of a new brand. This, in turn, would have involved a very substantial capital investment represented by promotion costs, with great uncertainty as to the likely degree of success. The tribunal considered that the prospects of increased sales of generic wines were so uncertain and the capital expenditure in launching them was so great that the claimants were quite justified in refusing to take the risk of losing their capital. There was therefore no breach of the duty to mitigate.

The application of the general rule that if the claimant acts unreasonably and does not attempt to mitigate his losses, he cannot recover the extra loss he suffers as a result, can be demonstrated by a case where the problem of mitigation of damages was considered in a situation relating to the performance of monetary obligations paid in a foreign currency. In this case, the tribunal dealt with the claim for damages allegedly incurred due to a change in currency value. The point of departure in his decision was the statement that the currency in which the debt was to be paid fluctuated because the rate of exchange was freely determined on the money market and the creditor was not entitled to expect that the exchange rate would remain stable and that consequently he would not sustain a loss of exchange.

The tribunal held in this case that obtaining a guaranty against exchange rate fluctuations (*Kurssicherungsgeschäft*) could have minimized the foreseeable risk of depreciation of the currency of payment. Such a guaranty could have been obtained for periods ranging from one day to five years. A domestic creditor is expected to hedge against the risk of the exchange rate, which entails relatively minor expenses. This also applied to the claimant in the present case, involving imports from East Africa. It was judged possible to foresee, not only that the currency would continue to decline, but also that a delay in the delivery of the goods might occur. To that extent, the claimant had a duty to mitigate damages. The claimant did not comply with this duty and had to bear the loss, which, incidentally, had become noticeably less as a result of the recovery of the exchange rate of the currency at a later stage.[29]

Another example of what was considered to be reasonable inactivity not contrary to the mitigation approach was found in an investment dispute involving a private investor and a host state. In this case, the argument of the state respondent that the claimant could have resumed its activities after the lifting of the ban which prohibited its activities in the host country was considered not to be persuasive by the tribunal. The tribunal was of the opinion that the investor, who had been subjected to a revocation of the essential licence for its investment activity three years earlier, had good reason to decide that, after that experience, it should not continue with the investment activity, after which the activity could be resumed.[30]

In another investment dispute where a foreign investor lost its licence to engage in business ventures in the host country, the state respondent contended before the tribunal that the investor could still have sold its interests in investment contracts to a third party and should indeed have done so to mitigate any loss sustained due to the decision to terminate its licence. It was said that both Indonesian and international law pointed to such a duty to mitigate. The investor did not contest that applicable national law and international law both acknowledged the principle of mitigation, but claimed that there was no realistic prospect of its being able to mitigate its loss. Finding that the assignment of corresponding interests was subject to limitations and certain relevant events that took place, the tribunal came to the conclusion that it would have been virtually impossible for the investor/claimant to find interested purchasers and held there was no failure on the part of the investor to mitigate damages.[31]

On the other hand, in another case[32] the tribunal found that the sudden, unexpected interruption of deliveries to the claimant caused harm to it, which took the form of difficulties in adapting to a new situation requiring changes in manufacturing arrangements during a period of time. But in the absence of indications as to the efforts and attempts made by the claimant during the alleged year of inactivity, the tribunal, considering whether the claimant took necessary steps to mitigate harm, held that the commercial inactivity of the claimant was caused in part by its inertia.

The circumstances surrounding the performance of the transaction can indicate that inactivity of an aggrieved party does not result in violation of the duty to mitigate damages. Subjective circumstances are taken into account to the extent of relieving an impecunious plaintiff from incurring expenditure, provided that such a situation does not betoken a reprehensible abdication of commercial responsibility on entering into the contractual adventure.[33]

The question of exactly when it is necessary for the aggrieved party to make the substitute contract is answered in some legal systems more or less directly. English law takes the position that it follows from the principle on which the "duty" of mitigation is based, namely that the duty will normally arise only when the claimant has become aware of the breach.[34] In the United States, the approach in dealing with this question, supported by relevant rules of the UCC and case law, is that the injured party is expected to act promptly after learning that the other party's performance will not be forthcoming.[35]

Arbitration practice unequivocally shows that, from a procedural point of view, reference to mitigation is ordinarily made by the respondent on whom rests the burden of proving that the claimant failed to mitigate avoidable damages by reasonable measures.

3. EVOLUTION OF THE RULE IN INTERNATIONAL INSTRUMENTS

The rules about mitigation of damages have recently appeared in a number of international documents produced for the purpose of unifying the legal regulation of international commerce. Among them are legal texts which have a different legal character, namely the instruments with binding effect, as well as those that are sources of so called "soft law".

Article 77 of the UN Convention on International Sale of Goods (CISG) provides that a party who relies on a breach of contract must take such measures as are reasonable in the circumstances to mitigate the loss, including loss of profit, resulting from the breach. It stipulates further that if he fails to take such measures, the party in breach may claim a reduction in the damages in the amount by which the loss should have been mitigated.

The case law on the application of this article collected in UNCITRAL CLOUT gives examples which facilitate a better understanding of the range of relationships covered by the article. As an example, in a court decision it was stated that if an aggrieved party does not request damages, whether by way of an affirmative claim or by way of set-off, Article 77 does not apply.[36]

In another case, the court with reference to the authority of the parties (Article 6 of CISG) to derogate from or vary the formula set out in Article 77, concluded that if an aggrieved party seeks to enforce a penalty clause in the contract, Article 77 does not require the aggrieved party to reduce the penalty in order to mitigate the loss.[37]

Addressing the question concerning the point in a legal proceeding at which the issue of mitigation must be considered by a court, the answer to which question is not provided in Article 77, the court, in one decision, concluded that the issue of whether mitigation should be considered in a proceeding on the merits or in a separate proceeding to determine damages was a procedural issue governed by domestic law rather than by the Convention.[38]

Article 77 does not expressly state when the aggrieved party must take measures to mitigate. Several decisions referred to in the UNCITRAL Digest of Case Law on CISG state that an aggrieved party is not obligated to mitigate in the period before the contract is avoided (i.e. at a time when each party may require the other to perform).[39] If an aggrieved party does take measures, however, he must do so within a reasonable time under the circumstances. In one of these decisions, the court found that the seller's resale of goods to a third party two months after they had been rejected, was reasonable within the context of the fashion industry.[40] In another case, it was found that the buyer's purchase of substitute goods approximately two weeks after the seller declared that it would not perform was not a failure to mitigate, even though the price in a volatile market had risen sharply.[41] It should be mentioned also that in this case the transaction was characterized as highly speculative.

Article 77 provides that the breaching party may claim a reduction in the damages to be awarded to the aggrieved party in the amount by which reasonable mitigation measures would have reduced the loss to the aggrieved party. The practice of applying this provision indicates that sometimes the reduction was calculated without specific reference to the loss that could have been avoided. In one case, in an award the tribunal found that the aggrieved buyer who failed to mitigate should be entitled only to 50 percent of the difference between the contract price and the price the buyer received when it resold the non-conforming goods to its customers.[42] In another arbitral award, the tribunal divided the loss between the aggrieved buyer and the breaching seller who was claiming payment for partial delivery because of the buyer's failure to mitigate damages.[43]

Since Article 77 does not explicitly require an aggrieved party to notify the other party of proposed steps to mitigate losses, it is worth mentioning one decision where lack of such notice led to the conclusion that the claimant lost the right to be awarded damages, which could have been avoided if the notice to the other party had been given. In this case, the buyer was denied compensation for the cost of translating a manual where the buyer had failed to notify the seller on the ground that if the buyer had done so, the seller could have supplied existing translations.[44]

Article 77 does not directly address the problem concerning which party bears the burden of pleading the failure to mitigate. This is probably one of the reasons why different approaches have emerged in dealing with this question in practice. In an arbitration case, it has been stated that the tribunal should review *ex officio* whether the aggrieved party complied with its duty to mitigate, but that the breaching party had the burden of establishing failure to comply.[45] On the other hand, the court addressing this question stated that no adjustment to damages would be made if the breaching party fails to indicate what steps the other party should have taken to mitigate.[46] The results of analysis of the current practice of applying Article 77 prompt the conclusion that decisions on who has the ultimate burden of establishing failure to mitigate consistently place the burden of establishing the failure of the amount of consequent loss on the breaching party.[47]

It is interesting to note that the idea of the contributory negligence of the aggrieved party, which reflects the traditional approach of continental civil law to the problem of mitigating damages, is also included in the CISG. Namely, Article 80 provides that a party may not rely on a failure of the other party to perform, to the extent that such failure was caused by the first party's act or omission.

The UNIDROIT Principles contain a separate Article 7.4.8 dealing with mitigation of harm, which reads as follows:

"1. The non-performing party is not liable for harm suffered by the aggrieved party to the extent that the harm could have been reduced by the latter party's taking reasonable steps.

"2. The aggrieved party is entitled to recover any expenses reasonably incurred in attempting to reduce the harm."

In this connection, it is useful to consider the Official Comments to the UNIDROIT Principles, since they play an important role in identifying the reasons and the logic of including in this informal codification a particular rule reflecting an internationally accepted general approach. The Comment to the above-mentioned article describes the duty of an aggrieved party to mitigate harm. The purpose of this article is to avoid the aggrieved party's passively sitting back and waiting to be compensated for harm which it could have avoided or reduced. Any harm that the aggrieved party could have avoided by taking reasonable steps will not be compensated. Evidently, a party who has already suffered the consequences of non-performance of the contract cannot in addition be required to take time-consuming and costly measures. On the other hand, it would be unreasonable from an economic standpoint to permit compensation for an increase in harm, which could have been reduced by taking reasonable steps. The steps to be taken by the aggrieved party may be directed either to limiting the extent of the harm – above all when there is a risk of it lasting for a long time if such steps are not taken (often they will consist in a replacement transaction: see Art. 7.4.5) – or to avoiding any increase in the initial harm.

The reduction in damages to the extent that the aggrieved party has failed to take the necessary steps to mitigate the harm must not, however, cause loss to that party. The aggrieved party may therefore recover from the non-performing party the expenses incurred by it in mitigating the harm, provided that these expenses were reasonable in the circumstances (§2).

The UNIDROIT Principles also contain the rule originating from civil law jurisdictions commonly used to deal with a situation implying the "duty" to mitigate damages. Article 7.4.7 (Harm due in part to aggrieved party) stipulates that where the harm is due in part to an act or omission of the aggrieved party, or to another event for which that party bears the risk, the amount of damages shall be reduced to the extent that these factors have contributed to the harm, having regard to the conduct of each of the parties.

Rules on mitigation of damages similar to those contained in the UNIDROIT Principles are also to be found in another informal codification of rules applying to the contracts in general: by the European Union. Article 9:505 (Reduction of Loss) of the Principles of European Contract Law includes two norms reflecting the commonly adopted approach. Making the distinction of the rule on mitigation from what may be called contributory negligence on the part of the aggrieved party, the commentary to the above-mentioned rules indicates that even where the aggrieved party has not contributed either to the non-performance or to its effects, it cannot recover for a loss it would have avoided if it had taken reasonable steps to do so. The Principles explain further that the failure to mitigate loss may arise either because the aggrieved party incurs unnecessary or unreasonable expenditures, or because it fails to take reasonable steps that would result in the reduction of loss or in offsetting gains.[48] It is also indicated that the aggrieved party will not necessarily be expected to take steps to mitigate its loss immediately when it learns of the breach; this will depend on whether its actions are reasonable in the circumstances.

END NOTES

1 G.H. Treitel, *Remedies for breach of Contract (Courses of Action Open to a Party Aggrieved),* International Encyclopedia of Comparative Law, Chapter 16, Vol. VII, Contracts in General, Arthur von Mehren / Chief Editor, 1976, pp.16-100.

2 *Bürgerliches Gesetzbuch*, § 254 par. 2.

3 See, for instance, the reference to Cass.civ 1, 29 April 1981, JCP 1982, 19730, where damages were reduced, as it was a "fault" of the creditor not to avoid loss due to the negligent performance of the debtor in *Principles of European Contract Law*, Parts I and II, prepared by the Commission on European Contract Law, edited by Ole Lando and Hugh Beale, 2000, p. 447.

4 Barry Nicholas, *French Law of Contract,* London, Butterworth, 1982, p. 226.

5 H. McGregor, *McGregor on Damages,* 17th ed., 2003, p. 217.

6 See G.H. Treitel, *The Law of Contract.* 11th ed., p. 976; E. Allan Farnsworth, *Contracts*, 3rd ed., pp. 806-807, *Restatement 2nd Contracts*, § 350, Comment, p. 127.

7 *McGregor on Damages*, p. 216.

8 Michael G. Bridge, *Mitigation of damages in contract and the meaning of avoidable loss,* Law Quarterly Review, 1989, pp. 398-399.

9 Clive M. Schmitthoff, *The Duty to Mitigate,* Journal of Business Law, 1961, pp. 362-364.

10 *Fouchard Gaillard Goldman on International Commercial Arbitration*, E. Gaillard and J. Savage eds., 1999, p. 817

11 Jean Thieffry, *Arbitration and the New Rules Applicable to International Sales Contracts under the United Nations Convention,* Arbitration International, Vol. 4 No. 1, 1988, p. 56.

12 *Middle East Cement Shipping and Handling Co. v. Republic of Egypt.* Award of 12 April 2002 in ICSID case No. ARB/99/6.

13 Award in case *Watkins-Johnson v. Iran* (No. 370 (429-370-1) 28 July 1989), *Yearbook Commercial Arbitration*, Vol. XV, 1990, p. 224.

14 Marc Blessing, *The New International Arbitration Law in Switzerland: A Significant Step Towards Liberalism,* Journal of International Arbitration, Vol. 5 No. 2, 1988, p. 61. See also Vanessa L.D. Wilkinson, *The New Lex Mercatoria Reality or Academic Fantasy?* Journal of International Arbitration, Vol. 12 No. 2, 1995, p. 110.

15 UN Compensation Commission, Governing Council, Eighth Session, Geneva, 14-18 December 1992, (S/AC.26/1992/15, 4 January 1993).

16 Schmitthoff, *The Duty to Mitigate,* p. 364.

17 G.H. Treitel, *The Law of Contract*, p. 977, Farnsworth, p. 809.

18 *Restatement 2nd Contracts*, § 350, Comment, p.128.

19 Arbitration Institute of the Stockholm Chamber of Commerce, Interim award of 17 July 1992 and final award of 13 July 1993, *Yearbook Commercial Arbitration*, A.J. van den Berg (ed.), Vol. XXII, 1997, pp. 197-210.

20 Final Award of 13 July 1998, *Yearbook Commercial Arbitration*, A.J. van den Berg (ed.), Vol. XXV, 2000, p. 216.

21 Partial Award in case No. 8782 of 1997, International Chamber of Commerce (ICC) Amsterdam, The Netherlands, *Yearbook Commercial Arbitration*, A.J. van den Berg (ed.), Vol. XXVIII, 2003, p. 39.

22 ICC Partial Award in case No. 5073 of 1986, *Yearbook Commercial Arbitration*, A.J. van den Berg (ed.), Vol. XIII, 1988, pp. 53-68.

23 *Restatement 2nd. Contracts*, § 350, Comment, p. 129.

24 G.H. Treitel, *Remedies for Breach of Contract*, pp. 16-103.

25 G.H. Treitel, *The Law of Contract*, p. 978.

26 *Restatement 2nd, Contracts*, § 350, Comment, ibid.

27 ICC Award (Second Partial Award) in case No. 7110 (1998), www.unilex, info.

28 ICC Final Award in case No. 5418 of 1987, *Yearbook Commercial Arbitration*, A.J. van den Berg (ed.), Vol. XIII, 1988, pp. 91-103.

29 Arbitral Tribunal of Hamburg Friendly Arbitration. Award of May 2 1977, *Yearbook Commercial Arbitration*, P. Sanders (ed.), Vol. IV, 1979, pp. 202-202.

30 *Middle East Cement Shipping and Handling Co. v. Republic of Egypt.*

31 ICSID Final Award of 5 June 1990 in case No. ARB/81/8 and Decision on Supplemental Decision and Rectification of 17 October 1990, *Yearbook Commercial Arbitration*, A.J. van den Berg (ed.), Vol. XVII, 1992, pp. 73-105.

32 Final Award in case 8817, ICC International Court of Arbitration Bulletin, Vol. 10 No. 2 , Fall 1999, pp. 77-78.

33 Michael G. Bridge, *Mitigation of damages in contract and the meaning of avoidable loss*, pp. 399-400.

34 G.H. Treitel, *The Law of Contract*, ibidem.

35 Farnsworth, p. 810.

36 CLOUT case No. 424 [Oberster Gerichtshof, Austria, 9 March 2000].

37 Reference in the *UNCITRAL Digest of Case Law on the United Nations Convention on International Sale of Goods* (A/CN.9SER.C/Digest/CISG/77) to Hof Arnhem, the Netherlands, 22 August 1995, Unilex (validity of penalty clause determined under national law).

38 CLOUT case No. 271 [Bundesgerichtshof, Germany, 24 March 1999] (applying German law).

39 CLOUT case No. 361 (Oberlandesgericht Braunschweig, Germany, 28 October 1999), CLOUT case No. 130 (Oberlandesgericht Düsseldorf, Germany, 14 January 1994).

40 CLOUT case No. 130.

41 CLOUT case No. 277 (Oberlandesgerich Hamburg, Germany, 28 February 1997).

42 CLOUT case No. 474 (Arbitration-Tribunal of International Commercial Arbitration at the Russian Federation Chamber of Commerce and Industry, award No. 54/1999 of 24 January 2000).

43 CLOUT case No. 265 (Arbitration Court attached to the Hungarian Chamber of Commerce and Industry, Hungary, 25 May 1999).

44 CLOUT case No. 343 (Landgericht Darmstadt, Germany, 9 May 2000).

45 ICC Award No. 9187, June 1999, Unilex.

46 Reference in *UNCITRAL Digest on CISG case law* (A/CN.9SER.C/Digest/CISG/77) to *FCF S.A. v. Adriafil Commerciale S.r.l.*, Bundesgericht, Switzerland, 15 September 2000, available on the Internet at http://www.bger.ch/fr/index/jurisdiction/jurisdiction-inherittemplate/jurisdiction-recht/jurisdiction-recht-urteile2000.htm.

47 *UNCITRAL Digest on CISG case law* (A/CN.9SER.C/Digest/CISG/77, § 19).

48 *Principles of European Contract Law,* p. 445.

3

The expectation model

By ***Jan Paulsson***
Partner, Freshfields Bruckhaus Deringer, France;
Council Member of the ICC Institute of World Business Law

Cole Porter's simple and yet unforgettable line, "Let's call the whole thing off!", ensured that his song lives on for generations, but it does not describe a satisfactory approach to deal with the breach of a contract.

It is all too convenient for the contract breaker. Once conditions change, performance may become more onerous, or it may become more profitable to reach a new bargain with a third party. At that point, it is unacceptable for a party wishing to escape contractual constraints to pretend that the contract has evaporated. This remains so even if that party reimburses expenses which the other may have incurred preparing for the contract. The most obvious case where this approach, which we may call the *rescission model*, would be intolerable is that of a downstream commitment to a third party; in a rising market, it may be ruinous for a buyer who is also a re-seller to be deprived of the benefit of a price set at a time when the buyer agreed to an on-sale price that has now become uncommercial.

But apart from the immediate economic loss in such circumstances, the rescission model is also intolerable because its effect is to destroy the reliability of promises. Contracts do not prove their value in stable markets. If markets were stable, each transaction might be endlessly repeated every day with unchanged terms – cash and carry; no need for contracts. The very fact that a bargain is likely to become less advantageous for one of the parties at some future time is what makes it so important that the law allows the other party to rely on its performance. To lose sight of this basic proposition would, one may say without fear of exaggeration, cause great harm to the very foundation of our economies.

In the international field, a dominant idea has for nearly a century been associated with the judgment of the Permanent Court of International Justice in the *Chorzów Factory* case,[1] namely that the victim of a breach should either be restored to its *ex ante* position or be given monetary compensation equivalent thereto. This does not tell us, however, whether the model is one of rescission or expectation. *Chorzów Factory* did not involve a breach of contract, but an expropriation without compensation. The notion of "rescinding a contract" has no meaning in such cases. And restoring a party to the financial equivalent of its position prior to an expropriation will mean to give it the value of the thing expropriated; in the case of business ventures, that value inherently reflects income-generating capacity – and therefore expected profitability.

A *locus classicus* of the expectation model in the common law is the venerable case of *Hadley v. Baxendale*, decided in 1854, where the Court of the Exchequer stated that:

> "the party breaking the contract, ... at the most, could only be supposed to have in his contemplation the amount of injury which would arise generally, and in the great multitude of cases not affected by any special circumstances, from such a breach of contract. For, had the special circumstances been known, the parties might have specially provided for the breach of contract by special terms as to the damages in that case; and of this advantage it would be very unjust to deprive them."[2]

In civil law countries, a typical formulation is that of Article 1149 of the French Civil Code, which establishes the general principle that a creditor is entitled to recover "the gain of which he was deprived". Since that gain is by definition hypothetical, here too the test must be one of legitimate expectation.

The aim of this paper is not to provide a comprehensive analysis of expectation damages; that would require a book-length treatment. The objective is rather to consider a few recurring topics, with no pretence of being systematic:
- recoverability of lost profits is a general principle
- claims for lost profits are not limited to some proportion of expenditure
- double counting and its avoidance

- the valuation of a loss of opportunity
- an illustration of the DCF method and its inherent uncertainties
- is there a role for the doctrine of abuse of right?

For illustrative purposes, I will cite extensively from a major case, *Himpurna v. PLN*, not because I happened to participate in it but because it confronts a series of important issues regarding quantum (and not just the sorry story of a party preventing an arbitrator from attending hearings, for which the case has become famous).

1. RECOVERABILITY OF LOST PROFITS IS A GENERAL PRINCIPLE

To set the stage for the rest of this paper – and perhaps to heighten anticipation of Professor Taniguchi's fuller exposition later in this programme – it may be useful to establish that the recoverability of lost profits is a general principle. It is not invalidated by the notions that *indirect, consequential* or *speculative* damages are excludable.

Adjudicators have struggled since time immemorial with the limits of compensable damages. At the one extreme are damages which demonstrably arise as the evident direct consequence of the wrongful act. At the other extreme, there are claims insufficiently established, either in fact or as a matter of causation. They are typically referred to as "too remote", "unforeseeable" or "speculative". In between there is an area of *indirect* damages that are controversial.[3]

That they may be recovered is beyond cavil. The difficulty is the permanent haze that overlies the boundary between what is *too remote* and what is merely indirect. In addition, there are contractual stipulations – or indeed treaty stipulations – that exclude the award of indirect compensation or compensation on account of lost profits. Such stipulations create their own difficulties of interpretation,[4] and moreover the risk that awards limited by them fail to be recognized as exceptions.

In principle, this passage written by Hersch Lauterpacht in 1927 has lost none of its cogency or authority:

> "The border line between direct and indirect damages, or between prospective and merely speculative profits, is seldom clear, and its determination is often dependent upon the subjective estimate of the arbitrator, who is, in fact, guided not so much by the technical distinctions between different kinds of damages, as by the wish, perfectly justified in law, to afford full redress to the injured. But to maintain that international law disregards altogether compensation for *lucrum cessans* is as repellant to justice and common sense, as it is out of accord with the practice of international tribunals."[5]

Courts and tribunals everywhere have understood that uncertainty about lost profits, since they are necessarily hypothetical, cannot allow the contract-breaker to escape liability. The important distinction to be made is between the question of whether the victim suffered loss at all and the question of the magnitude of a loss once it is established in principle. An excellent formulation may be found in a well-known case decided by a US federal court of appeal in 2002:

> "Evidence to establish [lost] profits must not be uncertain or speculative. This rule does not apply to uncertainty or speculation as to the *amount* of the profits which would have been derived, but to uncertainty or speculation as to whether the loss of profits was the *result* of the [breach] and whether any such profits would have been derived at all."[6]

This proposition may be usefully coupled with the admirable formulation of Art. 42 of the Swiss Code of Obligations to the effect that a loss "not ascertainable by calculation is determined by the judge at his discretion, having regard to the ordinary course of events and measures taken by the injured party".

Another way of putting this is that contractual morality requires that the risk of uncertainty should not fall on the victim of breach.

2. CLAIMS FOR LOST PROFITS ARE NOT LIMITED TO SOME PROPORTION OF EXPENDITURE

It is over-simplistic for a defendant to argue that claims should be dismissed as extravagant if they are in some sense disproportionate to the capital invested. As the arbitral tribunal in *Himpurna* reasoned:

"The trouble with this conclusion is that it applies to circumstances when the value of a contract is subject to the vagaries of all forms of risk, including the commercial risks of market share and price fluctuations, currency and inflation risks, and the risks of governmental interference. When these risks are extant, the notion of some form of proportionality – i.e. a sense of a 'normal' return on invested capital – may make sense. But the [Energy Supply Contract] in this case explicitly excluded each of these risks. That left only the far less troublesome risks of production, which on the evidence have to a large extent been resolved: the Claimant was able to mobilize the capital necessary to conduct operations and to build the physical plant; the Claimant had the know-how to generate electricity from the field; and the reservoir contained substantial energy resources – albeit debatable as to their volume – capable of sustaining production over the 30-year life of the purchase obligation. Indeed, these conclusions are conceded by PLN [the respondent] and its expert witnesses."[7]

The well-known *Aminoil* award is sometimes invoked as support for the proposition that the proper measure of recovery is that of "a reasonable rate of return" as opposed to the demonstrable profit stream from the particular venture that has been interrupted. Such reliance is misplaced. For while it is true that the *Aminoil* award applied such a standard (and on that basis rejected the claim based on a 30-year projection of profits under the relevant concession agreement), this was the consequence of that arbitral tribunal's having found that the parties had in fact "adopted" the standard of a reasonable rate of return in seeking to adjust the terms of their agreement in order to conform with an accord reached in 1974 between the Gulf States to harmonize their tax and royalty rates.[8] The tribunal was careful not to be seen to be making general pronouncements: " … the determination of the amount of an award of 'appropriate' compensation is better carried out by means of an enquiry into all the circumstances relevant to the particular concrete case, than through abstract theoretical discussion."[9]

The "relevant circumstances" in the *Aminoil* case – apart from the parties' mutual adoption of the reasonable-rate-of-return standard – included the fact that the concession agreement had been in force since 1948; by the date of the award 34 years later, the factors of risk, and reward for risk, were to a large degree played out. Recognizing the relevance of these features of the *Aminoil* precedent, the Tribunal in *Himpurna* concluded:

> "The significant controversies with respect to lost profits therefore relate to the quantities that should be deemed to be covered by PLN's take-or-pay obligations, and the discount rate that should be applied to the future income stream. To the extent that the claim is based on production volumes that appear certain, the issue of proportionality to invested capital does not arise; the lost profits flow directly from the contractual allocation of risk."[10]

3. DOUBLE COUNTING AND ITS AVOIDANCE

It is sometimes said that there are two kinds of lawyers: those who can count and those who cannot.

Like most jokes about lawyers, this is, of course, wicked and unfair, but it must be admitted that what one occasionally hears and reads about the danger of double counting when contemplating a combination of *damnum emergens* and *lucrum cessans* suggests that some lawyers are in urgent need of remedial education.

The central idea is surpassingly simple. Once there is an award of *damnum emergens*, there must be a corresponding debit before any *lucrum cessans* is recoverable.

To put it another way, if a tribunal begins with *lucrum cessans* and awards every bit of it, there is no room for *damnum emergens*. This is because *damnum emergens* represents the sunk costs of the victim of the breach, and *it would never have been recovered if there had been no breach*. This is no different from saying that if you lose a house that has a market value of $300,000, your loss is indeed $300,000 – and not $500,000 – because you originally paid $200,000 for it.

International tribunals may prefer to begin with *damnum emergens* for the very good reason that it relates to historical reality and may be proved by unquestionable written evidence of payments made and confirmed. Since *lucrum cessans* is, as a result of the breach, hypothetical (whether one considers the past that never was or the future which will never be), it is therefore awarded only if there is proof that profits would indeed be greater than sunk costs. (Further refinements may be necessary for costs of interim financing, staggered investments, taxes, and the like.)

This approach is illustrated by the following passage from the final award in *Himpurna*, which may be worth reproducing at some length:

> "In addition to asking for an award in the amount of unpaid invoices, the Claimant proceeds conventionally to quantify its damages under two headings, reflecting wasted costs and lost profits, respectively. The former, traditionally referred to as *damnum emergens*, represents the aggregate of what the Claimant lists as "capital invested and expended"; to this amount, the Claimant seeks to add interest. The latter, traditionally spoken of as *lucrum cessans*, assigns a present value to the expected future revenue stream; the nominal amounts are thus decreased by applying two discount rates: one reflecting the time value of money (i.e. the notion that a dollar to be received in the future is worth less than a dollar received today), the other a risk premium."

The conceptual approach is unremarkable and has been followed in countless international arbitrations.[11]

An initial general enquiry relates to the standard by which the Arbitral Tribunal should judge whether the amounts put forward are sufficiently reliable. In this respect, the Arbitral Tribunal turns to Asser's Handbook, the same Dutch authority on which [...] PLN's expert on Indonesian law was content to rely:

> "The creditor who demands compensation must claim, and if necessary prove, that the debtor is responsible for the damages caused by his non-performance ... If the debtor denies that damages have occurred due to his non-performance, the creditor has to prove them unless the judge, as is often the case, assumes that damages will naturally arise in the context of such non-fulfilment; it is then up to the debtor to rebut this assumption and to show that no damages have occurred. Similarly, if the amount of the damages claimed is disputed, the creditor must prove the amount. In determining the amount of damages the judge is not bound by the rules of evidence."[12]

In this case as in so many others, it is impossible to establish damages as a matter of scientific certainty. This does not, however, impede the course of justice. "It is well settled that the fact that damages cannot be settled with certainty is no reason not to award damages when a loss has been incurred."[13]

Approximations are inevitable. Moreover, considerations of fairness enter into the picture, to be assessed – inevitably – by reference to particular circumstances. The fact that the Arbitral Tribunal is influenced in this respect by equitable factors does not mean that it shirks the discipline of deciding on the basis of legal obligations. The *Sapphire* award was based on "general principles of law" but nevertheless decided *ex æquo et bono* when assessing damages.[14] And as the *Aminoil* award held: "It is well known that any estimate in purely monetary terms of amounts intended to express the value of an asset, of an undertaking, of a contract, or of services rendered, must take equitable principles into account."[15]

The *Sapphire* and *Aminoil* awards were on the firm footing of significant international precedents. The International Court of Justice in 1956 rejected a challenge against the judgment of an administrative tribunal which had awarded damages *ex æquo et bono*, finding no intent "to depart from principles of law" but rather the consequence of the fact that "the precise determination of the actual amount to be awarded could not be based on any specific rule of law."[16] The ICJ made the point even more limpidly in its judgment in the *North Sea Continental Shelf* case in 1969:

> "... in short, it is not a question of applying equity simply as a matter of abstract justice, but of applying a rule of law which itself requires the application of equitable principles."[17]

With respect to the evaluation of financial data, some introductory observations of a general nature may serve to clarify the Arbitral Tribunal's approach.

When a DCF method for evaluating damages in the context of a contractual breach is followed, any comparisons with precedents involving the evaluation of expropriated business ventures must be made with great care. In the latter situation, there is generally no basis to apply the *contractual* reliance damages (*damnum emergens*), but only the expectancy damages (*lucrum cessans*). An undertaking has been expropriated; the prejudice suffered by its former owner is simply the worth of the venture as a going concern. That worth is crystallised in an analysis that discounts the future revenue stream of the enterprise to establish its present value. Leaving aside special considerations justifying higher recovery in the case of *wrongful* expropriation,[18] there is no separate evaluation of sunk costs, whether or not represented by physical assets. That the Claimant has been dispossessed of the walls and machinery of a factory does not lead to a separate recovery on that account. Had there been no expropriation, past investments would have been recovered through subsequent revenues. Since those revenues are fully accounted for in the DCF going-concern evaluation, an award of lost investment as well would be an unacceptable double recovery.

In contractual cases such as this, it is usual that claimants seek recoupment of their entire investment as a discrete element of compensation. Claimants are on solid ground when they ask to be reimbursed monies they have actually spent in reliance on the contract; recovery of lost future profits is less certain. The value of the asset taken in an expropriation case may be higher or lower than the amounts the claimant expended in developing the asset. (Positive subsequent developments such as improved market conditions, or successful exploration campaigns, may have resulted in a higher value; negative developments such as failed exploration campaigns, or a fall in price, may have had the opposite effect.) In the case of a breach of contract, the wasted cost is what the claimant has spent in reliance on the agreement, without reference to how judicious or providential those expenditures turned out to be. No further explanation is necessary to understand why victims of contractual breaches tend first and foremost to articulate a plea for *damnum emergens*.

On this footing, however, the quantification of lost profits must result in a lower amount to avoid double counting. This is so because future net cash flow generally includes all the amortisation of investment there will ever be. To ask for the full amount of the future revenue stream when also claiming recoupment of all investments is wanting to have your cake and eat it too. If the DCF method is applied in a contractual scenario to measure nothing but net cash flows (thus excluding the accrual accounting notion of "income" which may cover non-cash items such as depreciation), there is no room for recovery of wasted costs. In other words, when the victim of a breach of contract seeks recovery of sunken costs, confident that it is entitled to its *damnum*, it may go on to seek lost profits only with the proviso that its computations reduce future net cash flows by allowing a proper measure of amortisation.[19]

4. THE VALUATION OF A LOSS OF OPPORTUNITY

A loss of opportunity (or chance) is a sub-category of lost profits where not only the magnitude but even the *existence* of monetary prejudice is doubtful. Ordinarily, this would be viewed as a matter of speculation and therefore not lead to recovery at all. What distinguishes this category of damages and rescues the claimant's prospects for recovery is that the possibility of profits itself has a value. The paradigm case is *Sapphire*,[20] which involved the cancellation of rights to explore and exploit any hydrocarbon resources found in a specific area. At the time of the breach, there was no way of knowing whether there would be any discovery of commercial value. Yet the chance itself had a value; a third party would have paid something for the licensee's rights.

But how does one measure that value? A one-dollar gambling chip may entail a chance to win a one-million dollar jackpot. The loss of the chip is therefore the loss of a chance to win one million. Yet there is no need to get into complicated probability calculations. The value of the lost chip is one dollar, because that is what it costs to buy another one.

Does that not mean that Sapphire's loss of a chance was represented by what it had spent to date in acquiring the license? If so, are we wrong in viewing this as a sub-category of lost profits, if the remedy is simply reimbursement of the wasted costs?

The answer to both questions is no. Just as the value of a one-dollar gambling chip may be less than one dollar if the word gets out that Fredo Corleone is running the casino, and just as its value will rise as gamblers are carried away in the frenzy of a compulsive intuition that the interval since the last jackpot has become abnormally long, so too events and information subsequent to the expenditure to procure a chance – e.g. Sapphire's license – have an impact on the value of the chance. If the price of oil goes up or down, the value of the license does too. (This is but another way of saying that the amount in the jackpot is *not* a stable one million.) If the government announces that it will grant no more licenses anywhere, the attraction of the *existing* license will tend to make it more valuable; and so also licenses in neighbouring countries.

5. AN ILLUSTRATION OF THE DCF METHOD AND ITS INHERENT UNCERTAINTIES

With respect to the DCF method, the *Himpurna* award reasoned as follows, explicitly recognizing the approximative nature of its outcome:

> "There was an air of unreality with respect to both Parties' arguments with respect to the DCF method. Each appeared determined to deny the undeniable; the Claimant seemed to ignore studiously that it had embarked on a venture in Indonesia, and PLN that it had signed a firm undertaking to pay in US dollars.
>
> "Thus, although one can hardly fault Professor Ruback's evidence [for the Claimant] as a matter of abstract financial analysis it was of limited value in this case.
>
> "His opinion was rightly offered on a hypothesis excluding breach. It would be improper for PLN to obtain a reduction of its debt by invoking a risk that it would violate its own contractual undertakings. Those undertakings include a provision to compensate for the effect upon the Claimant of any Governmental action to alter 'taxes or other exactions' (Section 5.5 of the Contract), and a force majeure clause which maintains PLN's obligations notwithstanding acts of Government. The Parties thus find themselves in a situation similar to that examined by the Iran-US Claims Tribunal in the *Philipps Petroleum* award, which accepted a DCF analysis and stated that there should be no reduction in the value placed on the venture on account of 'threats of expropriation or from other actions by the Respondents related thereto'."[21]

But the principle that PLN cannot reduce the amount of its liability by affirming the likelihood that it would not perform the contract goes only so far. Nor is it conclusive to say, as the Claimant justifiably does, that it negotiated a rigorous contract which protects the ESC revenue stream unconditionally. The fact remains that it is riskier to enter into a 30-year venture in Indonesia than in more mature economies. And it is no answer to say that the contract has allocated 99% of the risk to the Indonesian side. After all, there are documents which by their terms allot 100% of the risk to the debtor: bonds. Although they may be denominated in US dollars, although they may stipulate absolute obligations to pay, it still makes a difference whether the issuer is Switzerland or Swaziland.

Mr Cheng, on the other extreme, justified his high (47.8%) "risk-free rate" for investments in Indonesia by reference to a number of factors specific to his notion of the relevant country risk. (It should be understood that a risk-free rate is one which needs to be offered if one is to purge a capital placement of the perception of risk. Mr Cheng was very insistent on the point that the risk-free rate is not to be equated with the discount rate, which he ultimately believes should be 33.7%, because it derives from what he called a Weighted Average Cost of Capital calculation; transcript: 1236. In any event, risk factors clearly affect either figure.) His computations were unfortunately not only complex, but also obscure, as were his oral explanations. The Arbitral Tribunal concedes that it struggled unsuccessfully with his evidence, but has the impression that the same may also be true for the authors of both Parties' post-hearing briefs. Given the obvious competence with which Mr Cheng addressed other topics, the explanation for his impenetrable testimony with regard to the DCF issue may be that he had determined to seek to defend an indefensible thesis. The simple fact is that a dollar-denominated debt, even if it is owed by an Indonesian party, is not burdened with the full macula of the country risk; the factor of currency depreciation is removed.

To put it in a nutshell, PLN has failed to convince the Arbitral Tribunal that a US dollar paid from Indonesia is worth less than a US dollar paid in New York.

Nor does it avail PLN to stress repeatedly, as it does, the "probabilistic" nature of the estimates of the steam field reserves, as well as the risk of premature exhaustion or depletion through drilling. Given the fact that the Arbitral Tribunal has adopted reservoir estimates substantially inferior to the ones proposed by PLN's own expert, these risks must be put out of mind as amply covered by a generous margin of error. The Arbitral Tribunal is persuaded that the reservoir is more than twice as voluminous as what is necessary to justify its award.

On the other hand, PLN has raised a series of valid doubts to the effect that revenues could be diminished by, *inter alia*:

- a disruption, for technical or other reasons, of the rate of installation of Units;
- volcanic or hydrothermal eruptions;

- technical disputes as to the application of the price formula (for example, reference to a Unit Rate Capacity test in the absence of an operational Mechanical Gas Extractor could exaggerate the URC and thus the price);

and costs could be increased by, *inter alia*:

- unanticipated expenditures on account of such problems as scaling due to the chemical composition of brine affecting the state of pipes, wells and turbine blades; or the need to drill more so-called make-up wells than anticipated in order to maintain the steamfield pressure;
- insufficient clarity in the Claimant's computations as to the breakdown of costs in rupiah as opposed to US dollars.

Weighing the factors discussed [above] as well as the consideration – favourable to the Claimant – of the relative maturity and promise of the Dieng project, the Arbitral Tribunal holds that the most appropriate discount rate is 19%. The arbitrators make no pretence that this is the result of precise weighings of the discrete considerations that have influenced the arbitrators; nor do they wish to create the illusion that they have engaged in econometric modelling, or even calibrated costs and revenues with a time line that establishes hypotheses for the commissioning of generating Units, contingencies of reservoir evolution, and the like. Both the rate and its application reflect a series of adjustments made by the arbitrators in their equitable assessment of the evidence, and, in the circumstances of this case, resolving all doubts in favour of PLN, the debtor.

The Arbitral Tribunal is not aware of any instances of international arbitral tribunals carrying out their own DCF computations to replace those presented by one of the parties. Indeed, in the case of *Phillips Petroleum*, although the award clearly accepted the DCF methodology and contained a sophisticated discussion of its application in the context of a "careful and realistic appraisal of the revenue-producing potential of the asset" including levels of production, costs, taxes, other charges, prices, and risks,[22] Chamber Two of the Iran-US Claims Tribunal explicitly stated that it "does not intend to make its own DCF analysis with revised components, but rather to determine and identify the extent to which it agrees or disagrees with the estimates of both Parties and their experts concerning all these elements of valuation,"[23] and that in particular it would not "substitute the Claimant's discount rate with its own".[24]

It may be objected that this approach exposes the ostensible adoption of the DCF method as something of a fig leaf. Indeed, it is difficult to connect the criticisms raised by the tribunal in the *Phillips Petroleum* case against the claimant's computations with the lump sum announced as the result of that Chamber's having taken account, in the traditional formulation, of "all relevant circumstances".[25] True enough, the tribunal identified two kinds of factor that affected its view of the DCF calculation, namely general "equitable considerations"[26] and "verification" by means of an alternative valuation method[27] that looked to tangible investments and historic earnings. Nevertheless, it is legitimate to ask whether the result, in that case and often elsewhere, is not to create an illusion of scientific analysis to mask the reality of subjective approximations.

To be fair, there is nothing new under the sun. *Lucrum cessans* has always been an inexact science. As the arbitral tribunal put it in the *Delagoa Bay* case almost exactly one century ago, "such a computation made in advance on the basis of purely theoretical data cannot hope to be absolutely accurate but only comparatively likely".[28]

The present Arbitral Tribunal wishes to be transparent in both its reasoning and its computations, fully recognizing the limitations of an exercise where risks, costs, and revenues are conjectural, controversial, and imperfectly synchronized. The Arbitral Tribunal has followed three lodestars: (i) the DCF method is adopted in accordance with the understanding articulated above in paragraphs 438-448; (ii) the Claimant must bear the burden of demonstrating the validity of its hypotheses; (iii) the infirmities perceived by the Arbitral Tribunal with respect to those hypotheses have resulted in a recomputation which the arbitrators fully realize is imprecise, but which seeks to avoid arbitrariness by compelling a thorough consideration of all relevant factors, all the while being conscious of erring, whenever imprecision is inevitable, in favour of PLN. Thus doubts have been resolved equitably in favour of the debtor.

There is no reason to apologize for the fact that this approach involves approximations; they are inherent and inevitable. Nor can it be criticized as unrealistic or unbusinesslike; it is precisely how business executives must, and do, proceed when they evaluate a going concern. The fact that they use ranges and estimates does not imply abandonment of the discipline of economic analysis; nor, when adopted by the arbitrators, does this method imply abandonment of the discipline of assessing the evidence before them.[29]

6. IS THERE A ROLE FOR THE DOCTRINE OF ABUSE OF RIGHT?

In *Himpurna*, the arbitral tribunal was faced with a claim for many hundreds of millions of dollars representing profits lost on investments *not yet made*, but which nevertheless would have yielded a reliable income stream given the fixed quantities that had to be paid – in hard currency – on a take-or-pay basis. The tribunal was unwilling to allow that part of the claim, reasoning as follows:

> "True enough, damages for the loss of a bargain may in principle be granted even when the victim of a breach has not yet incurred significant costs. The *Sapphire* award provides an illustration. It arose from an oil concession agreement which had entered into effect in July 1958 but was held to have been breached by the National Iranian Oil Company within a matter of months, i.e. during an early stage of exploration and before any drilling, let alone extraction or sale. An expert called by the claimant gave his opinion that at most Sapphire might have made profits of US$ 46 million, but that if there were no commercial quantities it might have lost US$ 8 million. In addition to compensation for its limited costs during the short life of the contract, the sole arbitrator, fixing the quantum '*ex æquo et bono* by considering all the circumstances',[30] awarded the claimant a lump sum of US$ 2 million for its loss of chance, reducing the claimed amount of US$ 5 million because of uncertainties concerning the magnitude of oil reserves as well as the economic risks over the 25-year life of the concession."

But there are fundamental differences between the *Sapphire* agreement and the ESC. First of all, one can hardly overlook the fact that the Claimant seeks to be made whole for all of its expenditures, and to recoup a return thereon calculated over 30 years, before even getting to the issue of loss of bargain on investments not yet made at the date of the breach. In *Sapphire*, if the sole arbitrator had not allowed the latter head of recovery he would in fact have tolerated a breach with impunity; i.e. he would have allowed the defendant to put itself in the claimant's shoes merely by paying off its actual costs. And even more fundamentally, whereas in *Sapphire* the foreign investor had entered into the agreement on the basis of producing oil for export on the world markets, in the present case it was explicitly understood that the only purchaser for the energy produced would be PLN. In such circumstances, it strikes the Arbitral Tribunal as unacceptable to assess lost profits as though the Claimant had an unfettered right to create ever-increasing losses for the State of Indonesia (and its people) by generating energy without any regard to whether or not PLN had any use for it. Even if such a right may be said to derive from explicit contractual terms, the Arbitral Tribunal cannot fail to be struck by the fact that the Claimant is seeking to turn the ESC into an astonishing bargain in circumstances when performance of the Contract would be ruinous to the Respondent. (A US$ 2.3 billion return – including the unpaid invoices – would represent a 630% profit on a US$ 315 million investment.) What troubles the Arbitral Tribunal is less the level of profitability in and of itself than its contrast with the losses facing PLN. To extract the full benefit of the hard terms of the ESC with respect to investments *not yet made*, in a situation where that benefit will clearly exacerbate the already great losses of the cocontractant, strikes the Arbitral Tribunal as likely to constitute an abuse of right inconsistent with the duty of good faith that is fundamental to the Indonesian law of obligations.[31]

In an article published last year,[32] Professor Gotanda wrote that *Himpurna* misapplied the abuse of rights doctrine because:

> "It is not, as the tribunal stated, a general principle of private international law that precludes the awarding of lost profits whenever awarding such profits would cause a severe financial hardship to the party that has breached the contract."

Perhaps *Himpurna* misapplied the law, but certainly not for this reason. The award contains no statement like the one alleged by Professor Gotanda. To the contrary, the award cites *Socobelge* for the proposition that even extreme macroeconomic crises do not overcome explicit contractual undertakings. Both *damnum emergens* and *lucrum cessans* were awarded on account of breach. The doctrine of abuse of right was invoked because the claimant also had a contractual right to make *future* investments under terms which would have been ruinous for Indonesia. For every dollar spent by the investor, Indonesia would lose multiple dollars. For this purely executory part of the contract (i.e. future stages where there had been no investment at all), the tribunal found it would be an abuse of right to insist on pursuing a disastrous programme only to collect damages not yet incurred.

This may be debated, but the debate is unproductive if it is uninformed. Himpurna's approach is more completely understood if one considers the following additional passage in the award:

> "... in this matter [the Arbitral Tribunal] will apply the doctrine of abuse of right as an element of overriding substantive law proper to the international arbitral process. This is not an elaborate body of law. It has been applied notably when arbitral tribunals have upheld the principle of the autonomy of the arbitration clause[33] or refused to accept that a State invoke its internal law as an impediment to its consent to arbitration.[34] In *Benteler v. Belgium*, the arbitral tribunal considered that the rule had acquired the status of 'a substantive rule of private international law the observance of which is obligatory in international arbitration'.[35] Professor Böckstiegel has put it thus: 'where the state or one of its public entities has accepted an arbitration clause, it is considered as *part of international public policy* that they cannot later claim that they could not submit to arbitration due to their own national law'."[36]

The fact that such universal rules are few in number does not detract from their value when used to ensure the legitimacy of the international arbitral process.

In support of its inclusion in this limited corpus, it may be confidently said that the principle of abuse of rights (*abus de droit, Rechtsmissbrauch*) is universal. In his familiar study of general principles,[37] Bin Cheng devoted the entire Chapter 4 to this rule, which he also formulated in the obverse: "good faith in the exercise of rights". In the area of present interest, the doctrine has occasionally been applied to defeat the abuse of legal forms: *ex re sed non ex nomine*. Professor Böckstiegel writes that manipulation of the regime applicable to legal entities controlled by a State should not be effective to evade that State's obligations.[38]

If the general principle may be invoked *in favour* of the foreign investor so as to avoid the result that its legitimate expectations are frustrated by unworthy manoeuvres, so too, in the Arbitral Tribunal's view, may it be invoked in certain circumstances *against* claims for profits which would tend to impoverish the host State.

The principle is old; one need only recall Cicero's *summum jus, summa injuria*. To say that the blind application of a rule may lead to iniquitous results is to recognize that the search for justice would fail if the law could do no more than validate relative positions of strength, or consolidate the status quo indefinitely. Thus, the exercise of a particular right may be inhibited if it would abase the law.

The objection to the effect that this doctrine opens the door to subjective decision-making is to be taken seriously, but is not decisive. The Arbitral Tribunal notes that the Claimant has anticipated a risk of a finding of abuse of right, and argued vehemently against it, relying in particular on a treatise co-authored by a member of the Arbitral Tribunal. The Arbitral Tribunal does not believe that either Party has committed an abuse of right; rather, it wants to ensure that none occurs. It appreciates the difficulties of application to which the Claimant alludes, but believes they are surmounted in the particular facts of this case.

In the first place, the legal process necessarily depends, to some extent, on the personal convictions of the decision-maker. If this were not so, the common law could hardly accommodate the notion of implied terms, nor could the civil law give effect to the fundamental rule – reflected in Article 1338(3) of the Indonesian Civil Code – that contracts must be performed in good faith. Secondly, the principle must be applied with great prudence: only when necessary to correct obvious excess. In the present case, the advent of economic turmoil does not prevent the Claimant from seeking its *damnum emergens*; it is blameless, and entitled on a contractual basis to be made whole. Nor does this turmoil disentitle the Claimant from seeking damages reflecting the benefit of its bargain; as already affirmed, contractual morality demands that disincentives to non-performance be maintained (see § 495).

The Arbitral Tribunal believes that this is a case where the doctrine of abuse of right must be applied in favour of PLN to prevent the Claimant's undoubtedly legitimate rights from being extended beyond tolerable norms, on the grounds that it would be intolerable in the present case to uphold claims for lost profits from investment not yet incurred.

In reaching this conclusion, the Arbitral Tribunal is mindful of the status of PLN as an arm of governmental policy acting in pursuit of the public welfare. The ESC itself was not directed to the narrow ends of profitable trading but must be seen, in the words of the *Aminoil* award, as "one of the essential instruments in the economic and social progress of a national community in full process of development".[39] As noted above in distinguishing this case from *Sapphire*, the energy supplied under the ESC was not exportable; the only purchaser was PLN. To oblige PLN to foot the bill for massive future investments – in circumstances where 100% of the additional capacity supplied as a result thereof, at the contractual dollar prices, would not only have been useless but have caused direct injury – would be perverse.

Another consideration concerns the nature of the breach. The Respondent did not seek actively to dispossess the Claimant of valuable contractual rights; it has suffered helplessly from a precipitate deterioration in the macroeconomic value of a project with respect to which it had accepted the entire market risk. In this regard, this case stands in stark contrast with a number of illustrious arbitral precedents.[40]

Still, the application of the abuse of right was certainly controversial. One of the arbitrators, while not dissenting from the result as far as it went, appended a "statement" to the award in which he wrote:

> "I note that every doubt in respect of *lucrum cessans* has been determined favourably to the respondent. The imposition of a concept described as 'abuse of rights' in the absence of findings of malicious intent or lack of good faith on the part of the claimant to further reduce the entitlement to damages is in my opinion an inappropriate and unwarranted penalising of the claimant."[41]

Another approach leading to a similar result without resort to the abuse of right doctrine is reflected in ICC Award No. 7006, where the arbitral tribunal took into account the income stream of only one year beyond the breach on the footing that damages possibly arising in the course of the remaining contractual terms could have been mitigated.[42]

END NOTES

1 Factory at *Chorzów (Germany v. Poland)* (Indemnity), 1928 PCIJ (Ser. A) No. 17.

2 156 Eng. Rep. 145 (Ex 1854).

3 See the ILC Commentary under Article 36, in James Crawford, *The International Law Commission's Articles on State Responsibility: Introduction, Text and Commentaries*, Cambridge University Press, 2002, pp. 218-230.

4 Consider these hypothetical examples:

(A) Six ships are expropriated. Their replacement value is 100.

(B) A transportation company owning six ships is expropriated. It is established that a bona fide third party purchaser was prepared to purchase the company, which benefited from a portfolio of advantageous contracts, for 200.

(C) Same as B, but instead of proof of a third-party offer, there is an economically irreproachable demonstration that the going-concern value to the expropriated owners is 200.

A is not difficult. But how is B different from A? See Crawford, Articles, p. 226: *'The value of goodwill and other indicators of profitability may be uncertain, unless derived from information provided by a recent sale or acceptable arms-length offer'* (emphasis added). And if B is accepted, why not C? The demonstrable market value of a disposed asset has been accepted by international tribunals, as in the old *de Sabla* case (*US* v. *Panama*, 29 June 1933, VI RIAA 358) (proof of purchase offers for lots in Panama) and the more recent *SPP* v. *Egypt* case (*Southern Pacific Properties (Middle East) Limited* v. *Egypt*, decision on jurisdiction (No. 2), 14 April 1988, 3 ICSID Reports 131) (proof of willing purchasers of lots in the Pyramids Oasis project). But that may imply the recovery of anticipated lost profits; i.e. the purchasers are willing to go beyond the replacement value of the six ships (which are not for sale) to pay an enhanced value based on their expectations that the transportation company has demonstrable prospects of profitable operations. What then is the difference between B and C; or between enterprise value and lost profits?

5 *Private Law Sources and Analogies of International Law*, Longman, London/New York, 1927, reprinted in 2002, pp. 148-9.

6 *Kyocera v. Prudential-Bache*, 299 F. 3d 769, 790 (9th Cir 2002).

7 *Himpurna California Energy Ltd v. PT.* Persero Perusahaan Listruik Negana (PLN), and hoc, 4 May 1999, XXV *Yearbook Commercial Arbitration* 13, 2000, at 84.

8 *Aminoil v. Kuwait*, ad hoc award of 24 March 1982, 66 International Law Reports 518, 1984, at 605.

9 Ibid., at 602.

10 Ibid., at 85.

11 Nearly a century ago, the three Swiss arbitrators who rendered the award in *Delagoa Bay and East African Railway Co.* (*US and Great Britain v. Portugal*, 1900), extracts in English translation in M. Whiteman, *Damages in International Law*, pp. 1694-1703, 1943, determined damages for the premature cancellation of a 35-year railroad concession

"according to universally accepted rules of law, the *damnum emergens* and the *lucrum cessans*," ibid, 1698. After appointing experts to review financial performance and prospects, the arbitral tribunal projected the railroad's income over nearly 20 years, discounted it to a value at the date of the annulment (apparently using a discount rate of 6%) and granting compensation on that basis.

For a recent award containing a concise and pellucid exposition of this approach, see *Liberian Eastern Timber Corp. (LETCO) v. Republic of Liberia*, ICSID award of 31 March 1986, 26 International Legal Materials 647, 1987.

12 Asser's Handbook, op. cit. Note 12, at 231-232 (free translation).

13 *SPP* v. *Arab Republic of Egypt*, ICSID award of 20 May 1992, XIX ICCA Yearbook 84, 1994.

14 *Sapphire International Petroleums Ltd v. National Iranian Oil Company*, ad hoc award of 15 March 1963, 35 International Law Reports 136, 1967.

15 *Government of Kuwait v. American Independent Oil Company* (AMINOIL), ad hoc award of 24 March 1982, 66 International Law Reports 518, at 581 (1984). *Accord*, *Phillips Petroleum Company Iran v. Islamic Republic of Iran*, Iran-United States Claims Tribunal, award of 10 June 1989, 4 Mealey's International Arbitration Reports No. 11(C), § 112.

16 *Administrative Tribunal* case (ILO and UNESCO), advisory opinion, 23 International Law Reports 517, at 537.

17 41 International Law Reports 29, at 76.

18 See Factory at *Chorzów* (*Germany v. Poland*) (Indemnity), 1928 PCIJ (Ser. A) No. 17. The distinction established by the Permanent Court of International Justice between lawful and unlawful takings was explored by Chamber Two of the Iran-US Claims Tribunal in the *Phillips Petroleum* case, op. cit. Note 22, § 109-110.

19 XXV *Yearbook Commercial Arbitration*, 2000, at 70-73.

20 *Sapphire Int. Petroleum Ltd v. National Iranian Oil Company*, ad hoc, 15 March 1963, 35 International Law Reports 136, 1967.

21 Op. cit. Note 22, § 111.

22 Op. cit. Note 18, § 111.

23 Ibid., § 114.

24 Ibid., § 138.

25 Ibid., § 154. The same comment may be made with respect to the undifferentiated "overall determination of a global amount" used by Chamber One of the Iran-US Claims Tribunal to reduce another DCF evaluation, by the round figure of 350 million rial, in *Starrett Housing Corp. v. Iran*, Award No. 32-24-1, 1983, § 342.

26 Ibid., § 112.

27 Ibid., § 115.

28 Op. cit. Note 22, at 1699. In the *Starrett Housing* case, op. cit. Note 51, Chamber One of the Iran-US Claims Tribunal referred, § 338, to "the exercise of judgmental factors that are better expressed in approximations or ranges".

29 XXV *Yearbook Commercial Arbitration* at 97-103 (2000). For another case where the arbitral tribunal applied a 15% discount of the net present value of future losses, on account of "the uncertain nature of the calculations," see ICC Case No. 8445, XXVI *Yearbook Commercial Arbitration* 167, 2001.

30 35 International Law Reports 136, 1967, at 189.

31 XXV *Yearbook Commercial Arbitration*, 2000, at 89-90.

32 John Y. Gotanda, "Recovering Lost Profits in International Disputes", 36 Georgetown Journal of International Law 61, 2004.

33 See Stephen M. Schwebel, International Arbitration: Three Salient Problems, 1987, at 60.

34 See, e.g., *Benteler v. Belgium*, preliminary award of 18 November 1983, Journaux des Tribunaux (Bruxelles) No. 5289, 31 March 1984; extracts in English in [1985] European Commercial Cases 101.

35 Passage quoted in 2 Arbitration International, 1986, at 95.

36 Karl-Heinz Böckstiegel, Arbitration and State Enterprises, 1984, at 25.

37 General Principles of Law as Applied by International Courts and Tribunals, 1953.

38 Böckstiegel, op. cit., at 45.

39 66 International Law Reports, at 590.

40 XXV *Yearbook Commercial Arbitration*, 2000, at 91-93.

41 Ibid.

42 XVIII *Yearbook Commercial Arbitration*, 1993, at 58.

4

The obligation to mitigate damages

By ***Yasuhei Taniguchi****
Professor of Law, Senshu University Law School, Tokyo;
Of Counsel, Matsuo & Kosugi, Tokyo;
Member and former Chairman, Appellate Body of the WTO, Geneva;
Council Member, ICC Institute of World Business Law

INTRODUCTION

This short paper will discuss the following five subject areas that may be relevant in dealing with the obligation to mitigate damages in international commercial arbitration: (1) treatment of obligation to mitigate damages in national laws; (2) inclusion of obligation to mitigate damages in various non-national laws; (3) arbitrator's duty to apply law unless acting as *amiable compositeur* and arbitrator's choice of "law"; (4) possible conflict with rules of public international law; and (5) examination of some sample cases. Thereafter, a brief conclusion will follow.

The obligation to mitigate damages originates in English law. In order to simplify the matter, let us take an example of a sales contract. If the seller does not deliver the good sold, the buyer should not simply wait to see the damage he suffers increase, but should take an appropriate measure to mitigate the damage by purchasing, for example, the same good in the market. He can then claim the amount of damages, which is the difference between the purchase price and the price he has paid in the market. This rule seems quite simple and reasonable from the point of view of the good faith which must prevail in the area of contract law.

* The author thanks Ms Ana Rüsche of the law firm L.O. Baptista Advogados, Sao Paulo, for her valuable help in gathering materials for writing this paper.

National laws vary, however, for historical and other reasons. In order to overcome difficulties arising from varying national laws, efforts have been made to create certain non-national laws incorporating what is considered most appropriate and widely acceptable. The UN Convention for Contract for International Sales of Good (CISG) is the most successful legal document, and the UNIDROIT Principles of International Commercial Contracts is another achievement.

Our question is how an international commercial arbitrator must treat the obligation to mitigate damages. If the national law designated by the parties has provisions for such an obligation, he or she can simply resort to them. In doing so, can the provisions of CISG or UNIDROIT also be taken into consideration in order to implement and supplement the national law? When designated national law does not have such provision, what can be done? If no applicable law is designated, can an arbitrator resort directly to CISG or UNIDROIT? These are questions we must ask in this paper.

1. OBLIGATION TO MITIGATE DAMAGES IN NATIONAL LAWS

Common law systems

English law – Traditionally in common law, the remedy for a contractual breach has been damages. Specific performance is an exception. This seems to have been the background in which the very idea of the obligation to mitigate damages arose. In fact, it arises immediately when a non-performance (including anticipatory breach) occurs. The aggrieved party must immediately resort to the market in order to minimize his loss. Strangely, there is no leading case nor an abundance of judicial precedents on this point.[1] This principle is reflected in the manner in which the amount of damages is to be determined. Thus, the English Sale of Goods Act of 1979 (SGA) provides that when a seller neglects or refuses to deliver the goods to the buyer, the measure of damages is to be ascertained by the difference between the contract price and the market price at the time when they ought to have been delivered or at the time of the refusal to deliver (SGA 51(3). A similar provision is found for buyer's non-acceptance in 50(3)). The damages are determined without regard to whether the buyer actually bought a replacement. Obligation to mitigate damages expresses itself in a pure and abstract form.

American law – American law today, being based on the same principle, seems to take a more sophisticated approach. The Uniform Commercial Code, which has been adopted in most states, provides that the seller may resell the goods in case of the buyer's non-acceptance, or the buyer may purchase substitute goods ("cover") from elsewhere in case of the seller's breach. If such action has been taken in good faith and in a commercially reasonable manner or without delay, the difference between the two prices and incidental costs can be recovered by the aggrieved party (UCC §2-706, §2-712). The difference from English law seems to be that English law fixes the amount of damages as of the time of breach, while the American law depends on actual resale or purchase conditioned on good faith and reasonableness or promptness. Nevertheless, the basic principle of obligation to mitigate damages behind these rules is apparent. American law is more flexible than its English counterpart, because it introduces general principles like good faith and reasonableness. The Restatement of Contract 2d. of 1981 provides for a similar rule with a slightly different formulation.[2]

Civil law systems

German law – civil law contract law differs from its common law counterpart in that the specific performance is the rule, and a remedy of damages is rather subordinate and supplemental, at least in theory. If the seller does not deliver the goods, the seller should pursue obtaining the delivery through litigation. There may be damages resulting from late delivery, but there is normally no room, under such a system, for the obligation to mitigate damages to play a role. It has been pointed out, however, that "several Civil Law systems treat the aggrieved party's contributory negligence and his duty to mitigate his loss on an equal footing."[3]

Under German law, generally speaking, the buyer has no obligation to buy the same good from elsewhere in order to prevent or reduce the damage he is going to suffer, and likewise, the seller has no obligation to look for another buyer in order to prevent a loss, unless there are exceptional circumstances, such as a rising or falling market price or perishable goods involved. In this connection, German BGB Art. 254 deals with contributory negligence (*Mitverschulden*). In its first paragraph, it provides that the liability and scope of damages depend on the relative degree of contribution to the loss by the parties and, in the second paragraph, that the same applies when the aggrieved party neglected to prevent or mitigate the loss. Thus, the obligation to mitigate damages is included under the general principle of contributory negligence.

Further research is needed to understand the actual functioning of these provisions in practice and court decisions. But it can be assumed that, because of the priority of specific performance as remedy, the sphere in which such obligation works may be more limited than in common law.

Other civil law countries, such as Italy, Austria, Greece, Portugal, Belgium, Spain and Finland, are said to have similar provisions.[4]

French law – The French Civil Code does not have a provision similar to BGB §254, but the principle of contributory negligence seems well recognized by jurisprudence. It has been said in connection with Art. 1147 of the Civil Code, "At the present time, legal authors are almost unanimous in recognizing, in the areas both of contract and of delict, that whilst force majeure alone can totally exonerate the defendant, fault on the part of the victim remains a cause of partial exoneration [citing Mazeaud and Tunc …]. Case law has gone the same way …".[5] Another author has pointed out, citing Pothier, "Despite the absence of a direct reference to mitigation of damages, it is quite clear that the French classical writers whose work preceded the enactment of the Code Civil did not doubt that a party aggrieved by the wrong of another was expected at least to attempt to prevent the expansion of the damage he had sustained, and that the party would be denied recovery for a failure to do so."[6]

Under French law, however, damages are generally assessed as of the time of the judgment. If the seller is in default and the price of the good sold has been rising, it has been pointed out by a critical commentator that the result runs counter to the duty to mitigate damages.[7]

Incidentally, it is interesting to note that the Quebec Civil Code was amended in 1991 and introduced an express provision for the obligation to minimize damages (Art. 1479).[8]

Japanese law – Japan still belongs to the civil law camp. When a French-style civil code drafted by Gustave Boissonade, a French advisor, was rejected by the newly established parliament in 1890, the drafters turned to the first draft of the German BGB. Thus, the Japanese civil code is basically German, but some other elements are also found in it. It has been pointed out that the basic provision for damages (Civil Code Art. 416) is based on the English rule of *Hadley* v. *Baxendale* of 1854[9] and elements of French law. There is no specific provision for the obligation to mitigate damages. The only relevant provision is Art. 418 for contributory negligence and a general provision for the good faith principle (Art. 1(2)). Moreover, Art. 418 has an equivalent only in the first paragraph of BGB Art. 254. It simply says that the court determines the liability as well as the amount of damages by considering the negligence of the claimant. As in other civil law countries, specific performance is the primary contractual remedy. Therefore, a claim for damages arises only when the contract is formally avoided. This has caused serious controversy about the time at which the amount of damages should be assessed. When a specific performance is pursued in court, it is common that a claim for damages is joined on the condition that the specific performance proves futile at the time of execution. In this event, the court normally uses the time of the last date of hearing in court as the time for the assessment of damages. Although there is no statutory basis for the obligation to mitigate damages, there have been some court decisions that seem to adopt the same idea. A pre-war Supreme Court decision granted damages assessed at the time of termination of the contract by the aggrieved buyer. In view of the fact that the claim for damages arises only at the time of termination, this solution is ideologically similar to the English rule.[10] A more recent case was also decided in a similar way to UCC provisions. Because of breach by the seller, the buyer bought the good from elsewhere at a "reasonable price at the time" and was granted the difference between the prices.[11] These decisions do not depend on the principle of contributory negligence, because there was no negligence found on the part of claimant, who acted according to the "unspoken" obligation to mitigate damages.

Overview of civil law systems in comparison with common law – Traditionally, it is admitted, a civil law system did not have the doctrine of obligation to mitigate damages as such. Nevertheless, it has been asserted by various authors that the civil law jurisprudence has achieved similar, if not identical, results by resorting to other principles. A comparative analysis presented by Profs. Lando and Beale is illuminating: they distinguish three situations, namely: (1) where the aggrieved party's conduct was a partial cause of the non-performance; (2) where the aggrieved party, though not in any way responsible for the non-performance itself, exacerbated its loss-producing effects by its behaviour; and (3) where the loss resulting from the non-performance could have been reduced or extinguished by appropriate steps in mitigation. According to Lando and Beale, English law treats situations (1) and (2) as falling within the concept of contributory negligence and situation (3) within the concept of failure to mitigate damages. On the other hand, most civil law systems do not distinguish between these two concepts, but obtain similar results by using concepts such as causation.[12] I agree. Under the umbrella of the broad principle of good faith, failure to mitigate in a reasonable manner can either be construed as contributory negligence by itself or as outside of the *bona fide* expectation of the non-performing party. However, as much interpretative freedom may be available in theory, the contract law doctrines in each system are history bound, and not all theoretical possibilities can be exploited in practice. Thus, some kind of non-national system is needed to free national systems from their traditional bonds.

2. OBLIGATION TO MITIGATE DAMAGES IN NON-NATIONAL LAWS

Uniform Law on the International Sale of Goods of 1964 (ULIS)

The Hague Convention's Art. 88 concerns the obligation to mitigate damages as follows:

> "The party who relies on a breach of the contract shall adopt all reasonable measures to mitigate the loss resulting from the breach. If he fails to adopt such measures, the party in breach may claim a reduction in the damages."

Unfortunately, the Convention was acceded to by only nine countries, mainly European. Therefore, today it has only a historical importance in that it gave impetus to the adoption of the more popular Vienna Convention, adopted in 1980.

The UN Convention on Contract for the International Sale of Goods of 1980 (CISG)

This Convention (CISG), often referred to as the Vienna Convention, is now acceded to by almost 70 countries including all important trading countries, with the notable exception of two important trading nations, the UK and Japan. The rules set forth in the Convention have been widely accepted and applied. As a product of international cooperation from both common law and civil law sides, it represents an interesting integration of both systems.

Its Art. 77, which was derived from the earlier ULIS Art. 88, provides:

> "A party who relies on a breach of contract must take such measures as are reasonable in the circumstances to mitigate the loss, including loss of profit, resulting from the breach. If he fails to take such measures, the party in breach may claim a reduction in the damages in the amount by which the loss should have been mitigated."

This provision is the last in the series of provisions dealing with damages (Arts. 74-77). It is also inter-related with other provisions dealing with remedies. The whole scheme is admittedly "not free from difficulty" and "presents some substantial problems".[13] As a compromise or hybrid product between common law and civil law, the system has elements of both systems. Unlike common law, CISG emphasizes specific performance (Arts. 46, 62), and the avoidance of contract plays an important role in the assessment of damages (Arts. 75, 76) rather than just the breach. Not being a contract law specialist, I am not in a position to explain some of the problems. Thanks to the widespread applicability of CISG, its provisions are interpreted by the courts of many jurisdictions and by arbitrators.

In fact, CISG is applicable according to its Art. 1 when both parties to a sale of goods contract have a place of business in different contracting states, or when the rules of private international law lead to the application of the law of a contracting state. Therefore, it is possible that a company from a non-contracting state such as Japan can have a place of business in a contracting state subject to CISG. Moreover, if an action is brought in a Japanese court and the Japanese rules of private international law direct the court to apply the law of a contracting state such as France, CISG, as a part of French law, may be applied by the Japanese court. This point, however, is not entirely clear, and I am not aware of any court decision concerning this issue. In any event, we cannot ignore the fact that provisions of CISG are being interpreted and applied by the courts of the contracting states.[14]

UNIDROIT Principles of International Commercial Contracts 2004

The UNIDROIT Principles were first published in 1994 after a long preparation. The scope of their coverage is not limited to the sale of goods and was largely expanded in the 2004 version to include much new subject matter, but the provision for the obligation to mitigate damages is original. Its Art. 7.4.8, entitled "Mitigation of harm", provides:

> "(1) The non-performing party is not liable for harm suffered by the aggrieved party to the extent that the harm could have been reduced by the latter party's taking reasonable steps.
>
> (2) The aggrieved party is entitled to recover any expenses reasonably incurred in attempting to reduce the harm."

The gist of the provision seems the same as Art. 77 of CISG, but the wording of the provision better represents the nature of the rule. Despite the common term of "obligation" or "duty" to mitigate, there is admittedly no corresponding right. It only delimits the scope of damages to be granted. Apart from some differences in wording, such as "reduce" instead of "mitigate" and "harm" instead of "loss", an important difference is found in the second paragraph concerning recovery of expenses for reduction of harm, which is not found in CISG. It may be asked how this problem can be dealt with under CISG.

Generally speaking, however, there are basic similarities between the CISG's provisions and those of UNIDROIT regarding damages; both aim at the harmonization of common law and civil law principles of contract. Principles of European Contract Law prepared by the European Commission of European Contract Law (Art. 9:505) follow the UNIDROIT's formulation closely.[15] In any event, it is beyond my capacity to attempt a detailed comparison of these documents. It should be assumed that the UNIDROIT Principles, being the latest product, incorporate many improvements over the CISG. The preamble of the UNIDROIT Principles foresees various situations where the Principles are applied: First, "They shall be applied when the parties have agreed that their contract be governed by them." Then, they may be applied (1) when the parties have agreed that their contract will be governed by general principles of law, *lex mercatoria* or the like; and (2) when the parties have not chosen any law to govern their contract. Moreover, they may be used (1) to interpret or supplement international uniform law instruments; and (2) to interpret or supplement domestic law. The meaning of this will be considered in connection with arbitrator's task to apply law.

3. ARBITRATOR'S APPLICATION OF LAW – WHICH LAW?

General principle

It is well established today that the arbitrator must apply law unless the parties specifically request him/her to decide the dispute as *amiable compositeur* according to *aequo et bono*. Application of law guarantees the parties predictability and due process. My reasoning is as follows: the law's provision, by definition, specifies the requisite conditions for existence of rights and obligations. Each party to an arbitration, being aware of these conditions, presents allegations and evidence which will guide the arbitrator to a conclusion favourable to such party. The guarantee of procedural due process enables a party to rebut effectively the allegations and evidence presented by the other party, only because the arbitrator is bound by the rules of law under which the parties are litigating. In case of an *amiable compositeur*, the parties cannot know what allegation and evidence will effectively lead the arbitrator to decide favourably. They can only guess by using common sense. This point is particularly important in international arbitration. In domestic arbitration, because of the cultural affinity shared by both parties and the arbitrator, common sense may be more "common" than in an international context. It is understandable, therefore, why the principle of arbitration according to law has been established. In this respect, the arbitration is no different from litigation in a national court where the national judge must apply law. This aspect of arbitration has led to the often criticized modern trend of the "judicialization" of arbitration. It is interesting, however, to note that there have been some repercussions to such a trend by allowing the arbitrator a certain latitude in this respect, as discussed later.

Determination of applicable national law

The traditional rule is that the arbitrator must act like a national judge, that is, he must determine the applicable law by applying the rules of the private international law of the forum, namely the place of arbitration. The rules of private international law normally allow the parties to agree on the applicable law for matters outside of the mandatory regulation of *lex fori*; typically this involves contractual relationships. Thus, the parties to a contract are free to agree on the applicable law to the contract. Such a governing law clause is commonly found in an international commercial contract. It is generally admitted that the choice of law by the parties is not without limit, but its exact scope is not clear.[16]

This traditional formula creates many problems when the parties have not agreed to any law. Difficulties arise, among others, because the place (country) of arbitration is not always a good basis to start with. Its private international law may not be suitable for the particular case. The whole operation becomes very complex and unpredictable if the thus designated law of a state should include the private international law of that state. For these and other reasons, modern arbitral legislations have departed from the traditional formula and allow the arbitrator to pick a choice of law rule that he considers most appropriate for the case (UNCITRAL Model Law), or even to directly choose an appropriate substantive law (not including the choice of law rules) of a state.

The French law took a lead in adopting this "direct" approach as early as 1981. Its so-called New Code of Civil Procedure Art. 1496 provided that, in the absence of the parties' choice of law, the arbitrator decides the case according to the law that he thinks appropriate. It also provided that the arbitrator must take commercial usage into consideration. The purpose of this legislation is explained as freeing the arbitrator from an obligation to first select a conflict of law system. Some years later, the Swiss Private International law Act of 1989 (PILA or IPRG) took a slightly different approach. Its famous Art. 187(1) provided that, absent a choice of law made by the parties, the case shall be decided according to those rules of law with which the case has the closest connection.[17]

New arbitration laws of Germany (1988) and Japan (2002), for example, follow the Swiss example by using the idea of "closest connection", but their provisions seem fundamentally different from the Swiss model.[18] German-Japanese provisions direct the arbitrator to apply "the law of the State" with which the case is most closely connected and not "the rules of law" with which the case has the closest connection. This difference is significant because, under the Swiss formulation, the arbitrator can apply certain rules of law without going through a particular state, whilst in the German and Japanese approach the arbitrator must first find a state that is closely connected to the case. If any "rules of law" can exist without being the rules of law of any state, this difference would lead to an important difference in application of non-national law. This is discussed in the next section.

Application of non-national law – lex mercatoria

It is no coincidence that when the international arbitration started losing its "nationality" by being freed from the bind of its national *situs* with respect to the applicable law,[19] the possible application of a non-national law became more real. Arguments in favour of *lex mercatoria* have a long history. But a positivistic trend in legal thinking as well as in legal practice has long prevented its application from becoming a real practical issue. First, the contents of *lex mercatoria* were considered to be too vague to be used by the arbitrator as a clear standard for decision. Second, the fate of an award applying *lex mercatoria* was not certain before the national court. There was a risk of non-recognition. As a result, it was considered that there was not a sufficient degree of predictability that could be guaranteed by application of *lex mercatoria*.

The situation surrounding *lex mercatoria* began changing with the rising volume of international trade, expanding use of model contract forms such as Incoterms and active international cooperation to produce written rules applicable to cross-border commercial contracts. In effect, *lex mercatoria* has become more visible and its contents more acceptable and the outcome of its application more predictable. On the other hand, modern national arbitration laws have placed more restrictions on the ability of national courts to interfere with the arbitrator's application of substantive law.

If the parties are allowed to agree upon an *amiable compositeur* who is not bound by any law, there is no reason to prohibit the parties from agreeing that the arbitrator can apply *lex mercatoria*.[20] UNIDROIT Principles are not rules of law in the ordinary sense, but the parties are free to agree to their application to their case.[21] For a party from a non-contracting state adhering to CISG or ULIS, the rules laid down in these international documents are not binding in any sense. But a party is free to subject himself/herself to these rules on his/her own volition.[22]

A more difficult situation arises when the parties have not agreed to any national or non-national law. Does the arbitrator have the possibility to apply rules of *lex mercatoria*? In this connection, modern arbitral laws like the Swiss law can make a difference, because they allow the arbitrator to bypass any state law. On the other hand, the German and Japanese formulation directs the arbitrator to first find the state that has the closest connection to the case and then to apply its law. Therefore, there is ostensibly no opportunity for the arbitrator to apply *lex mercatoria* that is not the law of that state. However, there may be some interpretative avenues which make the application of rules of *lex mercatoria* possible. If the arbitrator is allowed or required to apply or to take into account the trade usage, as many arbitration laws today provide, he can take into account the rules of *lex mercatoria*. The good faith principle is recognized in most countries as the most important general principle in private law. The arbitrator may be able to find the expression of such a general principle in some *lex mercatoria* rules.

The most important question in the application of *lex mercatoria*, however, is how to satisfy the requirement of due process. As suggested earlier in this paper, due process is satisfied by adhering to the application of positive national law, because the parties know, or at least are able to know, its contents and to submit proper allegations and evidence accordingly. Even in the national courts, the opportunity to know the exact contents of the applicable law has become an important due process requirement. The ancient adage of *jura novit curia* is no longer entirely true. Surprise by a judgment is not allowed. The contents of applicable law must be known to the parties beforehand and submitted to the parties for discussion. Amended Art. 16(3) of the French Code of Civil Procedure now provides that the judge is not allowed to base his decision on a point of law raised by his own motion without having invited the parties to present their observations on it. In Germany also, the *Rechtsgespräch* between the parties and the judge has been emphasized in the same context.[23]

If this is correct, the arbitrator cannot so easily and lightly resort to *lex mercatoria*. The arbitrator must first identify the rules of *lex mercatoria* he/she thinks possibly apply to the case and present them for the parties' discussion.[24] This may cause confusion and delay when both parties refuse application of the particular rules that the arbitrator has proposed. But if the proposed rules are clear and reasonable, the parties will probably be willing to reformulate their arguments and to produce evidence accordingly. In order to obtain such a reaction from the parties, it is useful to propose well-reasoned rules of *lex mercatoria*, such as the UNIDROIT Principles or CISG where the latter is not legally applicable for some reason.

Possible conflict with public international law

In applying any law, national law or otherwise, that provides for the obligation to mitigate damages, is there any possibility of conflict with public international law as a result of which the arbitrator can be prevented from applying such a law? This question goes beyond my capacity. But a cursory reflection leads me to answer negatively. Public international law may prohibit traffic of certain products, such as narcotics, weapons, etc. If the obligation to mitigate damages compels one to violate such a prohibition, the obligation cannot be fulfilled. But this is not because of the rule of the public international law as such, but because of a national mandatory law that has incorporated the obligation of the state under the public international law. A final conclusion on this point, however, has to be reserved because, in view of the recent development of the public international law concept, there may be situations where a norm of the public international law directly affects a private legal relationship.

4. ARBITRATOR'S APPLICATION OF THE OBLIGATION TO MITIGATE DAMAGES

Various applications

Depending on a variety of situations, the arbitrator's mode of applying the obligation to mitigate damages may vary. If the applicable national law designated by the parties or by application of choice of law rules precisely provides for such obligation, the arbitrator can simply apply it. In common law countries where the principle is well established, it will be an easy task, but if the applicable national law is silent or ambiguous, the task will become more difficult. As I have noted earlier, however, most national laws now embrace the idea by utilizing various theories, such as contributory negligence, causation (reasonableness, foreseeability, etc.), the good faith principle, etc. Another clear situation is where CISG's provision for mitigation of damages is applicable because the parties originate from the contracting states or because the applicable choice of law rules lead to the application of the law of a contracting state.

When applicable national law does not somehow allow the arbitrator to apply the obligation to mitigate damages, or when an appropriate international convention like CISG or even ULIS does not apply, and when the arbitrator still thinks the obligation to mitigate damages should be applied to the case in order to reach a satisfactory outcome, what can be done? It can be admitted that the obligation to mitigate damages, being incorporated in the CISG and UNIDROIT Principles, has become a part of *lex mercatoria*. Therefore, if the arbitrator can resort to these documents as source of law, a solution can be obtained from them. Because the rules of these documents are relatively clear, well commented and studied and, in case of CISG, interpreted and applied by national courts, the parties will be able to argue and produce evidence in accordance with their respective interests, thereby satisfying the due process requirement in respect of the application of law. Whether the arbitrator can do so or not depends on the arbitration law by which he/she is bound. Under the Swiss type of law, it will be easier than under the German and Japanese kind.

The next question is how arbitrators have dealt with this problem in actual cases. A French publication in 1992 remarked,[25] citing Loquin, "*la* duty to mitigate damages *ou* mitigation *est, sans aucun doute, 'l'un des usages les moins contestés du commerce international' ... C'est dans ce cadre juridique que les arbitres du commerce international en ont fait un principe general de la lex mercatoria.*" Citing Yves Derains, the same author continued, "*En effet, l'obligation du créancier de minimiser le dommage qu'il subit 'reçoit application dans la plupart des sentences statuant sur des problèmes de responsabilité contractuelle sans que les arbitres ne s'appuient pour cela sur une loi nationale, et indépendamment du fait qu'ils aient ou non les pouvoirs d'amiable compositeurs'.*"[26] This is a sweeping statement. If this was already the situation in 1992, the present situation cannot be said to be different. We must then ask, on what basis can international arbitrators act in this way?

Some examples of application

It is necessary to review how international arbitrators have acted in actual cases.

■ ICC Case 8817 of 1997, Paris, reported in ICCA Yearbook XXV p.355 (2000)

This is a case arising from termination of a sole distributorship of a Spanish dealer by a Danish manufacturer. Because both Spain and Denmark are contracting States of CISG, Art. 77 was applied to limit the damages claim of the Spanish dealer. Apparently, there was no governing law clause in the contract. The arbitrator issued a procedural order on the law applicable to tell the parties that CISG and its general principles, as presently elaborated in the UNIDORIT Principles, were perfectly suited to the settlement of the present dispute. It was commendable from the point of view of due process to inform the parties of the arbitrator's determination of applicable law at an early stage. I understand the reference to the UNIDROIT Principles to mean that the latter would be used as an interpretative help in applying CISG.

■ ICC Case 8782 of 1997, Amsterdam, reported in ICCA Yearbook XXVIII p. 39 (2003)

This was a "partial" award in a case arising from a contract between the defendant Danish company, manufacture of a fish-sorting machine, and the claimant Belgian fish merchant, the purchaser of the machine. Because of UNECE Conditions included in the contract, which make the contractor's law applicable, the parties agreed that the Danish law should apply. They also agreed that CISG would also apply. It is not clear why CISG came into the picture. It may be because Denmark was already a contracting State (acceded in 1990) or because the parties just agreed to it. The arbitrator stated, "Apparently, the principles of Danish law either incorporate the relevant provisions of the CISG with respect to this question or Danish law is essentially the same as these provisions, without having incorporated them explicitly or officially." Without referring to Art. 77 of CISG, however, the arbitrator said, "In general, there is an obligation for a creditor who is suffering damages ... to limit or prevent same ... there may be other rules and principles under Danish law leading to – basically – the same result." The arbitrator in this case appeared to be uncertain as to which law precisely was applicable to the dispute. Since this was an interlocutory award, this might have been enough to motivate the parties to plead and prove in this way.

■ Merchant Arbitration in Hamburg of 1998, reported in ICCA Yearbook XXV p. 216 (2000)

The case involved a typical situation of a cover sale in the coffee trade. The arbitrator simply said, "the buyer breached its obligation under the Hamburg usages by failing to mitigate damages and to inform the seller of its intention to re-sell the coffee to a third party." The nationality of the parties is not known. But undoubtedly the Hamburg usage was established to include the obligation to mitigate damages, and such usage was directly applied by the arbitrator without any discussion of applicable law. In this kind of contractual relationship, an implied agreement of the parties to such a usage can easily be presumed.

■ ICC Case 5073 of 1986, Trinidad and Tobago, reported in Collection of ICC Arbitral Awards 1986-1990, p. 85

The dispute arose from the termination of a distributorship agreement. The American claimant (manufacturer) requested a declaration that the contract had been terminated, and the Argentine defendant (distributor) counterclaimed damages. In the contract, the parties agreed to use California law. The arbitrator said, "This result is entirely consistent with, and meant to be understood in light of, the rule of California law on mitigation of damages. [citing California cases] That rule required defendant [counterclaimant] to mitigate the damages flowing from claimant's abrupt termination of the contract. At a minimum, it appears that claimant's offer of 29 March 1984 to renew the contract for two years presented defendant [counterclaimant] with an appropriate opportunity to mitigate its damages." This case does not present a problem in the application of the obligation to mitigate damages, because it was clear that California law was applicable, and it no doubt included the rule.

■ ICC Case 4761 of 1987, Paris, reported in Collection of ICC Arbitral Awards 1986-1990, p. 519

This case arose from a construction project in Libya. A contract was entered into between a consortium of two Italian companies and a local Libyan company. The contract was expressly made subject to Libyan law. The arbitral tribunal gave a partial award in 1984 in which it held that the applicable law was, in principle, Libyan law, but that the arbitrators might apply a *lex mercatoria* where Libyan law had not been proved, or if it had *lacunae* or was incomplete. In the final award, the tribunal said, "Libyan law, in the same way as other national laws such as German or Swiss law or even the *lex mercatoria* [...] gives effect to the theory of the unforeseen (*imprévision*) which arises from the principle that the rule '*pacta sunt servanda*' is superseded by the higher principle of good faith [...]. The arbitral tribunal recalls also the provision of Libyan law which requires the creditor to take any measures within his power to reduce the extent of his loss (Art. 224, ch.2. Libyan Civil Code; in so far as reference is made to *lex mercatoria*: see awards I.C.C. 2103 and 2142 ... which apply the same rule.)" In this case, the role of *lex mercatoria* is not clear. Although the contents of the Libyan Civil Code provision are not known to us, this case seems to show that an arbitrator can interpret the applicable law as he/she likes by importing into it a certain desirable meaning.

■ ICC Case 5418 of 1987, Paris, reported in Collection of ICC Arbitral Awards 1986-1990, p. 123

This dispute arose from a sale contract of 1977 of Hungarian wine between a UK buyer and an Hungarian foreign trade company. The contract designated Hungarian law as applicable. The tribunal found that the Hungarian Civil Code Sect. 340(1) provides, "injured person shall make such effort in order to prevent or to mitigate the damage as might reasonably be expected generally in the given situation. Such part of the damages as has been caused by the injured person having omitted to comply with the said duty does not entitle him to compensation." Thus, it held, "the prospects of increased sales of generic wines were so uncertain and the capital expenditure in launching them was so great that the claimants were quite justified in refusing to take the risk of losing their capital. There was therefore no breach of the duty to mitigate." This is another case in which the agreed applicable law itself provided for the obligation to mitigate damages. I am curious about the origin of such a progressive Hungarian provision.

■ ICC Case 3880 of 1983, Paris, reported in Collection of ICC Arbitral Awards 1974-1985, p. 159

This dispute arose from a contract of sale of boots between two Belgian companies when the seller could not obtain the products from its Romanian supplier on time. The defendant asserted that the claimant should have done certain things "in conformity with its obligation to take all appropriate steps to limit its damage and reduce its losses". The applicable law under which such obligation arose was not identified. Without refuting the asserted obligation itself, the tribunal rejected this assertion on a factual basis. The applicability of the obligation to mitigate damages was not an issue. Both parties being Belgian, the applicable law was likely to be Belgian law, which probably embraced the rule of mitigation. However, it is also possible that the tribunal resorted to *lex mercatoria* and that the parties acquiesced to it.

■ ICC Case 2478 of 1974, Paris, reported in Clunet 1975, p. 925

This dispute arose from a contract between a French buyer and a Romanian company over the sale of a certain petroleum product. When the Romanian seller failed to deliver the product, an arbitration took place in Paris. There is no indication of the applicable law. For the calculation of damages, the tribunal remarked, "we should not lose sight of the fact that, by virtue of the general principle of law which is reflected in Art. 42(2) and 44(1) of the Swiss Federal Code of Obligation, it belongs to the aggrieved party to take all necessary measures in order not to increase the damage." The tribunal then blamed the French buyer for not accepting an offer by the seller of certain gas-oil at a lower price to compensate the initial non-delivery. It is characteristic of this case that the arbitrator directly applied the general principle of law. It may have been practice in East-West trade arbitration until the 1970s to resort to such an abstract principle in order to avoid attachment to a particular national legal system.

CONCLUSION

The obligation to mitigate damages is a part of many developed national legal systems and has been incorporated in documents that represent many supra-national endeavours to make a uniform rule of law by harmonizing varying national laws, such as CISG and UNIDROIT Principles. It has also become easier to talk about *lex mercatoria* as incorporated in these documents.[27] On the other hand, the theories about the methodology by which the arbitrator must reach the applicable law has become more and more sophisticated. It is generally accepted that the parties can agree to the application of *lex mercatoria*, general principles of law or the like. In practice, however, a designation of non-national law rarely occurs.[28] On the other hand, the designation of applicable law, even a national law, for various possible reasons does not always occur.[29] Thus, in many cases, the responsibility of arbitrators is heavy in selecting a proper law for the case. In view of the fact that the issue of mitigation of damages often arises in contractual disputes, how an arbitrator uses the doctrine of obligation to mitigate damages can be regarded as a touchstone for testing the validity of the methodology for selecting an applicable law. Whatever methodology may be used by the arbitrator, the important point is to procedurally guarantee due process and transparency in determining the applicable law.

END NOTES

1 The reason for this has been attributed to the fact that the issue of damages being considered as factual, the appellate courts paid deference to the trial courts. D. Harris, D. Campbell & R. Halson, *Remedies in Contract & Tort,* Butterworths, 2002, p. 108.

2 *Restatement of Contracts* 2d, Vol. 3 § 350, 1981, p.126.

3 Ole Lando and Hugh Beale, *Principles of European Contract Law Parts I and II*, p.447, Kluwer Law International, 2000.

4 Ibid., p.448.

5 Hugh Beale, Arthur Hartkamp, Hein Koetz & Denis Tallon, eds., *Cases, Materials and Text on Contract Law,* Hart Publishing, 2002, p. 834. Art. 1147 seems relied upon as the statutory basis, which provides (in official translation), "A debtor shall be ordered to pay damages, if there is occasion, either by reason of the non-performance of the obligation, or by reason of delay in performance, whenever he does not prove that the non-performance comes from an external cause which may not be ascribed to him, although there is no bad faith on his part." Cass. civ. 1re, 31 January 1973, D. 1973.149.

6 Saul Litvinoff, *Damages, Mitigation, and Good Faith*, 73 Tulane Law Review 1161, 1166, 1999.

7 G.H. Treitel, *Remedies for Breach of Contract – A Comparative Account*, p. 121, Clarendon Press, 1988.

8 Jean-Louis Baudouin, *Les Obligations* 4e éd., p. 438 (Les Editions Yvon Blais Inc., 1993). Its official English translation reads: "A person who is liable to reparation for an injury is not liable in respect of any aggravation of the injury that the victim could have avoided."

9 9 Exch. 341 (1854). This is said to have happened because one of the drafters had studied in England.

10 Great Court of Judicature, 5 February 1931, 4681 Horitsu Shimbun 15.

11 Tokyo High Court, 29 September 1958, 9 Tokyo High Court Special Civil Report 172.

12 Lando and Beale, supra No. 3, 444.

13 Jacob S. Ziegel, The Remedial Provisions in the Vienna Sales Convention: Some Common Law Perspectives, in Galston & Smit ed., *International Sales: The United Nations Convention on Contracts for the International Sale of Goods*, Matthew Bender, 1984, 9-1, 9-43.

14 Information is available, for example, at http:/www.cisg.law.pace.edu.

15 Lando and Beale, supra No. 3, p.445.

16 Generally speaking, the parties' autonomy cannot prevail over mandatory rules of law of the place of arbitration. But the exact extent of this rule is still uncertain. For example, the Japanese Supreme Court has decided that the enforcement of an American judgment granting punitive damages is not allowed as it was against public policy. Under this rule, can an arbitrator in Japan apply the American law agreed upon by the parties and grant punitive damages? The concept of international public policy may be relevant for solving this problem. W. Laurence Craig, William W. Park & Jan Paulsson, *International Chamber of Commerce Arbitration*, 3rd ed., p. 338, Oceana Publications, 2000.

17 For an analysis of the developments from traditional approaches to modern approaches, see Marc Blessing, Regulations in Arbitration Rules on Choice of Law, in Albert Jan Van den Berg, ed., *Planning Efficient Arbitration Proceedings – The Law Applicable in International Arbitration* (ICCA Congress Series) p. 391, 408 et seq., Kluwer Law International, 1996; see also for a thorough discussion of this Swiss provision, Joachim G. Frick, *Arbitration and Complex International Contracts – With Special Emphasis on the Determination of the Applicable Substantive Law and on the Adaptation of Contracts to Changed Circumstances*, p. 68 et seq., Kluwer Law International, 2001.

18 German Code of Civil Procedure Art. 1051 of 1988, Japanese Arbitration Law of 2002 Art. 36. Incidentally, the United Kingdom's new Arbitration Act of 1996 adopted the formulation of the UNCITRAL Model Law by providing that "the tribunal shall apply the law determined by the conflict of laws rules which it considers applicable".

19 "Absence of *lex fori*" in the modern theory of international arbitration is emphasized in Frick, supra No. 17, p. 48.

20 Wolfgang Kühn, *Express and Implied Choice of the Substantive Law in the Practice of International Arbitration*, in Albert Jan Van den Berg, ed., supra No. 17, pp. 380–382.

21 As mentioned earlier, the preamble of the UNIDROIT Principles make them applicable when the parties have so agreed. This provision raises no problem in arbitration. In litigation in a national court, the result can be the same, because the parties are deemed to have incorporated the contents of the Principles in their contract terms.

22 Note, General Principles of Law in International Commercial Arbitration, 101 Harvard Law Review 1816, at 1823 points out that the greatest weakness of the use of non-national law is in uncertainty and unpredictability, citing Redfern & Hunter, *Law and Practice of International Commercial Arbitration,* 1986. Thus, a choice of such a law by the parties is rare. See also infra No. 28 for recent statistics.

23 Cf. Hans-Willi Laumen, Das Rechtsgespräch im Zivilprozess (C. Heymann, 1984), Joachim Goebel, *Rechtsgespräch und kreative Dissens zugleich ein Beitrage zur Bedeutung der Sprache in der interpretativen Praxis des Zivilprozes*s (Dunker & Humblot, 2001).

24 Matti S. Kurkela & Hannes Snellman, *Due Process in International Commercial Arbitration*, p. 171 et seq. (Kluwer Law International, 2005) discusses the relationship between the principle "Jura Novit Arbiter" and due process, although the author's approach seems a little different.

25 Filali Osman, *Les principes généraux de la Lex Mercatoria*, p. 184 (L.G.D.J. 1992).

26 One of the famous protagonists Prof. Goldman mentioned the duty to mitigate damages as an actual content of *Lex Mercatoria*. Berthold Goldman, *La Lex Mercatoria dans les contrats et l'arbitrage internationaux: réalité et perspectives*, Journal du Droit International, 1979, pp. 475, 495.

27 Katherine Lynch, *The Forces of Economic Globalization: Challenges to the Regime of International Commercial Arbitration*, p 309 et seq., Kluwer Law International, 2003, points out the rising importance of *lex mercatoria* as a third legal system, but also mentions differing attitudes to it among countries, such as most active France and reluctant Germany. Japan rather belongs to the German camp.

28 Christopher R. Drahozal and Richard W. Naimark, eds., *Towards a Science of International Arbitration: Collected Empirical Research*, Kluwer Law International 2005, reveals that, from 2000 to 2003, only 1% to 2% of ICC arbitration clauses specified rules of decision other than national laws, such as EU law, general principles of equity, international law, international commercial law, ICSG. Ibid., p.200.

29 According to the statistics for the 1994-2003 period in Ibid., p. 197, between 77.8% and 82.1% of all ICC arbitrations specified applicable law. Blessing, supra No. 17, p. 396 points out, however, that the absence of an agreement may indicate an implied negative choice of law, meaning that the parties' will was clearly to avoid either party's national law.

5

Punitive and exemplary damages in international arbitration

By ***Jacques Werner***
Werner & Associés, Switzerland

The notes below give an overview of the subject and do not pretend to deal with it in an exhaustive manner. They draw heavily on the extensive analysis of punitive damages undertaken by Professor John Gotanda of the Villanova Law School in his lectures for the Hague Academy, which will be published in the Recueil des cours in 2007. Many thanks go to Professor Gotanda for having put his studies at my disposal.

Punitive damages, also called exemplary damages, are "sums awarded apart from any compensatory or normal damages, usually because of particularly aggravated misconduct on the part of the defendant". Punitive damages are of ancient origin. Examples can be found particularly in the Code of Hammurabi and in the Bible.

The usual justification for punitive damages is to punish and deter certain conduct, particularly wilful or malicious conduct. Opponents of such relief argue, however, that punitive damages are unfair because they constitute a windfall to the plaintiff. Award of punitive damages may also far exceed the maximum criminal penalty that can be imposed for the same behaviour.

Punitive damages differ from aggravated damages. Aggravated damages are compensatory in nature, and are awarded when high-handed conduct increases the injury to the plaintiff.

The common law tradition of awarding punitive damages traces its roots to England. However, unlike other common law countries, England restricts punitive damages to three categories of cases: (1) suits involving oppressive action by government servants; (2) suits involving conduct calculated to result in profit which may well exceed the compensation payable to the plaintiff; and (3) suits for punitive damages expressly authorized by statute. Recently, there have been efforts both to expand the availability of punitive damages and to limit the size of the awards.

European countries with civil law legal systems generally limit recovery of damages in private actions to an amount that restores a party to its pre-injury condition. In these countries, punitive damages are considered to be a form of punishment that is only allowed in criminal proceedings. The prohibition on punitive damages in private actions reflects the "strict separation of damages in civil law and punishment in criminal law". As said the Swiss Supreme Court in a 1998 decision:

> *"Le principe indemnitaire dans la répartition du dommage, selon lequel l'allocation de dommages-intérêts ne doit jamais conduire à l'enrichissement du lésé revêt un caractère fondamental en Suisse, aussi bien pour la responsabilité contractuelle que pour la responsabilité délictuelle. La prestation en dommages et intérêts doit être mesurée en ce sens que l'obligation du débiteur ne peut en aucune circonstance être supérieure à ce qui est nécessaire pour le réparation du dommage (Theo Guhl/ Alfred Koller/Jean Nicolas Druey, Das schweizerische Obligationenrecht, 8e éd., Zurich 1991, p.62). Vu son importance, le principe indemnitaire ou de l'interdiction de l'enrichissement relève de l'ordre public suisse ou interne, tel qu'il est défini par la jurisprudence (ATF 103 la 199 consid. 4a et les arrêts cités, p.204; Christian Lenz, Amerikanische Punitive Damages vor dem Schweizer Richter, thèse, Zurich 1992, p.113 et 143). La doctrine ne propose toutefois pas de le considérer comme un concept appartenant à l'ordre public international; la jurisprudence n'a pas davantage tranché cette question."*[1]

France, Germany and Switzerland are examples of countries in which damages for contract and tort claims are limited to restoring the parties to the position they would have been in had the damaging event not occurred. These countries allow recovery for non-pecuniary loss, which includes damages for pain and suffering, emotional distress, and moral harm, as well as reimbursement for legal fees. Such non-pecuniary damages, however, are not considered to be punitive in nature. This is because these damages are not imposed to deter or punish the wrongdoer, but rather to fully compensate the victim.

One of the basic characteristics of Asia is diversity. This is certainly true with respect to the availability of punitive damages in the region.

Japan, Korea and Taiwan do not permit awards of punitive damages in private actions. These countries, like the European civil law countries upon which their laws are modelled, limit recovery to compensatory damages.

In China, the General Principles of the Civil Law provide for compensatory damages in tort and contract actions, but do not provide for punitive damages.

India and the Philippines allow awards of punitive damages. In India, exemplary relief is limited to tort actions, such as assault, false imprisonment, trespass, negligence, libel and slander. Punitive damages are not available in breach of contract cases.

In sharp contrast to most civil codes, the Civil Code of the Philippines authorizes awards of punitive damages. Contrarily to India, punitive damages may also be imposed in a breach of contract action if the defendant acted in a fraudulent, reckless, oppressive or malevolent manner. Moreover, the Civil Code of the Philippines makes null and void prior stipulations between parties renouncing to punitive damages.

The most widespread use of punitive damages is, of course, in the United States, where the award of exemplary relief is governed both by state and federal law. In the United States, punitive damages typically serve two purposes: (1) to punish a party that has engaged in wrongful, malicious or outrageous conduct, and (2) to deter that party and others from engaging in the prohibited behaviour in the future.

As an illustration of how extensive punitive damages awarded by US Courts can be, let us remember the *Loewen* case[2] which, last year, was heavily discussed in arbitration circles.

Loewen, a Canadian company operating funeral homes, had a business dispute with a competitor in the US state of Mississippi. The amount of the dispute was about US$ 4 million. During the trial before the Mississippi State Court, Loewen was subjected to a constant barrage of xenophobic and racist attacks by opposing counsel, without the presiding judge interfering.

The jury rendered a verdict in the amount of US$ 500 million, including US$ 74 million for emotional distress suffered by Loewen's competitor and US$ 400 million in punitive damages.

Mississippi law required an appeal bond of 125 percent of the judgement as a condition of staying execution, and Loewen could not comply with that. Finally, one day before the start of the forced execution, Loewen settled with the opposite party for US$ 175 million. Then Loewen filed an investment arbitration claim against the United States under Chapter Eleven of the North American Free Trade Agreement (NAFTA). In the end, their claim was turned down by the NAFTA tribunal.

1. PUNITIVE DAMAGES IN ARBITRATION

In the United States, there are different views, varying from state to state, as to whether an arbitrator has the authority to award punitive damages. The first of these views is that arbitrators do not have the power to award punitive damages. This view has become known as the "*Garrity* rule" after being set forth initially in the New York Court of Appeal's decision in *Garrity v. Lyle Stuart, Inc.*[3] The rationale is that a punitive damages award is a socially exemplary remedy that can be imposed *only* by a judicial authority that is an instrumentality of the state.

The second view is that arbitrators may not award punitive damages absent an express provision in the arbitration agreement authorizing this relief. Courts following this view argue that, because punitive damages are an extraordinary remedy, the authority to award such damages cannot be implied from broad language providing for the arbitration of all disputes.

The third view is that arbitrators may award punitive damages unless the parties expressly prohibit the award of this relief in the arbitration agreement. Courts adopting this view reject the premise that an arbitrator has no power to award punitive damages; they presume that the scope of arbitral issues includes claims for exemplary relief.

As far as interstate and foreign commerce is concerned, a federal statute allows arbitral awards of punitive damages. The controlling legislation is the Federal Arbitration Act (FAA), which applies to actions involving interstate commerce and to international arbitrations. The Supreme Court has interpreted the FAA to provide arbitrators with the power to award punitive damages if the arbitration agreement authorizes such an award.

With respect to domestic arbitration, conflict between federal and state law arises when a contract governed by the FAA contains both an arbitration clause that is broad enough to permit punitive damages and a choice-of-law clause designating the application of a state law that prohibits arbitrators from awarding exemplary relief. The United States Supreme Court addressed this issue in its 1995 decision *Mastrobuono v. Shearson Lehman Hutton, Inc.*[4]

In *Mastrobuono*, the Supreme Court ruled that parties are generally free to define the scope of their arbitration agreement and that the FAA ensures that such an agreement will be enforced according to its terms notwithstanding state law limits on arbitrability. Thus, when the parties expressly provide in the arbitration agreement that the arbitrators shall have the authority to award punitive damages, the FAA will pre-empt state laws prohibiting arbitrators from awarding such relief. Conversely, when the parties exclude such claims from arbitration, that agreement will operate to preclude an award of exemplary relief. If an agreement is ambiguous on the issue of arbitrator-awarded punitive damages, the Court ruled that the arbitrator will be deemed to have the authority to award such damages.

The *Mastrobuono* decision also implicitly addressed the issue of whether United States courts will enforce foreign arbitral awards of punitive damages. Before this decision, a few federal courts either refused to enforce or showed a reluctance to enforce foreign arbitral awards containing punitive sanctions because they viewed these awards as violating public policy. Because the Court in *Mastrobuono* explicitly approved arbitral awards of punitive damages, it seems clear that foreign arbitral awards granting exemplary relief can no longer be denied recognition.

The cases where arbitrators have awarded punitive damages in US arbitral proceedings are few. However, some SMA[5] panels have awarded punitive damages in certain limited circumstances.

The decision in *Octonia trading, Ltd v. Stinnes Interoil GmbH* was the first SMA arbitration to award punitive damages. In *Octonia*[6] the claimant sought, *inter alia*, punitive damages on the ground that the respondent wrongfully stole its petroleum cargo from the ship's bunkers and used it to fuel the ship. The tribunal awarded the claimant US$ 100,000 in punitive damages, ruling that the governing law permitted arbitrators to award punitive damages and that the reprehensible conduct of the owner justified such extraordinary relief.

Following the *Octonia* decision, the SMA panel in *Triumph Tankers Ltd v. Kerr McGee Ref. Corp.*[7] awarded treble damages of US$ 368,495 to the claimant under RICO on the ground that the respondent had converted part of the claimant's petroleum cargo. The panel reasoned that the parties' agreement, which stated that all disputes arising out of the charter would be submitted to arbitration, was broad enough to encompass an award of punitive damages and that such relief was necessary to punish the egregious conduct of the respondent.

Let us also mention the *Sawtelle v. Waddell & Reed, Inc.*[8] case of 2003, where an NASD[9] arbitration panel had awarded the plaintiff, Steven Sawtelle, a mutual fund broker, US$ 25 million in punitive damages.

The record showed that, immediately after he was terminated by his former firm, Waddell & Reed, Mr Sawtelle found employment with another firm, retained the lion's share of the clients he serviced while at Waddell, and earned as much, if not more, than when at Waddell. Nevertheless, in August 2001, a NASD arbitration panel found that Waddell & Reed had been guilty of unfair trade practices in seeking to retain its clients, and awarded Sawtelle a total of US$ 1.8 million in compensatory damages and US$ 25 million in punitive damages based on the reprehensible nature of Waddell's conduct.

After the panel's award was upheld by the New York Supreme Court, Waddell finally prevailed on its appeal to the Appellate Court, which rendered a decision vacating the award of punitive damages on the grounds that: (1) the US$ 25 million award was irrational; and (2) the panel had manifestly disregarded controlling law by awarding punitive damages in an amount wholly disproportionate to the actual harm suffered by Sawtelle.

The Appellate Court decision in *Sawtelle* established that arbitrators' remedial powers, though broad, are not unlimited, and that punitive damages awards that are so excessive they defy rational analysis can be set aside by courts.

International tribunals, such as ICSID or the Iran-US claim tribunal, traditionally have not awarded punitive damages in disputes between transnational contracting parties.

Let us mention in this respect the *Sedco Inc. v. NIOC*[10] case. In *Sedco*, an American company claimed that the Iranian government had wrongfully expropriated its interests in an oil drilling operation. The tribunal awarded the claimant the full value of the expropriated interest. Although the majority did not discuss exemplary relief, in a separate opinion Judge Brower stated that punitive damages may be warranted for an unlawful taking in addition to compensatory damages. In a subsequent case, *Amoco Int'l Fin. Corp.* v. *Iran,*[11] the tribunal rejected Judge Brower's suggestion on the availability of exemplary relief. The tribunal stated that punitive damages are inappropriate in cases of unlawful expropriation and that the measure of damages for such claims is limited to the claimant's actual loss.

Several civil law countries also prohibit arbitrators from awarding punitive damages even if the substantive law governing the dispute is a foreign law that allows such relief. The Swedish Arbitration Act expressly prohibits an arbitrator from awarding penalties or fines. In Germany and Switzerland, arbitral awards that are incompatible with domestic public policy may be set aside. Tribunals and commentators have stated that both Germany and Switzerland consider punitive damages to be contrary to public policy and, as a result, an arbitrator sitting in either country would not be able to award punitive damages even if the applicable law would permit exemplary relief.

2. RECOGNITION AND ENFORCEMENT OF FOREIGN PUNITIVE DAMAGES AWARDS

There is little authority on whether, in a country not permitting punitive damages, courts will enforce a foreign arbitral award of such damages. As a general rule, foreign arbitral awards are more readily enforced than foreign court judgements, thanks to the New York Convention, stipulating that arbitral awards rendered in signatory countries are enforceable in all other signatory countries, subject to a narrow list of defences.

Under article V(2)(b) of the New York Convention, a court may refuse to recognize and enforce a foreign arbitral award if it "would be contrary to the public policy of that country". This public policy exception has been read by some countries, such as France, as referring to international public policy, not national public policy. Unlike domestic public policy, which includes all of the imperative rules of the state in which enforcement is sought, international public policy encompasses only those basic notions of morality and justice accepted by civilized countries.

Because international public policy is much narrower in scope than the domestic public policy of the enforcing state, some commentators have argued that civil law countries applying an international public policy standard to New York Convention article V(2)(b) would recognize and enforce arbitral awards of punitive damages. According to these commentators, while such damages may violate a mandatory rule of the enforcing state, they arguably would not be contrary to generally accepted principles of morality and justice. If it is so, foreign arbitral awards of punitive damages could still be denied enforcement on other grounds, such as the amount awarded is "excessively disproportionate to the loss suffered".

Swiss courts have rendered diverging decisions on this, once refusing enforcement, once granting it.[12] Germany will not recognize or enforce a foreign court judgement containing punitive damages. In a case involving an American state court judgement which included punitive damages, the German Supreme Court refused to recognize and enforce the punitive damages award on the ground that it violated German *ordre public*.

CONCLUSION

Should an arbitral tribunal deciding a transnational dispute award punitive damages?

Let us return to Professor Gotanda's analysis (I am quoting him from his above draft):

> "I believe the answer depends on a number of factors. An arbitrator deciding a transnational dispute in which a claim for punitive damages is raised should first determine if there exists an agreement containing an express clause either including or excluding punitive damages from the issue to be arbitrated. If it does, that clause should be enforced unless it violates an applicable mandatory rule of law. This procedure would

respect the principle of party autonomy – the right of parties to define the process by which any future contractual dispute will be settled. It also respects the limits of party autonomy by providing that parties are not permitted to exclude the application of mandatory rules of substantive law.

"In the absence of an express provision, the arbitrator should determine whether the parties intended to give the arbitrator the authority to award exemplary relief. In ascertaining the parties' intent on the issue, the arbitrator may consider (i) whether the parties have explicitly chosen a law to govern the despite that either prohibits or permits awards of punitive damages, (ii) whether awards of punitive damages are customary in the particular trade and (iii) whether other contractual provisions evidence the parties' intent to include or exclude arbitral awards of punitive damages. The purpose of this process is also to effectuate the intent of the parties.

"Even if the arbitrator is satisfied that the tribunal legitimately possesses the authority to award punitive damages, there may be circumstances under which such authority should not be exercised because to do so would jeopardize the enforceability of the award. This procedure would enable the arbitrator to fulfill his or her obligation to the parties to render an enforceable award. And if the arbitrator decides to award punitive damages, the arbitrator should make clear that such an award is separate and distinct from the other damages. This would allow a foreign domestic court that is asked to enforce the award, at a minimum, to recognize and enforce the award of compensatory damages even if it determines that the punitive damages award cannot be enforced because its violates the public policy of the jurisdiction."

Shall a court called upon to enforce a foreign arbitral award of punitive damages do so?

"As noted, there is no consensus on whether a court called upon to enforce a foreign arbitral award of punitive damages should do so. I believe the answer should depend on whether the award violates international public policy. I agree with those who believe that the New York Convention's public policy exception, under which a country has the right to refuse enforcement of an arbitral award on the grounds of public policy, should be constructed narrowly by applying the 'international public policy test'.

> Although there is no precise definition of the contents of international public policy, it has often been said to mean that a foreign award should be denied 'only where enforcement would violate the forum State's basic notions of morality and justice'. An International Law Associate Report recommended that international public policy of any State includes: (i) fundamental principles, pertaining to justice or morality, that the State wishes to protect even when it is not directly concerned; (ii) rules designed to serve the essential political, social or economic interests of the State, these being known as '*lois de police*' or 'public policy rules'; and (iii) the duty of the State to respect its obligations toward other States or international organizations. I believe that, as a general principle, an award of punitive damages should not violate international public policy because the recognition and enforcement of such an award would not manifestly disrupt the essential political, social or economic interests protected by the rules. The fact that an award of damages may be penal in nature should not in-and-of-itself be grounds to refuse enforcement. Indeed, I suspect that many countries would enforce an award of attorneys' fees and costs event if the tribunal assessed these fees and costs because the party engaged in reprehensible behaviour."

Probably because they are well thought-out and carefully phrased, Professor Gotanda's views will highlight even more what seems here the irreconcilable opposition of common law to civil law, for which the strict differentiation between civil remedies and criminal remedies is intangible.

END NOTES

1 *Asmidal* decision of 17 July 1998, TF Ière Cour civile, 4P.7/1998.

2 ICSID Case No ARB. (AF) 1998/3, 26 June 2003. See as well *Making Investment Arbitration More Certain, a modest Proposal*, Jacques Werner in The Journal of World Investment, Vol.4 No. 5, October 2003.

3 *Garrity* v. *Lyle Stuart, Inc.* (353 N.E. 2nd 793 (N.Y. 1976)).

4 115 S. CT., pp 1215-19.

5 Society of Maritime Arbitrators.

6 Society of Maritime Arbitrators, No. 2424, 1987.

7 Society of Maritime Arbitrators, No. 2642, 1990.

8 N.Y. App. Div. 1st Dept. Feb. 13, 2003.

9 National Association of Securities Dealers.

10 See *Sedco, Inc.* v. *NIOC*, 10 Iran-US Cl. Trib. Rep. 180, 1986.

11 See *Amoco Int'l Fin. Corp.* v. *Iran*, 15 Iran-US Cl. Trib. Rep. 189, 1987.

12 SJZ 1986, 309 (denied) and BJM 1991, 31 (granted).

6

Damages in investor-state arbitration

Applicable law and burden of proof

By **Hugo Perezcano Díaz**
General Counsel for Trade Negotiations,
Ministry of the Economy, Mexico

INTRODUCTION

This paper addresses the standards of applicable law and burden of proof in the context of international investment agreements (IIAs).[1]

It should be noted at the outset that investor-state proceedings arising under IIAs are essentially damages proceedings. An investor is entitled to bring to arbitration a claim that the host state of the investment has breached an obligation contained in a IIA, which has caused the investor or its investment to suffer losses or damages in connection with, or arising out of, that breach.

The International Law Commission *Articles on responsibility of states for internationally wrongful acts* (the ILC Articles on state responsibility) contemplate the following types of remedy in the event that the responsibility of the state has been established: cessation of the internationally wrongful act and assurances of non-repetition (Article 30), and the requirement that a responsible state make full reparation for the injury caused (Article 31), which may take the forms of restitution (i.e. to re-establish the situation that existed before the wrongful act was committed), compensation (which shall cover any financially assessable damage – i.e., the damage capable of being evaluated in financial terms – that is established, and generally consists of a monetary payment) or satisfaction (which may consist in an acknowledgement of the breach, an expression of regret, a formal apology or another appropriate modality), and interest on any principal sum due in order to ensure full reparation (Articles 34-38).[2]

This is not always the case in international arbitration. For instance, international commercial agreements such as the Marrakesh agreement establishing the World Trade Organization or the North American Free Trade Agreement (NAFTA) do not contemplate an obligation to make full reparation in disputes involving the states. The aim of the WTO dispute settlement mechanism "is to secure a positive solution to a dispute." In this context, the Understanding on rules and procedures governing the settlement of disputes (the WTO DSU) establishes a hierarchy of remedies, with a clear preference for a "solution mutually acceptable to the parties to a dispute" that is "consistent with the covered agreements" (i.e. the WTO Agreements).[3] The WTO DSU then goes on:

> "In the absence of a mutually agreed solution, the first objective of the dispute settlement mechanism is usually to secure the withdrawal of the measures concerned if these are found to be inconsistent with the provisions of any of the covered agreements. The provision of compensation should be resorted to only if the immediate withdrawal of the measure is impracticable and as a temporary measure pending the withdrawal of the measure which is inconsistent with a covered agreement. The last resort which this Understanding provides to the Member invoking the dispute settlement procedures is the possibility of suspending the application of concessions or other obligations under the covered agreements on a discriminatory basis vis-à-vis the other Member, subject to authorization by the DSB [the WTO Dispute Settlement Body] of such measures."[4]

Compensation under the WTO DSU does not involve financial compensation, i.e. the payment of damages, but rather usually takes the form of tariff reductions or other types of improved access to the responsible WTO Member's market. It is voluntary and a temporary relief in the event that the WTO Member concerned does not implement the recommendations and rulings of the DSB within a reasonable time. Therefore, it may only be maintained while such situation lasts. The suspension of the application of concessions or other obligations is a form of treaty-regulated countermeasure where no satisfactory compensation has been agreed to. It is also temporary and it is subject to the authorization of the DSB. The NAFTA and other commercial agreements establish somewhat similar rules.

In private commercial arbitration there is a menu of available remedies:

Arbitration awards may cover a range of remedies including:
- monetary compensation;
- punitive damages and other penalties;
- rectification;
- adaptation of contracts and filling gaps;
- restitution and specific performance;
- declaratory relief;
- interest; and
- costs.[5]

IIAs typically limit available remedies to restitution of expropriated property or payment of monetary damages, where the host state may choose to pay compensation in lieu of restitution. However, restitution is frequently unavailable or inadequate, and compensation is, thus, the form of reparation most commonly sought in international practice.[6] In Mexico's experience, awards against a host state have been limited to ordering payment of monetary damages.

While the Convention on the settlement of investment disputes between states and nationals of other states (ICSID Convention) gives the Centre a broader jurisdiction such that it extends to "any legal dispute arising directly out of an investment, between a Contracting State … and a national of another Contracting State, which the parties to the dispute consent in writing to submit to the Centre" (Article 25) – and disputes are not limited to claims of breach of an IIA, nor are remedies limited to awarding damages – in practice this has been the case. The majority of investment disputes involving the ICSID Convention are disputes arising under IIAs where a claim for damages is made against the host state in respect of alleged breaches to certain provisions of specific IIAs.

1. APPLICABLE LAW

The ICSID Convention provides that a tribunal shall decide a dispute in accordance with such rules of law as may be agreed by the parties or, in the absence of such an agreement, the tribunal shall apply the law of the contracting state party to the dispute (including its rules on the conflict of laws) and such rules of international law as may be applicable (Article 42). A tribunal would thus first turn to the contract between the investor and the host state. In the absence of a clause indicating the choice of law, a tribunal would apply the law of the disputing state and applicable rules of international law.

In *LETCO v. Liberia*, the tribunal recognized:

> "Under the doctrine of party autonomy, parties to a contract are free to choose for themselves the law which is to govern their relationship. This doctrine has gained almost universal acceptance, particularly in international commercial transactions (see Law, 'Applicable Law in International Commercial Arbitration' (1978), p. 71 *et seq.*) and it is adopted by the ICSID Convention which provides, in Article 42: 'The Tribunal shall decide any dispute in accordance with such rules of law as may be agreed by the parties'."[7]

The tribunal added that, "in the absence of any express choice of law by the parties, the Tribunal must apply a system of concurrent law" and explained: "The law of the contracting state is recognized as paramount within its own territory, but is nevertheless subjected [under the ICSID Convention] to control by international law."[8]

As already noted, however, IIAs are generally more limited in scope. They usually provide that the governing law shall be the treaty itself, and applicable rules of international law (see, for instance, NAFTA Article 1131). In the absence of such a provision, a tribunal would have to look at the specific rules of procedure: Where the claim is subject to the ICSID Convention, Article 42 would apply; the ICSID Additional Facility (arbitration) rules (Article 54), the UNCITRAL arbitration rules (Article 33) and the Permanent Court of Arbitration optional rules for arbitrating disputes between two parties of which only one is a state (Article 33), *inter alia*, similarly provide that disputing parties are free to designate the governing law and, failing a designation by the parties, leave it to the tribunal to determine, under conflict of law rules, what such applicable law is.

It should be noted that all those rules refer to a choice of law by the disputing parties, while in IIAs the choice is made by the contracting states, only one of which would eventually become a disputing party in any given case. Thus, a question could arise as to what is the governing law, since one of the disputing parties would have made no such choice. The NAFTA and other international agreements to which Mexico is a party clear up any doubt by providing that "the applicable arbitration rules shall govern the arbitration except to the extent modified by" Section B of Chapter 11 (which regulates investor-state dispute settlement, see NAFTA Article 1120). Since it is Section B that grants private investors access to international arbitration – i.e. the right of action conferred can only be exercised in accordance with the provisions of Section B – there is no room for doubt. If a specific IIA does not contain a similar provision, the issue would nevertheless have to be resolved in the same manner for the same reasons, namely that it is the IIA that grants investors a right of action, which right is subject to the other rules established in the IIA.

Whatever the case, the governing law as determined under the corresponding rules equally applies to issues concerning damages. In the case of IIAs that contain a governing law provision similar to NAFTA Article 1131, where a tribunal has found that a state is liable for breach of the international agreement, then it must look to the corresponding treaty and applicable rules of international law to determine the measure of damages.

At risk of being overly simplistic, it can be said that IIAs generally contain the same types of investment protection: they establish national and most-favoured nation (MFN) treatment clauses; provide for the minimum standard of treatment, including fair and equitable treatment; and include disciplines regarding expropriation. Some agreements also contain other types of protection, for instance, a prohibition against imposing certain performance requirements and restricting transfers.

Yet, only in the case of expropriation do IIAs contain rules regarding the quantification of damages. Whatever the formula used – whether it refers to the fair market value of the investment; full, fair and adequate compensation; prompt, and effective compensation, etc. – IIAs and international law contain specific rules that allow a tribunal to calculate damages in the case of an expropriation that has been carried out in breach of the IIA. While some IIAs may be more specific than others, they generally contain rules for determining the quantum in a case involving an expropriation.

That is not to say that calculating damages in expropriation cases is therefore simple. It may indeed turn out to be a complicated exercise, but there are rules and other guidance to turn to. This is not so in the case of breach of other provisions of IIAs, for instance, a breach of the national treatment obligation.

In *S.D. Myers v. the Government of Canada*, the tribunal noted in this respect that "by not identifying any particular methodology for the assessment of compensation in cases not involving expropriation, the Tribunal considers that the drafters of the NAFTA intended to leave it open to tribunals to determine a measure of compensation appropriate to the specific circumstances of the case, taking into account the principles of both international law and the provisions of the NAFTA."[9] The *S.D. Myers* tribunal referred to a "general principle of international law that compensation should undo the material harm inflicted by a breach of an international obligation" and cited the *Chorzów Factory* case which concluded:

> "The essential principle contained in the actual notion of an illegal act – a notion that seems to be established by international practice and in particular by the decisions of arbitral tribunals – is that reparation must, as far as possible, wipeout all the consequences of the illegal act and re-establish the situation which would, in all probability, have existed if that act had not been committed. Restitution in kind, or, if this is not possible, payment of a sum corresponding to the value which a restitution in kind would bear; the award, if need be, of damages for loss sustained which would not be covered by restitution in kind or payment in place of it – such are the principles which should serve to determine the amount of compensation for an act contrary to international law."[10]

The *S.D. Myers* tribunal added that there must be a sufficient causal link between the loss or the damage suffered and the breach complained of, a principle accepted also by the *Pope & Talbot* tribunal.[11] The breach of the IIA must be the proximate cause of the loss or damage. Indeed, the *Pope & Talbot* tribunal, while faced with a claim for damages for over US$500 million , awarded damages for a little over US$400 thousand , this having been the only harm suffered in connection with the breach of the duty to provide fair and equitable treatment in what it called "the verification episode."[12]

While the *S.D. Myers* tribunal cautioned that it was not attempting to set out detailed, exclusive principles for calculating the compensation payable, it enumerated the principles it applied as follows:

- the burden is on SDMI [the claimant] to prove the quantum of the losses in respect of which it puts forward its claims;
- compensation is payable only in respect of harm that is proved to have a sufficient causal link with the specific NAFTA provision that has been breached; the economic losses claimed by SDMI [the claimant] must be proved to be those that have arisen from a breach of the NAFTA, and not from other causes;
- damages for breach of any one ... provision can take into account any damages already awarded under a breach of another NAFTA provision; there must be no "double recovery".[13]

It then summarized: "the Tribunal will assess the compensation payable to SDMI [the Claimant] on the basis of the economic harm that SDMI can legally establish."[14]

2. BURDEN OF PROOF

A claimant, therefore, needs to prove the economic harm it alleges to have suffered. There is a general principle that the burden of proof rests on the party asserting a proposition or a fact. Durward Sandifer has so noted in his book, *Evidence Before International Tribunals*: "The broad basic rule of burden of proof adopted, in general, by international tribunals [...] may be simply stated: that the burden of proof rests upon him who asserts the affirmative of a proposition that if not substantiated will result in a decision adverse to his contention."[15] The tribunal in *Asian Agricultural Products v. Sri Lanka,* "in order to handle the legal issues related to evidence", referred to a set of "established international law rules" and recognized that, with regard to "the proof of individual allegations advanced by the parties in the course of proceedings, the burden of proof rests on the party alleging the fact".[16] International tribunals have consistently accepted this principle. In *United States – Measures Affecting Imports of Woven Wool Shirts and Blouses from India*, the WTO Appellate Body noted: "[...] various international tribunals, including the International Court of Justice, have generally and consistently accepted and applied the rule that the party who asserts a fact, whether the claimant or respondent, is responsible for providing proof thereof".[17] This principle applies to damages as well, as damages are issues of fact that require proof. Because it is the claimant who asserts that it has suffered damages, it is incumbent on it to show that such is the case.

3. SUFFICIENCY OF PROOF

The *Asian Agricultural Products* tribunal, citing Bin Cheng, noted that "a party having the burden of proof must not only bring evidence in support of his allegations, but must also convince the tribunal of their truth, lest they be disregarded for want, or insufficiency, of proof."[18] International tribunals have accepted that a claimant need only go so far as to establish a *prima facie* case of breach. In other words, a claimant need only establish a presumption that a treaty obligation has been breached, and then the burden of proof shifts to the responding party to rebut the case. The WTO Appellate Body stated:

> "... it is a generally accepted canon of evidence in civil law, common law and, in fact, most jurisdictions, that the burden of proof rests upon the party, whether complaining or defending, who asserts the affirmative of a claim or defence. If that party adduces evidence sufficient to raise a presumption that what is claimed is true, the burden then shifts to the other party, who will fail unless it adduces sufficient evidence to rebut the presumption."[19]

The tribunal in *Asian Agricultural Products*, quoting Sandifer, acknowledged that "in case a party 'adduces some evidence which *prima facie* supports his allegation, the burden of proof shifts to his opponent'."[20]

In *Autopista Concesionada de Venezuela v. Venezuela*, the tribunal stated that the concessionaire had not satisfied the burden of proving all of the damages alleged, and found that Venezuela had cast sufficient doubt to rebut the *prima facie* evidence presented by the concessionaire in respect of some of the losses allegedly incurred regarding certain issues.[21] The tribunal seems to have accepted that, just as in respect of liability, only a *prima facie* case need be established regarding damages.

A question arises, nonetheless, as to whether that proposition applies to damages, or should a claimant fully satisfy a tribunal that it has incurred the loss or damage alleged. The question is one of sufficiency of proof.

Liability naturally involves conduct imputed to the state. Therefore, it can be presumed that the state will normally be able to respond to a *prima facie* case concerning its own conduct. To the contrary, damages involve information generated and business practices followed by the claimant. Thus, by the same token, it can be presumed that a claimant will be able to furnish sufficient evidence on the damages alleged. Also, such information may not be readily available or even accessible to the responding state.

The fact that these proceedings involve sovereign states is significant as well. Where state responsibility has been established, reparation will almost certainly involve the use of public funds. It is thus incumbent on international tribunals to provide certainty and ensure transparency in the quantification of damages.

In this context, it should be noted that international tribunals have declined to award damages for want of proof. In the *Chorzów Factory Case*, the Permanent Court of International Justice (PCIJ), while noting that the German Government had not failed to draw attention to circumstances that were said to prove damage to the German company that had been deprived by the Polish Government of the Chorzów factory – arising from injurious competition of the factory under Polish management since it had become acquainted with, and obtained the means for using, the German company's production processes – declined to award damages alleged to have resulted from such competition because they had been insufficiently proved.[22]

In *Generation Ukraine v. Ukraine*,[23] the tribunal severely criticized the claimant for its shortcomings in proving the nature and quantum of its expenditures in the investment project. It began by noting that the claimant was severely handicapped in its efforts to discharge its burden of proof because all the primary documentation evidencing expenditures had been accidentally destroyed, and added that in such a case it was expected that "the claimant would have done everything in its power to furnish the tribunal with other forms of evidence to corroborate its statements on the nature and quantum of its expenditures", but "[i]t transpired that the claimant both comprehensively and conclusively failed to meet this expectation".[24] It criticized the witness and other evidence tendered by the claimant for its lack of credibility and reliability and noted that "no further reliable evidence was forthcoming from the Claimant in relation to its expenditure [...] despite the fact that several avenues appeared to be open to the Claimant to obtain such evidence."[25] The tribunal concluded that "the absence of information that must surely have been available to a party making reasonable endeavours" had further undermined the claimant's case.[26]

The standard expressed by the *Generation Ukraine* tribunal also holds true where evidence on the nature and quantum of investments or damages for some reason or other is not available, even absent the extraordinary circumstances of that case. It follows that if a claimant that has lost the evidence supporting its claim for damages must do "everything in its power to furnish the Tribunal with other forms of evidence to corroborate its statements on the nature and quantum of its expenditures", under normal circumstances a claimant should be required to comprehensively support its claim for damages and not be allowed to hold back evidence or even aim at making only a *prima facie* case in the hope of gaining an advantage and, perhaps, recovering more that the actual economic prejudice suffered.

In *GAMI Investments Inc. v. The Government of the United Mexican States*,[27] the tribunal in essence dismissed the claim, because GAMI failed to prove the actual damages purportedly suffered. GAMI was a minority shareholder in a Mexican company, GAM, that owned five sugar mills, all of which were directly expropriated by the Mexican Government. Under Mexican law, the government offered compensation at the fair market value of the mills, but GAM chose to challenge the expropriation decree before the Mexican courts (GAM, being a Mexican company owned and controlled by Mexicans, could not bring a NAFTA claim against the Government of Mexico). GAM ultimately withdrew from the judicial proceedings concerning two of the mills – which were then definitively expropriated – and successfully challenged the expropriation of three mills that the government subsequently returned.

GAMI alleged violations to the national treatment (NAFTA Article 1102), minimum standard of treatment (NAFTA Article 1105) and expropriation (NAFTA Article 1110) provisions. It is worth reviewing the tribunal's full reasoning concerning damages in relation to Article 1105:

> "83. One cannot fail to observe that GAMI's complaint of alleged unfair and inequitable treatment is not connected with a demonstration of specific and quantifiable prejudice. Mexico's alleged wrongdoing would

doubtless have resulted in some short-term decline in the value of its shares in GAM. (There would have been no loss of dividends: GAM's business strategy has never been to distribute earnings to shareholders.) The ultimate duration of this unspecified decline in value is uncertain. It was bound to be reversed to some degree by the return of the three wrongfully expropriated mills and by the prospect of compensation for the two others (the expropriation of which GAM did not challenge). Above all there is consensus as to the positive effect of the more vigorous application of Mexico's Sugar Program.

"84. GAMI did not attempt to prove or even present a theoretical financial analysis of what the short-term decline might have been. GAMI rather proceeds on the basis that the entire value of its investment has been destroyed. This is demonstrably untrue. GAMI's shareholding in GAM remains intact. GAM's principal productive assets have either been restored to it or are the subject of negotiations to determine compensation. The sugar industry is now operating on a better footing. Mr Pinto testified that a tax on soft drinks sweetened by fructose 'has turned out to be a very beneficial measure for the Mexican sugar industry'. GAM has declared itself to be optimistic for the future. Counsel for GAMI declared flatly in final oral submissions that 'the system is working now'. GAMI's failure to make good on its claim of total destruction will be dealt with in detail below when examining its claim of expropriation. But also with respect to the Article 1105 claim it must be noted that GAMI has not sought to quantify the alleged prejudice arising from particular alleged acts or omissions.

"85. GAMI's approach seems to be all or nothing. But no credible cause-and-effect analysis can lay the totality of GAMI's disappointments as an investor at the feet of the Mexican Government. Both sides agree that the economics of sugar are highly distorted and subject to powerful international market forces. No one has suggested that NAFTA entitles an investor to act on the basis that a regulatory scheme constitutes a guarantee of economic success. GAMI can assert only that maladministration of the Sugar Program caused it some prejudice. But the prejudice must be particularized and quantified. GAMI has not done so. The Tribunal does not know if such a demonstration would even be possible in the circumstances given the problem of timing. There are years when

> the sun shines on the sugar industry. In Mexico in particular the industry has had its ups and downs. Recent developments have apparently been positive. GAMI presumably benefits from them. Absent a complete destruction of its investment GAMI has not identified a particular point in time when a metaphorical snapshot of its prejudice should be taken. It may be that such a demonstration is impossible in this case. At any rate the Tribunal would have been in no position to award damages even if it had found a violation of Article 1105. The Tribunal will nevertheless explain its conclusion that GAMI also failed to establish its claim in principle under Article 1105."[28]

Thus, the tribunal dismissed GAMI's 1105 claim having found that its allegation of total destruction of the investment was "demonstrably untrue". The tribunal, perhaps for the sake of completeness, went on to "explain" that GAMI was also unsuccessful in establishing a claim in principle under Article 1105; but it is clear from its award that the fact that it failed to particularize and quantify the actual damage suffered was enough to reject its claim, as it "would have been in no position to award damages even if it had found a violation of Article 1105."

GAMI also alleged that the direct expropriation of GAM's mills had destroyed the value of its shares in GAM and thus resulted in an indirect expropriation of said shares. It claimed damages amounting to the full value of its original investment, even though during the arbitral proceedings GAM successfully recovered three of the five expropriated mills (and began negotiations with the government regarding compensation for the other two).

The tribunal concluded that it did not need to:

> "... decide whether partial destruction of shareholding interests may be tantamount to expropriation. It would in any case be necessary to assess the value of shareholdings in GAM at the time of the Expropriation Decree. GAM was and remains in the hands of its owners. Its principal assets had been taken. But Mexican law gave it substantial protections."[29]

It added:

> "GAMI may have had subjective apprehensions that Mexican judicial remedies would be insufficient. But this Tribunal can only act on the basis of objective findings justified by evidence that GAM's value as an

> enterprise had been destroyed or impaired [...] GAMI has staked its case on the proposition that the wrong done to it did in fact destroy the whole value of its investment."[30]

The tribunal noted that GAMI sought to lend credibility to its position by agreeing to relinquish its shares in GAM as a condition of the award it sought. "It [GAMI] suggests that any residual value is therefore of no moment." The tribunal concluded:

> "This posture is untenable. The Tribunal cannot be indifferent to the true effect on the value of the investment of the allegedly wrongful act. GAMI has neglected to give any weight to the remedies available to GAM. Assessment of their effect on the value of GAMI's investment is a precondition to a finding that it was taken. GAMI has not proved that its investment was expropriated for the purposes of Article 1110."[31]

4. SPECULATIVE DAMAGES

The ILC has noted that international tribunals "have been reluctant to provide compensation for claims with inherently speculative elements".[32] In his separate opinion on the issues at the quantum phase of in *CME v. The Czech Republic*, Professor Brownlie concurred: "The principle denying recovery for speculative damages has long been recognized in the practice of international tribunals."[33] There is considerable support for this conclusion. The Iran – US Claims Tribunal stated in *Amoco v. Iran*:

> "One of the best settled rules of the law of international responsibility of States is that no reparation for speculative or uncertain damage can be awarded. This holds true for the existence of the damage and of its effect as well. Such a rule, therefore, applies in the case of unlawful expropriation. *A fortiori*, the reasoning on which it rests must also apply in the case of compensation for a lawful expropriation. It does not permit the use of a method which yields uncertain figures for the valuation of damages, even if the existence of damages is certain."[34]

In the *Chorzów Factory* case, the PCIJ concluded that the damages alleged to have been caused by injurious competition "would come under the heading of possible but contingent and indeterminate damage which, in accordance with the jurisprudence of international tribunals, cannot be taken into account."[35]

In this context, while recognizing the validity of certain valuation methods that factor in different elements of risk and probability, such as the discounted cash flow (DCF) method, international tribunals have exercised caution because "[t]he method analyses a wide range of inherently speculative elements, some of which have a significant impact upon the outcome (e.g. discount rates, currency fluctuations, inflation figures, commodity prices, interest rates and other commercial risks)."[36] The Iran – US Claims Tribunal in *Amoco* questioned whether the method could be used at all: "As a projection into the future, any cash flow projection has an element of speculation associated with it, as recognized by the Claimant. For this very reason it is disputable whether a tribunal can use it at all for the valuation of compensation."[37] The tribunal explained:

> "The element of speculation in a short-term projection is rather limited, although unexpected events can make it turn out to be wrong. The speculative element rapidly increases with the number of years to which a projection relates. It is well known, and certainly taken into account by investors, that if it applies to a rather distant future a projection is almost purely speculative, even if it is done by the most serious and experienced forecasting firms..."[38]

The tribunal addressed the sufficiency of proof supporting the calculation of the discount rate. It questioned certain adjustments made to take into account the differences between the company in question and other oil companies that were used as reference, as well the adjustments made in order to properly weigh certain risks. The tribunal said that it was unable to test the veracity or the importance of the adjustments made for the purpose of comparing the company in question to similar oil companies, and that "no precise information was provided by the Claimant on the technique used in order to translate into figures the general qualitative considerations presented in the expert's report on each of the specific risks" that were taken into account. It added that these "these considerations, indeed, were relatively succinct and not very elaborated" and that "the mere mention that a risk was higher or lower than the average" was "too vague to furnish a valuable indication and to assist the Tribunal to assess the validity of the adjustment" made.[39] The tribunal went on to say:

> "In the words of the Claimant's expert, 'there necessarily will be room for some variations in detail and the exercise of expert judgment in applying the [DCF] analysis in a specific instance'. It appears that 'the exercise

of expert judgment' is at a peak for the determination of the adjustment of the reference discount rate. With all respect for the undoubted experience of such a distinguished expert, it remains true that expert judgment means subjective judgment, and that the reasons on which it rests in relation to this specific issue have not been fully disclosed."[40]

A crucial element in a DCF analysis is the operating record of a company as a going concern. The tribunal in *Metalclad Corporation v. The United Mexican States* noted:

> "Normally, the fair market value of a going concern which has a history of profitable operation may be based on an estimate of future profits subject to a discounted cash flow analysis [...] However, where the enterprise has not operated for a sufficiently long time to establish a performance record or where it has failed to make a profit, future profits cannot be used to determine going concern or fair market value."[41]

It agreed with the tribunal in *Asian Agricultural Products v. Sri Lanka* that an enterprise "requires the prior presence on the market for at least two or three years, which is the minimum period needed in order to establish continuing business connections."[42] The *Metalclad* tribunal considered a discounted cash flow analysis in the circumstances of that case inappropriate because the investment in question (a hazardous waste landfill) had never operated and thus lacked a track record on which future profits could be assessed. It concluded that any award based on future profits would therefore be wholly speculative.[43]

In *Autopista Concesionada de Venezuela*, the tribunal stated that it was disinclined to award lost profits because the claimant had not shown future lost profits with a sufficient degree of certainty under the relevant standards (of both Venezuelan and international law). It referred with approval to a number of cases cited by Venezuela and asserted that international tribunals are reluctant to award lost profits for a beginning industry and unperformed work. It concluded:

> "In the present case, the fact remains that Aucoven [the company in question] had no record of profits and that it never made the investments in the project nor built the Bridge required by the Concession Agreement.

> In these circumstances, the Tribunal considers that Aucoven's claim for future profits does not rest on sufficiently certain economic projections and thus appears speculative. Hence, it does not meet the standards for an award of lost profits under Venezuelan law, nor would it meet these standards under international law, if the latter were applicable."[44]

Other relevant circumstances need to be taken into account. The tribunal in *Autopista Concesionada de Venezuela* held that "a claim cannot be valued without consideration of its environment, i.e., without consideration of social, economic, political or other factors which may affect it."[45] In *Phelps Dodge v. Iran*, construction of the factory in question, owned by an Iranian company, SICAB (in turn owned in part and controlled by Phelps Dodge), began in 1976 and concluded in 1978. By late 1978 almost all the equipment was on site and had been installed, and the factory began limited production of certain product lines. Commercial production of all product lines would have been able to begin in mid-1979, but growing unrest in Iran and, ultimately, the outburst of the Iranian Revolution prevented it. In mid-1979 stock of SICAB owned by Iranian nationals was nationalized, as were two Iranian banks that were investors in the company. In November 1980, management of SICAB was transferred to Iranian Government agencies. In light of these circumstances, the tribunal could not agree that at the time of the taking the factory was a going concern "so that elements of value as future profits and goodwill could confidently be valued" and determined that "any conclusions on these matters would be highly speculative." It noted that, "while no diminution in value should be made because of the anticipation of a taking, the Tribunal could not properly ignore the obvious and significant negative effects of the Iranian Revolution on SICAB's business prospects, at least in the short and medium term."[46]

The Iran-US Claims Tribunal in *Amoco* ultimately rejected using the DCF method. It stated that while "projections can be useful indications for a prospective investor, who understands how far it can rely on them and accepts the risks associated with them; they certainly cannot be used by a tribunal as the measure of a fair compensation".[47] Nonetheless, the DCF method has been accepted as an adequate valuation method. Its applicability to a specific case, however, will depend on the specific circumstances, including the performance record, and the degree of certainty provided by the experts, which in turn will greatly depend on the available data and the information concerning the specific techniques employed and decisions made by them.

CONCLUSION

The question of damages in the context of investor-state arbitration under IIAs has important implications. First, access to international arbitration is contingent on (1) an investor making an allegation of breach of the provisions of an IIA, where (2) that breach has caused the investor or its investment to suffer economic prejudice. This is no trivial matter: as the *GAMI* case shows, while an investor may get over the access hurdle by simply alleging that it has incurred loss or damage, a substantive claim – not just a particular claim for damages – may be entirely thrown out for failure to prove such prejudice. To paraphrase the *GAMI* tribunal, even if a claimant were to successfully establish a breach of the agreement, a tribunal may not be in a position to make an award for damages.

Also, because one of the parties will always be a sovereign state – something that is relevant for many other reasons – international tribunals have a responsibility of providing certainty and ensuring transparency in the quantification of damages. Payment of damages in compliance with an award involves the use of public funds, and a state will be accountable to its citizenry. This, in my view, imposes a greater onus on claimants to satisfy tribunals of the actual prejudice suffered, and a greater onus on tribunals as well to accurately and transparently quantify the prejudice.

END NOTES

1 The UNCTAD uses the term international investment agreements. They include "treaties for the promotion and protection of investment (or bilateral investment treaties), treaties for the avoidance of double taxation (or double taxation treaties), other bilateral and regional trade and investment agreements, as well as various multilateral agreements that contain a commitment to liberalize, protect and/or promote investment." See, for instance, *World Investment Report 2005*, Chapter 1, Note 45. As used in this paper, they exclude double taxation of agreements.

2 See also International Law Commission: *Report of the International Law Commission on the work of its Fifty-third session.* Official Records of the General Assembly, Fifty-sixth session, Supplement No. 10 (A/56/10), Chapter IV.E.2, p. 244.

3 *Understanding on rules and procedures governing the settlement of disputes*, Articles 7(3) and 22.

4 Ibid.

5 Redfern, Alan and Martin Hunter: *Law and Practice of International Commercial Arbitration.* 3rd ed., Sweet & Maxwell, London, 1999, p. 365.

6 See International Law Commission, *Report of the International Law Commission on the work of its Fifty-third session,* p. 244.

7 *Liberian Eastern Timber Corporation (LETCO)* v. *the Government of the Republic of Liberia*, Award of 31 March 1986 (rectified on 14 May 1986), 26 I.L.M. 647, 1987, p. 658.

8 Ibid.

9 *S.D. Myers* v. *the Government of Canada*, Partial Award of 13 November 2000, § 309.

10 *Case concerning the factory at Chorzów (Claim for indemnity) (The merits)*, Judgment No. 13 of 13 September 1928, Publications of the Permanent Court of International Justice, Collection of Judgments, Series A.– No. 17, p. 47.

11 *S.D. Myers,* § 316. *Pope & Talbot* v. *the Government of Canada*, Award in respect of Damages of 31 May 2002, § 80.

12 *Pope & Talbot,* § 81-85.

13 *S.D. Myers,* § 316-317.

14 Ibid.

15 Durward Sandifer: *Evidence before international tribunals.* University Press of Virginia, Procedural Aspects of International Law Series, 1975, p. 127.

6 *Asian Agricultural Products Limited* v. *Republic of Sri Lanka*, ICSID Case No. ARB/87/3, Award of 27 June 1990, § 56, Rule (H).

17 *United States – Measures Affecting Imports of Woven Wool Shirts and Blouses from India*, Report of the Appellate Body, adopted 23 May 1997, WT/DS33/AB/R, p. 14.

18 *Asian Agricultural Products,* § 56, Rule (I).

19 *United States – Measures Affecting Imports of Woven Wool Shirts and Blouses*, p. 14.

20 *Asian Agricultural Products*, § 56, Rule (L).

21 *Autopista Concesionada de Venezuela, C.A.* v. *Bolivarian Republic of Venezuela*, ICSID Case No. ARB/00/5, Award of 23 September 2003, § 268.

22 *Chorzów Factory*, pp. 56-57. The court did award damages for the deprivation of the factory.

23 *Generation Ukraine, Inc.* v. *Ukraine*, ICSID Case No. ARB/00/9, Award of 16 September 2003.

24 Ibid., § 19.1-19.4.

25 Ibid., § 19.5 *et seq.*

26 Ibid., § 19.26. The tribunal went on to analyze the merits of the claim and rejected all the allegations of breach. It concluded that it could not discern a breach of the BIT by Ukraine and dismissed the claim in its entirety.

27 *GAMI Investments Inc.* v. *The Government of the United Mexican States*, Final Award of 15 November 2004.

28 Ibid., § 83-85.

29 Ibid., § 132.

30 Ibid., § 132-133.

31 Ibid. The tribunal also dismissed GAMI's 1102 claim on the merits.

32 International Law Commission, *Report of the International Law Commission on the work of its Fifty-third session*, p. 259.

33 *CME Czech Republic B.V. (The Netherlands)* v. *The Czech Republic*, Separate opinion on the issues at the quantum phase of, § 66 *et seq.*

34 *Amoco International Finance Corporation* v. *Islamic Republic of Iran*, Partial Award of 14 July 1987, 27 I.L.M. 1320, 1988, § 238.

35 *Chorzów Factory*, p. 57.

36 International Law Commission, *Report of the International Law Commission on the work of its Fifty-third session*, p. 258.

37 *Amoco*, § 238.

38 Ibid., § 239.

39 Ibid., § 241-243,

40 Ibid., § 244.

41 *Metalclad Corporation* v. *The United Mexican States*, ICSID Case No. ARB (AF) 97/1, Award of 30 August 2000, § 119-120.

42 Ibid., § 120.

43 Ibid., § 121.

44 *Autopista Concesionada de Venezuela,* § 362. The tribunal held that, under the terms of the concession agreement, Venezuelan law was applicable but that it would resolve conflicts between Venezuelan law and international law, if any, in accordance with the latter. It based this conclusion on the parties' agreement that Venezuelan law was consistent with international law and their acceptance that the latter prevailed over the former in case of conflict.

45 Ibid., § 364.

46 *Phelps Dodge Corp. and Overseas Private Investment Corp.* v. *The Islamic Republic of Iran*, Award of 19 March 1986, 10 Iran-U.S.C.T.R. 121, § 30-31.

47 Ibid., § 239, *in fine.*

7

Recovery of damages for breach of an obligation of payment

By **Nayla Comair-Obeid***
Professor, Faculty of Law, Lebanese University; Partner, Obeid Law Firm, Lebanon; Chartered Arbitrator; Council Member of the ICC Institute of World Business Law

INTRODUCTION

This topic is extremely wide, so I shall devote my paper to interests which represent the main compensation for damages resulting from failure to fulfill an obligation of payment. In this respect, there would appear to be nothing more simple for an international arbitrator than deciding any question about damages due for failure to fulfill an obligation of payment. However, the practice shows that the lack of uniformity in the rules related to interest applied by arbitral tribunals does in fact lead to uncertainty in arbitration jurisprudence.[1] On one side, the requests for arbitration sometimes omit any demand for the judgment to include payment of interest, or at least formulate it in an incomplete way that leaves it to the discretion of the arbitrator to fix the rate of interest that he deems appropriate.[2] On the other side, it happens that at the end of a difficult ruling, the arbitrator does not attach sufficient importance to the problem of interest.

The interest meant to indemnify a creditor for the temporary absence of the funds due to him[3] is the result of failure to fulfill an obligation of payment of a sum of money, one which arises from a contractual obligation or, alternatively, from an extra-contractual obligation that will be converted into a monetary obligation.

* Author of *Arbitration in Lebanese Law – A Comparative Study*, Delta, Beirut 1999, *The Law of Business contracts in the Arab Middle East*, Kluwer Law International, London, May 1996, *Les Contrats en Droit Musulman des Affaires*, Economica, Paris, 1995.

But whatever the nature of this pecuniary obligation (whether obligation of giving or of doing),[4] there can be no doubt that by engaging himself to pay the debt due, the debtor also takes on the obligation of a precise and determined result and cannot be exonerated even because of force majeure, in application of the principle *genera non pereunt.*

Compensation due from another party's failure to fulfill a monetary obligation is made good at a fixed rate in international commercial arbitration by the allocation of moratory interest, by the allocation of compensatory interest provided for by national legislation[5] and/or is also recognized in jurisprudence and doctrine.[6] In this respect, compensatory interest presupposes that the person responsible should make partial or total reparation for the prejudice caused, with the further addition of the moratory interest. We shall limit our study to the question of moratory and compensatory interest granted by international arbitrators.

The difficulty arises with the inconsistent positions adopted by arbitral tribunals concerning the interest to be granted, and also with the challenges confronting such tribunals concerning the choice of the appropriate legal system. What are the solutions to be adopted by arbitral jurisprudence in the absence of such a stated choice and what is the solution to be recommended for possible unification in this matter?

1. DIFFICULTIES AND CHALLENGES

Arbitral jurisprudence confirmed the principle accepted in international law that the parties winning a suit on the merits have the right to receive interest on the granted principal.[7]

However, the position of arbitrators concerning the means at the disposal of the creditor of a sum of money to obtain reparation for loss imposed by absence or delay of payment is far from uniform.

Arbitrators have to settle delicate questions about the law applicable (1) concerning interest, in particular as to the qualification of the interest to be granted (moratory, compensatory, punitive, damages and interest for delay, etc.), its rate, its starting-point and its computation. In the absence of an expressly stated choice of the law to be applied (2), they will also have to decide what rules should be applied in allocating interest, entirely using their own discretion. This is a particularly sensitive issue for arbitration in view of the importance of the sums involved. The amount of interest due sometimes exceeds the principal itself.[8]

1. Concerning application of the law chosen by the parties

The choice of the law to be applied in fixing the interest takes on great importance in view of there being consideration for the legal system chosen by the parties. The arbitrator will have to pronounce the award according to the contractual agreement between the parties if there is a choice expressed, (a) and in the absence of such stated agreement between the parties, (b) he will have to settle various questions concerning the function of the law to be applied for the interest (i) whether the latter should be moratory or compensatory and what its rate should be, (ii) as well as its starting point and date for computation (iii).

a) If the intention of the parties is clear, it appears from an examination of the arbitral awards that the parties, having made their choice[9] concerning the law to be applied to the merits, have also agreed on an appropriate interest. In such a case, the arbitrators should respect the agreement of the parties and apply the agreed rate of interest.[10]

The autonomy of the parties is a fundamental principle in private international law, and sacred to international arbitration. In arbitration, the arbitral tribunal must take the provisions of the contract into account.[11]

In this respect, an international *ad hoc* arbitral tribunal has adopted in its award the agreed conventional rate, which is higher than the rate provided for in the law applicable to the contract. A challenge has been made, based *inter alia* on the fact that the amount of the interest, being 75% of the principal, constitutes a Ribawi interest, which would be contrary to the international public policy and, as such, considered as a cause of annulment of the award. Beirut Court of Appeal[12] rejected such allegation in its decision of 14 February 2002, based on the parties' autonomy to decide on their contractual commercial relationship, especially noting that the Lebanese Commercial law in this matter did not provide for an interest rate ceiling.[13]

However, in a final award rendered under ICC Rules of Arbitration in Case 8874, the arbitral tribunal, acting as *amiable compositeur*, considered "according to the principles of equity" that, despite the parties' initial contractual agreement on a monthly rate of 1.4% and despite the principle that the allowance of interest is a cornerstone of economic and commercial relations, the initial interest rate, if applied to the considered amount and period of time, would be disproportionate with the economic and commercial conditions of this case. Therefore, the arbitral tribunal substituted the US prime rate recommended by the Principles of Unidroit for the initial contractual rate of 1.4% per month, for the delayed payment owed to the claimant by the respondent.[14]

The first challenge which arises in the above-mentioned case is whether an *amiable compositeur* arbitrator, in disregarding the parties' contractual provision and based on its own consideration of equity, could have stayed within the limits of the *ultra petita*.

b) In the absence of such stated agreement between the parties to be applied in fixing the interest, in case the parties have omitted to fix a conventional interest, the qualification of the interest should be resolved by the arbitral tribunal in accordance with the applicable law to the dispute. The issue to be examined is: how to apply this *lex contractus* under the different approaches adopted by the various juridical systems (i).

As to the rate at which interest should be awarded (ii) and to the starting point of interest (iii), decisions of arbitral tribunals have not revealed a unanimous solution in this regard.

i. Qualification of interest under the *lex contractus*

Moratory interest is defined as being interest related to monetary debts, drawn up in local or foreign currency. It compensates on an inclusive basis, regardless of a debtor's fault, for the loss of a sum of money by the creditor due to the debtor's delay in fulfilling his payment obligation. It constitutes an inclusive compensation indemnifying the capital withholding.[15] Compensatory interest refers to a pre-contractual, contractual or extra-contractual liability of the defaulting party. It aims to restore the injured party to the proprietary situation that would have been his if the damage relief had occurred immediately.[16]

Many juridical systems have adopted this distinction.[17] Unlike moratory interest, the allowance of compensatory interest requires the proof of the debtor's fault[18] and of the damage suffered by the claimant; moreover, some legislations require the proof of the debtor's bad faith[19] or an unjustified resistance.[20]

The difference between compensatory damages and moratory damages has been underlined by many civil law specialists.[21] Interest qualification, whether moratory or compensatory, depends on the legal system chosen by the parties. In a civil law system, this distinction remains applicable, which is not the case in a common law system, where interest is regarded as a procedural matter and not a matter of substantive law.

In fact, in Japanese law, the matter of interest is a substantive issue. If there is no provision on interest, courts award no interest. Article 420 of the Japanese Civil Code (CC) provides that parties can agree on an estimate of damages in the case of breach of contract, and in such circumstances the court cannot change the amount of the estimate of damages. This provision is based on the principle of freedom of contract.

In Russia also, the matter of interest is regarded as a substantive issue. If there is an agreement on interest by the parties, arbitrators must determine interest based on the agreement. In the absence of such an agreement, the rules of the law applicable to substantive issues are applied.

In regard to Scotland and England, the matter of the award of interest is procedural. Since there is no particular provision allowing an arbitral tribunal to award interest in the Law on Arbitration, arbitrators may have discretionary power in this regard.

Under the Scots Late Payment of Commercial Debts (Interest) Act 1998, statutory interest and a contractual remedy following late payment of a debt are terminologically distinguished (Part II, Section 8). Therefore, interest is a special kind of damages, but must be distinguished from "damages", which must be proven by the party.

If there is an agreement on liquidated damages, which is regarded as a pre-estimate of damages, interest can therefore be claimed on such damages. Under the Arbitration Act of 1996, the parties can freely agree on the power of the arbitral tribunal as regards interest (Article 491).

In the absence of such an agreement, the arbitral tribunal may award simple or compound interest from such dates and at such rates as it considers meets the justice of the case.

In order to impose interest, arbitrators must fix the principal sum on which interest is imposed. As a pre-condition for this, arbitrators must decide whether the damages that had been agreed by the parties are to be classified as liquidated damages or penalty.[22]

Furthermore, there is a wide range on the ground of applicable law with respect to the provision of interest, starting from a total prohibition, passing by a partial prohibition based on a distinction between civil and commercial contracts, up to a total recognition of the principle of interest, as will be detailed below.

- ***Total prohibition***

Saudi Arabia is the only country that has not adopted regulations governing interest rates in commercial matters. On the one hand, this is because interest, in whatever form, is considered as *Riba* and, on the other hand, because in the absence of a civil code, the *Sharia* takes the place of a constitutional civil code and is therefore the basis of all rules of law.[23]

As a consequence, and unlike the other Middle Eastern countries, which have adopted the distinction between civil and commercial law in order to render interest rules more flexible, Saudi Arabia has maintained the prohibition on usury in commercial matters, in accordance with the general principles of the *Sharia*. Courts in Saudi Arabia do not mention interest in their judgments, as it is forbidden by *Sharia*. The same applies in respect of arbitral tribunals, which disregard in domestic cases the allowance of interest as being contrary to the *Sharia*, the provisions of which are of public policy.[24] Therefore, an international award dealing with interest could be annulled on this ground by the Board of Grievances in charge of the enforcement of arbitral awards.

Moreover, in an arbitral award rendered in Saudi Arabia, the official position of the Kingdom can be summarized as follows: "The Sharia's Islamic law forbids usury in any form or manner whatsoever, whether or not it is gained or in secret. The defendant asserted that a portion of the amount claimed by the claimant [...] is illegal. If the defendant's contention properly invokes Sharia provision, then the Arbitral Tribunal must apply it since it relates to the public order of the Kingdom."[25]

■ ***Partial prohibition***

This partial prohibition is based on the one hand on the nature of the legal relation, and operates a distinction between civil and commercial disputes and, on the other hand, on the function of interest, some systems allowing moratory interest without stipulating any provisions as to compensatory interest, yet providing for an integral compensation of the damage.

– The Kuwaiti legislature for instance, has taken the view that the rules which govern civil matters are not appropriate for commercial matters. As a result, the rules of the *Sharia* in general, and the prohibition against *Riba* in particular,[26] which are observed in civil matters, are not observed in commercial matters, because they are deemed not to be appropriate to the world of business.

  Thus Article 102, subsection 1 of the Kuwaiti Commercial Code fixes at 7% the legal rate of interest, and enables contracting parties to stipulate interest rates for commercial loans; in the absence of an agreement as to the interest rate, the legal rate shall apply.[27] In banking transactions, term deposits earn interest as in all traditional banks. Furthermore, under Article 364 of the Commercial Code, a customer who is granted a credit facility will be required, not only to repay the capital, but also to pay the interest agreed upon in the contract or, failing this, the legal rate. In addition, the Central Bank has the power to regulate and set ceilings for interest rates concerning bank credits and loans.

– The same distinction applies in Bahrain between civil and commercial debts, where the law allows moratory interest in commercial matters on the following conditions: " ... in no case shall the total interest payments charged by the creditor be in excess of the principal debt amount on the basis of which interest has been charged in the cases of debts the repayment period of which does not exceed 7 years."[28] Such ceiling is only applicable to commercial transactions in local currency and does not apply to commercial transactions in foreign currency. However, moratary interest is not permissible under civil obligations.[29]

  As to the compensatory interests, they are allowed by the Bahraini law without any distinction between civil and commercial obligations.[30]

- Another example of legislation providing for partial prohibition is the Code of Commercial Transactions of the United Arab Emirates, promulgated by the Federal law of 7 September 1993, relating to the parties' obligations in commercial contracts. Article 76 of the aforementioned Code stipulates that the creditor is entitled to charge interest on commercial loans according to the interest agreed in the contracts. If the rate of interest is not specified in the contract, the rate prevailing on the market at the time of the agreement will apply, on condition that it does not exceed the ceiling of 12% at the time of repayment.

  Article 399, paragraph 1, relating to current accounts, stipulates that interest on current accounts is not paid to customers unless otherwise agreed by the parties. The interest is then calculated on the official rate basis. However, if the interest rate is not set, it should be calculated on the basis of the prevailing price on the market, but may not exceed the rate of 12%.

- The Sultanate of Oman also does not have a civil code and, therefore, applies the *Sharia* in civil matters.[31] The Commercial Code stipulates in Article 1 that its provisions apply to merchants and to commercial activities that may be undertaken by any individual, including those who do not have the status of merchant. Article 5 stipulates that, in the absence of statutory provisions, precedence is granted to custom, special or local custom being preferred to general custom, but in the absence thereof, the *Sharia* shall apply. Where none of those exist, the rules of equity shall apply. This Commercial Code follows the example of western codes and regulates all commercial and banking activities (documentary credits, cheques, bills of exchange, bankruptcy and so on) as well as commercial loans. Article 80 of the Omani Commercial Code grants the lender the right to receive a return as consideration for the debtor having obtained a loan or a commercial facility. The rate of this return is set by mutual agreement between the two parties within the limits laid down each year by the Minister for Trade and Industry, after agreeing thereon with Oman's Chamber of Commerce and Industry, and having regard to the loan's maturity date, its purpose and risks. In a case where the debtor delays settling his debt after maturity date, the creditor will be entitled to the return agreed for the delay. The creditor may claim complementary damages, to be added to the return agreed in the loan or commercial facility, if the delay has caused the creditor damage in excess of the return. The court will assess those damages.

- As to Iranian law, the Iranian Constitution prohibits *Riba* and such prohibition has been confirmed by the decision of the Council of Guardians and by the arbitral tribunal's decision in the ICC Case 7263.[32]

  However, it should be noted that the Iranian law allows an important exception to the strict prohibition of interest in the case of transactions between Iranian nationals and foreigners whose laws permit the payment of interest.

  In addition, in a decision rendered in the ICC Case 7373,[33] the arbitral tribunal gave liberal interpretation to the Iranian law, by considering that such law allows compensatory interest in the event of late payment. The arbitral tribunal based its decision on equity, considering that it would be unfair in international commercial relations not to award interest to the claimant.

  And in a recent decision, the arbitral tribunal referred to the Iranian Civil Code, which allows courts to order debtors to pay an indemnity to creditors for losses incurred due to late payment, if such indemnity is provided for in the contract.[34]

- It should be also noted that some Islamic countries, such as Egypt and Iraq, have moved away from *Sharia* and expressly allowed the payment of interest at a certain rate.[35]

  However and despite the admission of interest in Egyptian Law, the arbitral tribunal, having applied on the matter of interest the Libor rate + 3% instead of the interest rate as fixed in Article 226 and sequence of the Egyptian Civil Code, has seen its award annulled by the Appeal Court of Cairo,[36] which considered as contrary to public policy the award rendered in the ICC Case 9982, on 21 December 1999, where the arbitral tribunal did not compute the interest in conformity with the provisions of Article 227 of the Egyptian Civil Code, whereas the parties had agreed to solve the dispute according to the Egyptian law.

The challenge that arises in cases where a ceiling is imposed by certain legal systems somehow binds the arbitrator in the matter of interest because of a potential challenge which could be made on the ground of his award infringing public policy.[37]

Furthermore, there is no relevant provision concerning compensatory interest in several Middle Eastern legislations. However, compensation for delay in settling a civil debt is permitted only if the delay has caused damage to the creditor. On the other hand, compensation for delay in settlement of a commercial debt is not linked to the damage caused to the creditor; it is expressly stipulated that the creditor may receive damages over and above the interest on overdue payment that is awarded, without being required to prove the existence of fraud or gross negligence on the part of the debtor. The same provision related to the full compensation of prejudice is stipulated in several other Middle Eastern countries.[38]

It should be noted that some arbitrators, in the presence of a total or partial prohibition in the above-mentioned countries, are confronted with the challenge represented by the parties' agreement on a conventional rate higher than the one stipulated by the law of the contract. This would lead to the risk of annulment of the award, or to the refusal by the competent judicial authorities to give the exequatur for non-conformity with the mandatory laws. If the case arises, whenever the arbitrator admits the rate fixed in the law applicable to the substance and not the agreed conventional rate, he takes the risk of having his award censured on the ground that he has ruled without conforming to the mission entrusted to him and will have then ruled, in our opinion, *ultra petita*.

■ *Recognition of the principle of interest*

In Europe, the practice of awarding interest is well established among European countries.[39]

In a final award rendered in the ICC Case 8711,[40] the arbitral tribunal considered it fair under German law to allow the claimant a compensation for the valuable services made to the respondent. However, the arbitral tribunal referred to the exclusion set by German law related to a presupposed fault of the commercial agent.

The English Arbitration Act of 1996 best illustrates the awarding of interest under a common law system. Interest has been customarily awarded under the Act of 1950 whenever a claimant has been deprived of the use of money, unless the parties have expressly agreed otherwise.[41]

Asian countries such as China, Taiwan, India, Japan and the Republic of Korea generally allow interest to be paid when a debtor is in default on a money payment.[42]

Therefore, having reviewed the different legal systems and noted the different approaches adopted thereto in the matter of interest,[43] with respect to their qualification and function, these being a matter of substantive or procedural law, difficulties confront an arbitrator when dealing with this issue, even if the parties have chosen an applicable law on the substance of the case. Furthermore, another challenge arises when dealing with the interest rate, where a wide diversity of solutions has been adopted by international tribunals.

ii. The rate of interest

The classic solution consists in fixing the rate of interest on the basis of the applicable law to the contract. However, a review of the most recent awards shows that there are different methods currently used by international arbitration tribunals to determine the rate of interest, and not a uniform one. This plurality of methods results from the general trend that comes out in doctrine and international arbitral practice, which consists in leaving the arbitrator, when fixing this rate, free not to refer to the legal rate of a national legal system.[44]

■ *Lex contractus*

The arbitral jurisprudence referred in many awards to the applicable law to the contract in order to determine the applicable rate of interest. In an arbitral award of the ICC rendered by a unique arbitrator,[45] the latter mentioned that "this was the more correct and appropriate solution." In fact, until 1980, tribunals fixed the interest rate following the law of the contract.[46]

■ *Lex fori*

Arbitral tribunals seem inclined to apply the legal rate of the place of arbitration, as such rate is related to the procedure and not to the substance.

The application of *lex fori* provides the arbitrators with a large power of appreciation concerning the appropriate rate to be assessed.[47]

- ***The rate of the place of payment***

In some awards, arbitral tribunals have applied the interest rate of the place of payment.[48] However, "in many cases, the currency of the debt is preferred to that of the place of payment".[49]

- ***The reasonable rate as determined by the arbitral tribunal***

Arbitral tribunals have in some awards disregarded the law chosen by the parties for determining the interest rate, using their discretion to determine the reasonable rate on a case by case basis.[50] In a final award in Case 8769,[51] the sole arbitrator considered that it was appropriate to apply a commercially reasonable interest rate.

- ***The market rate in the currency of the award***

Another method of determining the interest is based on the market rate of the currency in which the award is rendered.[52]

- ***The rate corresponding to the discount bank interest rate of the creditor's domicile, at the date of performance of the obligation***

An ICC Case 9771 (2001)[53] considered that, as Russian law[54] does not set up a fixed legal rate of interest, but provides as main rule that the creditor is entitled to a rate corresponding to the discount bank interest rate prevailing at its domicile at the date of performance of the obligation, "the default interest starts to run from the time when the Request for Arbitration was submitted until the payment date on the official Italian discount rate as applicable from time to time."

iii. The starting point of interest

As to this matter also, arbitral jurisprudence has not revealed a uniform position, as different starting points have been adopted:

- ***Date of failure to execute the contractual obligation***

This date can be chosen because it reflects the date on which the defaulting party should have made the payment. Thus, the non-defaulting party should have had the use of the money from that date.

In an ICC Final Award rendered in Case 6281,[55] the arbitral tribunal considered that defendant's default began on any date at which he should have delivered but did not perform the delivery, and applied Article 277, paragraph 1, of the Yugoslav Law on Obligations according to which interest is due to the creditor on the amount of damages as of the date at which the debtor begins to default.[56]

■ ***Date of the request for payment***

Most often, arbitral tribunals decide that interest will be payable as from the first request of payment.

In the award rendered under ICC Case 6531,[57] the arbitral tribunal decided that interest must be calculated at the French legal rate, and that it started running as from the moment when the creditor gave the debtor formal notice to pay (*mise en demeure*) (Article 1153 CC). In a partial award rendered in 1996 in Case 7983, the arbitral tribunal considered that monetary interest at the legal rate requested by the claimant ran only as from the date of the notice service.[58]

In several awards, arbitral tribunals referred to the date of the request for payment.[59]

■ ***Date of the claim filing***

The date of submission of a request for arbitration has been adopted by several arbitral awards and constitutes the most frequently adopted solution.

In an ICC Case 6162 (1990),[60] the arbitral tribunal decided that the claimant was entitled to an interest of 5% as from the filing date of the request for arbitration. In the final award in ICC Case 10329 (2000),[61] the arbitral tribunal considered that the awarded amount should bear an interest of 5% *per annum* from the filing date of the request for arbitration until full payment.[62]

An ICC award rendered in Case 5864 (1989),[63] based on Article 229 of the Libyan Law on Damage for Delay,[64] decided that, pursuant to the applicable law (Iranian Law) and in the case circumstances, interest should run only from the date of commencement of the arbitration.

- ***Date of the award***

The latest of the four starting points is the date of the award itself. In ICC Case 8264 of 1997, the arbitral tribunal rejected the claimant's claim for pre-award interest, stating that the respondent's delay in payment could have been explained by the claimant's reluctance to provide certain information to the respondent. The arbitral tribunal decided that interest should run as from the 30th day after notification of the award.[65]

- ***Date of the damage occurrence***

Some awards fix, as the starting date for damages, the date of occurrence of the event that caused the damage. Such is the case in the *Starret affair*, in which the Irano-American Arbitral Tribunal fixed the starting date for damages as from the expropriation date.[66]

2. In the absence of the choice of law applicable to the substance

When the parties have not expressly chosen the applicable law to the substance of the case, it is up to the arbitrator to determine the applicable law, in conformity with the chosen mode of arbitration, by adopting either the conflictual method or the direct one. The arbitrator certainly enjoys a large freedom at this stage: "the extent of the arbitrator's freedom depends on the *lex arbitri* which may allow an arbitrator to implement not only the national law but rules of law".[67] However, he will have to make sure that the chosen law does not infringe international public policy of the country in which the execution of the award will take place. This freedom is implicitly confirmed by Article 5 of the New York Convention, Article 7-1 of the European Convention, Article 28 of the UNCITRAL Model Law, Article 17 of the ICC Rules, Article 31-1 of the UNCITRAL Rules of Arbitration, Article 46 of the English Law and the Arbitration Act of 1996.[68]

a) The conflictual method

In numerous arbitral awards, the tribunal resorted to the conflictual method to determine the applicable law in the field of interest.

For example, in ICC Case 8175 of May 1996,[69] the Arbitral Tribunal was of the view that if the conflict of laws rules were to be applied at all, the appropriate law in relation to these questions as to interest was French law. Application of that law resulted in this case in the application of Indian law, since questions relating to interest are treated as substantive under the French conflict of laws rules.

Furthermore, in ICC Case 8501, the arbitral tribunal, applying Article 13 (3) of the ICC Rules, decided that "the Arbitral Tribunal will apply the law designated by the conflict of laws rules that it deems appropriate for the case."[70]

Recently, a final award of the Hague Permanent Court of Arbitration,[71] dated 19 September 2003, ruled that international law does not prescribe a specific rate of interest, but that several other juridical systems could be relevant. In circumstances in which laws of several different juridical systems could be applied to a particular transaction or event, it is a frequent practice to select the law of the legal system with which the question to be decided in the specified case has the closest connection. In this case, the tribunal noted that the Swiss legal system is the one having the closest connection with this question. (Switzerland was the place where the registered office of the bank was situated, as well as the seat and operational center of the activities of the bank. In addition, the bank made dividend payments in Swiss francs, and the currency in which interest had to be paid was the Swiss franc. Moreover, the private shareholders dealt with the bank in Switzerland and their dividends were paid in Swiss francs.) Therefore, the tribunal referred to Article 73 of the Code of Obligations, which states: "Where the object of an obligation is the payment of interest, and no rate is fixed either by contract, by law, or by custom, then the interest shall be paid at the rate of five percent per annum. This shall not affect provisions of public law regarding usury." Furthermore, Article 104 (relating to moratory interest) provides: "If an obligor is in default as to the payment of a financial debt, he shall pay default interest at five percent per annum, even if the contract provides for a lower rate. If a higher interest rate than five percent has been agreed upon in the contract, whether directly or by stipulation of a periodic bank charge, such higher interest may also be claimed during the period of the default. Among merchants, when the usual bank discount at the place of payment is higher than five percent, default interest may be calculated at such higher rate."

Accordingly, the tribunal decided that the rate of interest to be paid by the bank was 5% simple interest.

The application by the arbitral tribunal of the conflictual method is confirmed by Article 33-1 of the UNCITRAL Arbitration Rules, prescribing that "the Arbitral Tribunal shall apply the law designated by the parties as applicable to the substance of the dispute. Failing such designation, the Arbitral Tribunal shall apply the law determined by the conflict of laws rules which it considers applicable."

It should be noted that the arbitral practice reveals that arbitrators prefer not to adopt the conflictual process. Pierre Lalive stated in this context in the ICC case No. 1512[72] that, "the international arbitrator does not have a lex fori from which to derive conflict of laws rules".

b) The direct method

Several arbitrators have considered that no national law could meet the rightful expectations of the parties in international transactions to the same extent as transnational rules or the *lex mercatoria*.[73] Indeed, a new trend in the field of international arbitration consists in the application of the direct method, this being by reference either to the law deemed by the arbitrator to be the most appropriate, or by reference to the "general principles and normal usages of international trade".[74]

In the final award rendered in ICC Case 6219,[75] the arbitral tribunal considered that the general trend arising out of the legal literature and international arbitral practice is to grant the arbitrator a large measure of freedom in fixing such rates, the arbitrator not being obliged to refer to the legal rate of any national legal system, whether that of the law of the contract or the *lex fori* of the place of arbitration.[76]

In addition, the inappropriateness of the legal rate application, as fixed in the various national laws, has been indicated by arbitrators.[77]

This need to meet the parties' rightful expectations has been emphasized by Yves Derains,[78] who referred to the award of ICC Case 8385, in which the arbitral tribunal decided that the law that should be implemented was the law that best meets the needs of the community of international commerce. The one that does not conflict with the parties' rightful expectations, brings about uniform results and offers a reasonable solution to the dispute [...] Furthermore, he held that application of international principles offers a lot of advantages. They are applied uniformly and independently of the distinctive characteristics of each national law. They take into consideration the needs of international relations and allow a fruitful exchange between the systems that are sometimes exaggeratedly bound to conceptual distinctions and those looking for a fair and pragmatic solution to particular cases. Thus, it was an ideal opportunity to apply what is more and more frequently designated as *lex mercatoria*. The same author has often reiterated his position, considering that whatever the process used, the international arbitrator applies the law that best meets the rightful expectations of the parties. Indeed, UNIDROIT principles illustrate that trend, as will be shown below.

In light of the above, it appears that, except in cases where the parties have expressly designated the applicable law to interest, international arbitrators do not adopt a standard solution whenever the parties file a claim in relief of the damage deriving from the debtor's failure to execute his obligation of payment.

On one side, in case of the choice of a *lex contractus*, arbitrators were not unanimous in applying it to the interest issue. And in cases where the parties did not choose the law to be applied on the substance, different solutions were decided.

No matter the method used, conflictual or direct, the outcome is similar: in both cases, the general trend that comes out in doctrine and international arbitral practice is to leave to the arbitrator a great freedom in the field of interest, particularly when the parties show a lack of concern at this level upon their filing of the request for arbitration.[79] Yet, disregarding this issue is unjustified, given the substantial interests which are at stake.

If this observation derives from the characteristic flexibility of arbitration, it remains that the free faculty of appreciation left to the arbitrator in this field, which reflects in many awards the lack of motivation,[80] constitutes an additional challenge imposed by the issue of interest in the field of international arbitration.

How to remedy such a *de facto* situation?

PROPOSED SOLUTIONS

Examination of the above-mentioned international arbitral awards allows one to distinguish the criteria adopted by the arbitral tribunals for the allocation of moratory and compensatory interests.

As for the moratory interest, this is a question of a fixed-rate indemnity sanctioning delay in fulfilling the obligation to pay. Delay in the fulfillment of the obligation to pay is the only condition required for such interest to be due for payment. As for compensatory interest, a study of the relevant jurisprudence allows a list to be drawn up of the various criteria considered by the arbitration tribunals to make it due for payment, to fix its amount and to fix the date from which it should be calculated (1).

The diversity to be seen in the many criteria adopted in jurisprudence makes it necessary to consecrate a material rule for fixing interest in conformity with the expectations of the parties concerning the best law (2).[81]

1. The various criteria in jurisprudence for compensation due on account of non-fulfillment of the obligation to pay

Many criteria have been adopted by arbitral jurisprudence. On the one hand, some arbitral decisions simply look for the existence of a loss borne by the creditor as a result of non-fulfillment (a); others require bad faith on the part of the debtor (b); while yet others make reparation conditional on the absence of fault on the part of the creditor (c).

a) The existence of a damage suffered by the creditor on account of non-fulfillment of the obligation to pay

The awarding of compensatory interest is conditional on the proven existence of a damage caused to the creditor. This condition is however not required for the allocation of moratory interest, which comes as a matter of course.[82]

Several arbitral awards have laid down the features of the damage which open the way to reparation.

The classic solution has been the attribution of reparation covering not only actual loss but also profit that might have been gained. Arbitral jurisprudence has, however, required the presentation of proof of the loss suffered for compensation to be admitted. At this level, therefore, proof is required concerning the harm done and the amount of profit lost. So it was that in the award pronounced by the ICSID Tribunal on 25 February 1988 in the case *Soabi* v. *Senegal,*[83] the arbitral tribunal considered that only "real, certain and special" prejudice is reparable. The arbitral tribunal had recourse to the concept of loss of an opportunity implying identification of prejudice that is reparable according to the degree of probability of the event occurring and considered that the loss of possible profit was in fact the loss of an opportunity to gain the profit expected. The arbitral tribunal then proceeded to calculate the prejudice thus understood by comparing the agreed price with the cost of execution initially foreseen, reduced by the hazards of an economic and financial nature likely to affect the carrying out and profitability of the projects in the long term.[84]

More explicitly, in a decision of 17 July 2003 rendered in the ICSID case of *CMS Gas Transmission Company* v. *Argentina,*[85] the arbitral tribunal declared that the granting of any particular compensation supposes that the investor proves that he has truly suffered loss.[86] This has been justified by the tribunal's concern that the investor should not be in a position to be indemnified twice over, particularly when the investor took advantage of the provisions of an instrument of protection of investments in order to sue, in his own name, a host state.[87]

In the case *Asian Agriculture Products Ltd (AAPL)* v. *Sri Lanka*, in its award of 27 June 1990,[88] the arbitral tribunal based its decision on the principle that any future loss is reparable, but only on condition that such loss is certain. Therefore, the arbitral tribunal fixed compensation according to the then value of the shares held by the investor, but refused to take into account the profit that the investor claimed he would be making in the coming years. The award considered that future profit for a business company of only recent foundation, under-capitalized, relying on just one product and with only one market outlet, was too uncertain for it to be open to compensation.

In a more recent ICSID decision of 30 August 2000 in the case *Metalclad Corporation (Metaclad)* v. *Mexico,*[89] the arbitral tribunal considered that the correct market value of an active business that had always been profitable could be judged on the basis of an estimation of the future profits, subject to an analysis in terms of discounted cash flow. However, it also considered that when a business firm had not been exploited enough, over a period long enough to allow analysis of the evolution of its results, or when it had not been profitable, the future profits could not be taken into consideration in order to determine the value of its business or its market value. According to the arbitral tribunal, any award based on supposed future profits would be purely speculative; therefore it was an indemnity equal in value to what had been invested that should have been awarded to the plaintiff. The reason was that reparation on behalf of the plaintiff should as far as possible simply make good all the consequences of the illicit act and re-establish the state of things that would presumably have existed if the said act had not been committed (*statu quo ante*).

A final award in Case 10346 (December 2000)[90] stated that it was necessary to consider the consequent compensation for loss and damage that respondent must pay to claimant. The question of compensation would appear to be resolved merely by applying the concepts of *damnum emergens* and *lucrum cessans*, the first of which means a reduction in net worth, and the second a frustrated gain (income not received). Thus, the tribunal should proceed to evaluate the figures proved in the proceedings as making the *damnum emergens* and *lucrum cessans* using the parameter of fullness of the compensation, referable to the need to place the aggrieved party in the position it would have been in, absent the loss. However, for a loss to be compensated, it must be "certain" rather than "contingent loss", which only gives the right to compensation.

In the above case, the classification of damages as certain or contingent constituted for the arbitral tribunal a necessary filter for the determination of the reasonable losses and was based on the degree of seriousness and the scientific or technical solidity possessed by the prediction of what would have occurred had the harmful event not intervened, and from there to go on to quantify the loss which will amount to 100% if there is legal certainty that the situation would have occurred.

In a final award in ICC Case 9771 of 2001,[91] the arbitral tribunal examined first the claimant's entitlement to damages, as the goods delivered were not in conformity with the contractual specifications and, therefore, since respondent breached its obligation under the contract to deliver goods of a specific quality, the claimant was entitled to compensation for the damages suffered. However, the arbitral tribunal rejected the claimant's claim related to the loss of reputation, as it had not presented any evidence in this respect.

Likewise, in the case *Aucoven* v. *Venezuela*, the arbitral tribunal recalled in its decision of 23 September 2003[92] that loss of profit can be made good only if the expected profit presents a sufficient degree of certainty. The applicable law was Venezuelan law, but the arbitral tribunal stressed that the solution would have been the same even under international law.

So also in the ICSID case *Amco Asia Corporation (Amco)* v. *Indonesia* of 20 November 1984,[93] the arbitral tribunal pointed out that according to the principles and rules common to the main juridical systems, damages should be limited to reparation for direct and foreseeable harm. The requirement that it should be direct is the consequence of the need for a causal link between the fault and the prejudice.

As per Anglo-Saxon juridical systems, the reparation for the loss cannot impose exaggerated burdens on the liable party. Article 1616 of the Spanish Civil Code also states that the debtor is only liable for direct losses, i.e. losses that are the necessary and strict consequence of his unlawful act. In contrast, the debtor has no liability if the loss is not the certain and necessary result of his conduct, or if there is no causal relationship.[94] Therefore, the loss should have a direct character, that is to say resulting from the cause-effect relationship.

However, as per jurisprudence[95] and ICC Case 10346 (December 2000),[96] it is not enough to denote a loss as direct, as regard must also be had to the distinction between "foreseeable" and "unforeseeable" losses, with compensation being payable in relation to the former but not in relation to the latter, save where the debtor had acted fraudulently. The distinction between "foreseeable" and "unforeseeable" losses presents difficulties, and the judge who follows the "foreseeability" standard will have to conduct investigations into the type of losses which, ordinarily and reasonably, should have been within the contemplation of the party as associated with its breach, in order to decide from there whether or not compensation should be ordered and, if so, the amount of such compensation. Foreseeability, referring to the harmful consequences of their actions being within the reasonable contemplation of the parties, is therefore an additional condition to allow compensatory interest: both elements of damages must be foreseeably caused by the fundamental breach.

b) Bad faith on the part of the debtor

In an award rendered in ICC Case 6162,[97] the arbitral tribunal dismissed the claimant's claim for damages as the claimant had not alleged that the defendant would have acted in bad faith.

In a final award in Case 9032 (January 1998),[98] the arbitral tribunal granted the agent a right to indemnity on the grounds of loss of profit in addition to indemnity for cessation or non-renewal of contract, further to a right to interest as from the date of summons of the debtor. This was because of unjustified failure to execute the contract on the part of the mandatory, so causing a loss of possibilities of sales and therefore a loss of earnings for the agent.

This requirement of bad faith is set out by certain national legislations, including French legislation (Art 1153 of the French Civil Code stipulates that the creditor to whom its defaulting debtor has caused a prejudice due to bad faith unrelated to this delay, may receive damages distinct from the moratory interest). These texts reflect this moralizing function sought through the allocation of compensatory damages.

c) Absence of fault on the part of the creditor

In a final award in Case 8711 (March 1998),[99] the arbitral tribunal considered that to allow a compensation was fair because the claimant had provided the defendant valuable services.

In a final award in ICC Case 10329 (2000),[100] the arbitral tribunal based its decision on Article 75 of UN Convention on Contracts for the International Sale of Goods (CISG), which states that, if the seller has resold the goods within a reasonable time from contract avoidance, the party claiming damages may recover the difference between the contract price and the price in the substitution transaction.

In this case, after having requested the respondent to perform its obligations under the contract, the claimant advised him that it was taking measures to mitigate its loss. Article 77 of the above-mentioned Convention provides that a party who relies on a breach of contract must take such measures as are reasonable in the circumstances to mitigate the loss. The arbitral tribunal noted, therefore, that the claimant's claim for damages should be admitted because it had taken the necessary and appropriate measures in time and place to mitigate its damages.

In a final award in Case 10274 of 1999,[101] the arbitral tribunal considered that according to Article 75 of UN Sales Convention, the party claiming damages may recover the difference between the contract price and the price in the substitute transaction, as well as any further damages recoverable under Article 74 of UN Sales Convention, if the contract was avoided and if, in a reasonable manner and within a reasonable time after avoidance, the seller has resold the goods. However, the goods should be resold in a reasonable manner, if the seller acted as a prudent and reasonable seller would have acted. In this case, the claimant tried to resell the goods for more than 20% less than the price agreed with the respondent. Thus, the arbitral tribunal considered that the claimant acted as a prudent and reasonable seller.

2. For a material regulation concerning interest: consecrating the principle of integral reparation for prejudice

Behind the diversity of solutions retained, one rule is, in our view, evident, concerning the integral reparation of prejudice suffered by the creditor because of failure on the part of the debtor to fulfill his obligation to pay a certain sum of money.

According to Article 78 of the Vienna Convention, failure to pay the price gives a right to interest on the sum due, without affecting the damages which might be demanded in the event of basic breach as in non-basic breach of contract. In his commentary on an ICC award given in 1994 in Case 7585, Heuze considered that it resulted from Article 78 of the said Convention that any sum is productive of interest.[102]

In Case 64 of 1985,[103] the Iran-US Tribunal considered that "in the absence of a contractually stipulated rate of interest, the Tribunal will derive a rate of interest based approximately on the amount that the successful claimant would have been in a position to have earned if it had been paid in time and, thus, if it had the funds available to invest in a form of commercial investment in common use in its own country."

In the ICC Case 7197 of 1992,[104] the arbitrator, by invoking Article 14 of the Vienna Convention (Article 78), granted the entire indemnity claimed.

In ICC Case 7710 of 1995,[105] the arbitral tribunal considered UNIDROIT principles to be the main component of the general rules and principles concerning international contractual obligations, enjoying as they did wide international consensus.

In the ICC Award No. 8501,[106] the arbitral tribunal considered that application of the appropriate commercial usages was compatible with Article 12(5) of the ICC regulations and with arbitral practice; in a growing number of international suits, the arbitrators are deciding that the obligations of the parties should be determined according to the usages and customs of international commerce or to the general principles of law without reference to any one particular national law. In many cases, these principles are a more exact expression of the true intention of the parties than would be the application of a conflictualist approach tending to impose the way of any one national law.[107]

For these reasons, the arbitral tribunal concluded in the above case that it would decide the case by applying to the contracts concluded between the parties the generally accepted usages of commerce and the principles of international commerce. In particular, the arbitral tribunal would refer, as circumstances required, to the dispositions of the Vienna Convention of 1980 concerning contracts for international sale of merchandise (Vienna Convention) or to the principles relating to contracts of international commerce laid down by UNIDROIT concerning practices admitted in international commercial law.

As for the law applicable in the question of reparation, the arbitral tribunal considered that, as stated above, the parties had expressed their common intention to have their relations regulated by the general principles of international commerce.

In the ICC Case 5835 of 1996,[108] the arbitral tribunal decided that Kuwaiti law was applicable on the basis of the method of combined application of different systems of conflict of laws. It also stated that Kuwaiti law limited the rates of interest only if there was a contractual rate or a rate of interest applicable when the payment of sums of money whose amount was known to the debtor was overdue,[109] and further if the interest intended to compensate the injured party because the damages his adversary was condemned to pay him were handed over a certain time after the deadline and the creditor had had to accept financial obligations in order to survive while awaiting compensation (...). Kuwaiti law provides that compensation should include "the prejudice suffered by the creditor (...) on condition that it is the natural result of the non-execution of the obligation or of delay."[110] The arbitral tribunal considered that the financial costs could be qualified, given the circumstances of this case, as the "natural result" of the debtor's delay in paying the damages due to his contractual partner. In particular, if the basis of the debtor's responsibility is "a grave fault" (...), the limits normally applicable to rates of interest no longer exist.[111]

As per Yves Derains, "this interpretation of Kuwaiti law is in conformity with the internationally accepted principles which otherwise would become applicable in conformity with the first interim Award handed down by the Tribunal. Reference may also be made to the UNIDROIT Principles of 1994, which lay down in their Article 7.4.9 (3) that the creditor further has a right to supplementary damages if the rate of interest normally applicable is not sufficient to cover the prejudice that the debtor's failure to pay has caused him. There was recourse to UNIDROIT Principles in this case as a means of showing that the decisions came up to the level of what was to be expected in the case of an international transaction." [112]

Based on the above, the survey of legal literature reveals that, in spite of the persisting controversies with regard to cases involving monetary interest, the case law elaborated by international arbitral tribunals strongly suggests that, in assessing the liability due for losses incurred, the interest becomes an integral part of the compensation itself.

As is reflected in various arbitral awards, interest is awarded to compensate the damage resulting from the fact that, during the period of non-payment by the debtor, the creditor is deprived of the use and disposition of the sum that he was supposed to receive.

CONCLUSION

In conclusion, the development of arbitration and promotion of international commercial transactions compel a basic rule: arbitration flexibility; granting the arbitrator freedom of action, along with a commitment to the basic rules governing the arbitral procedure and international litigation, in such a way as to conform with, and achieve, international trade prosperity.

Arbitration is the natural jurisdiction of international commercial agreements and the competent judicial private power for the world of trade. Given the above, the question arises: is it not high time we thought of laying down independent material rules governing interest in arbitration, in a way that helps achieve this aim within the mentioned criteria?

The time has come to establish internationally recognized guiding rules, far from any conflictual method.

Arbitral practice has shown, as developed above, a great diversity in both orientations and solutions, both as much in the application of the *lex contractus* as in the absence of such choice of law, and revealed lack of uniformity in respect of interest, its rate, computations and starting point.

This situation leads to uncertainty in this field, which has a negative impact on international trade practice, the operators being confronted to the various challenges either in having the award annulled because of violation of public policy, or in having an *ultra petita* or a non-motivated ruling in the matter of interest. The solution would be the adoption of a material rule that gives the arbitrator freedom to decide integral compensation of the damage, based on a case-by-case ruling in the matter of interest, which is of crucial importance in view of the important amounts involved.

END NOTES

1 *Sylviana Technical Systems, Inc.* v. *Iran*, Case No. 64 of the Iran-US Tribunal, Award No.180-64-1 of 27 June 1985, *Yearbook of Commercial Arbitration*, Vol. XI, 1986, pp. 290-305.

2 See *Sylviana Technical Systems, Inc.* v. *Iran*, op. cit., in which the Iran-US Tribunal stated that "in the absence of a contractually stipulated rate [...] the Tribunal has exercised its discretion, applying rates varying from 8.5% to 12%, which it determined to be 'fair rates'."

3 Herbert Schönle, *Intérêts moratoires, intérêts compensatoires et dommages-intérêts de retard en arbitrage international*, Etude de droit international en l'honneur de Pierre Lalive, p. 250.

4 Yves Picot, in *Encyclopédie Dalloz*, Répertoire de droit civil, Obligations, No. 39.

5 Jérôme Ortscheidt, *La réparation du dommage dans l'arbitrage commercial international*, Dalloz, No. 482, p. 220.

6 Herbert Schönle, op. cit., p.650.

7 ICC Case No. 7331 in 1994, JDI 1995 p. 100, obs. D. Hasher. Likewise, see also *Mc. Collough & Company, In. v. Ministry of Post, Telegraph and Telephone, National Iranian Oil Company*, Bank Markazi 22 April, 1986, *Yearbook of Commercial Arbitration* XVII, 1987, p. 316, especially p. 321.

8 Yves Derains, *Intérêts moratoires, dommages-intérêts compensatoires et dommages punitifs devant l'arbitre international*, Etudes offertes à Pierre Bellet, Paris, Litec, 1991, p. 120.

9 Lara Hammoud and Matthew Secomb, *Interest in ICC Arbitral Awards: Introduction and Commentary*, ICC Bulletin, Vol. 15 No. 1, Spring 2004, p. 2.

10 In ICC Case 10696 (ICC International Court of Arbitration Bulletin, Vol. 15 No. 1, Spring 2004, p. 96), the Arbitral Tribunal bases its decision to award interest to the claimant on the intention of the parties as expressed in their contract, stating that it is a duty to abide by the Parties' agreement.

11 ICC Rules of Arbitration, Article 17 (2). See ICC Cases 10696 (op. cit.), 7373 (ICC International Court of Arbitration Bulletin, Vol. 15 No. 1, Spring 2004, p. 74), 5597 (ICC International Court of Arbitration Bulletin, Vol. 3, 1992, p. 16). See also *Sylviana Technical Systems, Inc.* v./ *Iran*, op. cit.: "The rates stipulated in the contract and thus agreed by the parties are usually accepted by the Tribunal."

12 Beirut Court of Appeal, Case No. 1725/2001, dated 29/11/2001, The Lebanese Review of Arab and International Arbitration, No. 33, p.52.

13 Article 257 of the Lebanese Code of Commerce, providing for an interest rate of 9%.

14 Final Award rendered in Case 8874, ICC International Court of Arbitration Bulletin, Vol. 10 No. 2, Fall 1999, p. 85.

15 Final Award rendered in ICC Case 7153, JDI, 1992, p. 1005, Obs. Dr. Hascher.

16 Herbert Schönle, op.cit., p. 650.

17 Articles 104 and 106 of the Swiss Civil Code; and Article 1153 of the French Civil Code.

18 Article 106 of the Swiss Civil Code.

19 Article 1153 al. 4 of French Civil Code.

20 Lebanese Civil Code: Article 265, par. 2: However, if the debtor is of bad faith, the creditor who has been harmed by an unjustified resistance may be allocated complementary damages.

21 Yvaine Buffelan-Lanore, *Droit Civil*, 9th ed., 2004, No. 303, p. 697, Muriel Fabre-Magnan, *Les Obligations*, Thémis, 1st ed. 2004, No. 213, p. 575.

22 Ikko Yoshida, *Comparison of awarding interest on damages in Scotland, England, Japan and Russia*, Kluwer Law International, p. 2.

23 Nayla Comair-Obeid, *Charging interest in the Arabian Peninsula,* Middle East Commercial Law Review, Sweet & Maxwell, Vol. 1, issue 3, May-June 1995, p. 92.

24 The Lebanese Review of Arab and International Arbitration, No.16, p. 48.

25 Nathalie Najjar, *L'arbitrage dans les pays arabes face aux exigences du commerce international*, LGDJ, 2004, p. 350.

26 Article 547 of the Kuwaiti Civil Code. See Nayla Comair-Obeid, *The Law of Business Contracts in the Arab Middle East,* Kluwer Law International, 1996, p. 194 and seq.

27 Article 102, subsection 2 of Kuwaiti Commercial Code.

28 Article 81 (2) of the Law of Commerce (Legislative Decree No. 7 of 1987).

29 Article 228 of the Bahraini Civil Code (Legislative Decree No. 19 of 2001) provides that (a) "any agreement for interest in consideration of utilizing a sum of money or against delay in settlement thereof shall be void".

30 Concerning commercial debts, the above-mentioned Article 81, § 4 stipulates that "A creditor shall have the right to claim supplementary damages to be added to the delay interest without the need for proving that the damages in excess of such interest have been caused by the debtor's deceit or gross failure". Also Article 228 of the Bahraini Civil Code allows the Court, "when the object of an obligation is the payment of a sum of money and the debtor fails to pay after he was formally summoned whilst he is able to do so", "...to order the debtor to pay a compensation as required by the law if the creditor proves that the loss is caused to him due to such failure".

31 Decree of Sultan Qabus, No. 550/90, put into effect in 1991. See Nayla Comair-Obeid, op. cit. under 26, p. 190.

32 Final Award of September 1996 rendered in ICC Case No. 7263, ICC International Court of Arbitration Bulletin, Vol. 15 No. 1, Spring 2004, p. 73.

33 Final Award of February 1997 rendered in the ICC Case 7373, ICC International Court of Arbitration Bulletin, Vol. 15 No. 1, Spring 2004, p. 74.

34 Final Award of June 1989 rendered in ICC Case 5082, *Yearbook of Commercial Arbitration*, Vol. XXII, 1997, p. 87.

35 Articles 226 of Egyptian Civil Code and 171 of Iraqi Civil Code.

36 The Lebanese Review of Arab and International Arbitration, No. 26, p. 73. In the same sense, the Egyptian Court of Cassation in its decision rendered on 31 May 1990 considered as contrary to public policy the Award which computed the interest at 8% whereas the Egyptian law provides for an interest rate ceiling of 5%.

37 Article 114 of Kuwaiti Commercial Code.

38 Article 171 of the Syrian Civil Code, 173 of the Libyan Civil Code, 207 and 208 of Iraqi Civil Code, 170, 221 and 222 of Egyptian Civil Code.

39 Article 1153 of Belgian Civil Code and Article 345 of Greek Civil Code. See in this respect ICC Case 5485 of 1987, *Yearbook Commercial Arbitration*, XIV 1989, p. 157.

40 ICC International Court of Arbitration Bulletin, Vol. 12 No. 1, Spring 2001, p. 124.

41 Ikko Yoshida, *op. cit.*

42 Article 23 of the Law of the People's Republic of China on Economic Contracts involving foreign interest; Article 419 of Japanese Civil Code, Article 548 of Korean Civil Code, Article 203-05 of Taiwanese Commercial Code, Article 224 of Thaï Commercial Code.

43 See in this respect *Lesotho Highlands Development Authority* v. *Impregilo SPA and others*, 31 July 2003, ASA Bulletin, Vol. 22 No. 2, 2004, p. 411-431.

44 ICC Final Award – Case No. 6219, JDI, 1990, p. 1047, obs. Yves Derains. See also *ICC Arbitral Awards 1986-1990*, p. 428.

45 ASA Bulletin, 1993, p. 373.

46 ICC Final Award of April 1995 rendered in Case 8123, ICC International Court of Arbitration Bulletin, Vol. 15 No. 1, Spring 2004, p. 84.

47 ICC Final Award of 1989 rendered in Case 5731, International Court of Arbitration Bulletin, Vol. 3 No. 1, 1992 and ICC Final Award rendered in Case 7078, ICC International Court of Arbitration Bulletin, Vol. 15 No. 1, p. 70 and ICC Final Award of 1995 rendered in Case 8123, op. cit.

48 ICC Final Award of 1989 rendered in Case 5324 of 1989, ICC International Court of Arbitration Bulletin, Vol. 3 No. 2, 1992, p. 53.

49 James Otis Rodner, *The Applicable Interest Rate in International Arbitration*, ICC International Court of Arbitration Bulletin, Vol. 15 No. 1, Spring 2004, p. 47.

50 ICC Final Award of September 1999 rendered in Case 10079, ICC International Court of Arbitration Bulletin, Vol. 15 No. 1, Spring 2004, p. 94. See also ICC Final Award rendered in Case 8123, op.cit., ICC Final Award rendered in Case 6219, ICC International Court of Arbitration Bulletin, Vol. 3 No. 1, 1992, p. 22, ICC Final Award of March 1995 rendered in Case 7622, ICC International Court of Arbitration Bulletin, Vol. 15 No. 1, Spring 2004, p. 81.

51 ICC International Court of Arbitration Bulletin, Vol. 10 No. 2, Fall 1999, p. 77.

52 ICC Final Award rendered in Case 7063 (1993), *ICC Arbitral Awards 1996-2000*, p. 75.

53 ICCA YB Final Awards in Case 9771 (2001), *Yearbook of Commercial Arbitration*, Vol. XXIX, 2004, pp. 46-65.

54 Article 395 of the new Russian Civil Code.

55 *ICC Arbitral Awards 1986-1990*, p. 394.

56 See also the Final Award rendered in the ICC Case 7114, ICC International Court of Arbitration Bulletin, Vol. 15 No. 1, Spring 2004, p. 72 and the Final Award rendered in the ICC Case 7373, *op. cit.*

57 *Yearbook of Commercial Arbitration*, Vol. XVII 1992, p. 221.

58 JDI, 4, 2004, p. 1271.

59 ICC Case 6754 of 1993, *ICC Arbitral Awards 1991-1995*, p. 600, ICC Case 7331 of 1994 (op. cit.), ICC case 7078 (*op. cit.*). See also Lara Hammoud and Matthew Secomb, op. cit., p. 58, item 33.

60 ICC Case 6162, *Yearbook Commercial Arbitration of 1990*, p. 84.

61 ICC Case 10329 of 2000, ICCA YB Final Awards.

62 See also ICC Final Award (1998) rendered in Case 9333, ICC International Court of Arbitration Bulletin, Vol. 10 No. 2, Fall 1999, p. 105.

63 ICC International Court of Arbitration Bulletin, Vol. 3 No. 1, 1992, p. 19.

64 Which states that when the object of an obligation is the payment of a sum of money, the amount of which is known at the time when the claim is made, the debtor shall be bound, in case of delay in payment, to pay to the creditor, as damages for the delay, interest at the rate of 4% in civil matters and 5% in commercial matters.

65 ICC International Court of Arbitration Bulletin, Vol. 15 No. 1, Spring 2004, p. 86.

66 *Yearbook Commercial Arbitration*, 1988, p. 271. See also ICC Case 6281, *Yearbook Commercial Arbitration*, 1990, p. 96.

67 Yves Derains, op. cit , p.106.

68 Yves Derains, *The Role of Unidroit principles in the International Commercial Arbitration: A European view*, ICC International Court of Arbitration Bulletin, 2002, p. 10.

69 ICC International Court of Arbitration Bulletin, Vol. 15 No. 1, 2004, p. 85.

70 ICC Case 8501, JDI No.4, 2001, p. 1164.

71 *Yearbook Commercial Arbitration*, Vol. XXVIII, 2003, pp. 100-168.

72 *Yearbook Commercial Arbitration,* 1976, pp. 128-129.

73 In the ICC Case 8874 published in ICC International Court of Arbitration Bulletin, Vol.10 No. 2, Fall 1999, p. 85, the Arbitral Tribunal considered that the initial interest rate, if applied to the considered amount and period of time, would be disproportionate with the economic and commercial conditions of this case.

74 ICC Final Award of 1989 rendered in Case 5881, ICC International Court of Arbitration Bulletin, Vol. 3, 1999, p. 51.

75 ICC International Court of Arbitration Bulletin, Vol. 3 No. 1, 1992, p. 22.

76 See also ICC Final Award of April 1997 rendered in Case 8521 (ICC International Court of Arbitration Bulletin, Vol. 15 No. 1, Spring 2004, p. 90) in which the arbitral Tribunal applied the rate which it considered is general practice in International Arbitration and may be considered as a relevant trade usage within the meaning of Article 13 (5) of the ICC Rules.

77 Reference is to be made to ICC Final Award of September 1999 rendered in ICC Case 10079 (ICC International Court of Arbitration Bulletin, Vol. 15 No. 1, Spring 2004, p. 94), in which the sole arbitrator decided to award on the approximate rate applicable to accounts held in US dollars, as both parties agreed that the legal rate was not appropriate for a disposition in US dollars.

78 Yves Derains, op. cit. under 67, p. 13 and also for the same author, *Attente légitime des parties et droit applicable au fond en matière d'arbitrage commercial international*, Travaux du Comité français de droit international privé, 1984-1985, Paris, CNRS, 81.

79 See ICSID Award *AGIP S.p.A.* v. *Government of the Republic of Congo*, 30 November 1979, Rev. Crit. DIP ,1982, p. 92, especially p. 104 ; ICSID Award *Benvenutti et Bonfante v. Government of the Republic of Congo*, 8 August 1980, *Yearbook Commercial Arbitration*, 1983, p. 144, especially p. 151.

80 In a Final Award of 1992 rendered in ICC Case 7006 (*ICC Arbitral Awards 1991–1995*, p. 199), the arbitral tribunal considered that a judge's award of interest in a monetary condemnation from a date prior to the judgment must be motivated and finally that the motivation, while not restricted in any particular way, cannot flow from an arbitrary discretion that the judge is empowered to exercise but must be enrooted in the circumstances that the disposition of the substantive issues reveals.

81 ICC Final Award of 1995 rendered in Case 1170, JDI, IV, 2001, p. 858.

82 In an ICC Final Award of 1990 rendered in Case No. 6162, op. cit., the arbitral tribunal dismissed the claimant's claim for damages, as the claimant had not alleged that the defendant would have suffered an exceptional prejudice. Also in the ICC Final Award of 1992 rendered in Case 6962 (*ICC Arbitral Awards1991-1995*, p. 306), the arbitral tribunal stated that "no evidence of a loss is required under French law for claiming interest on overdue interest on overdue amounts at the legal rate of interest...".

83 Revue de l'Arbitrage, 1994, No.1, p. 192.

84 Emmanuel Gaillard, *La Jurisprudence du CIRDI*, ed. Padone, 2004, p. 286.

85 JDI 2004, No. 131, pp. 236-254.

86 In the same sense, see the Case *American Manufacturing & Trading Company (AMT)* v. *Zaïre* of 21 February 1997, JDI 1998, No. 125, p. 243 and the Case *Azurix* v. *Argentine*, JDI 2004, No. 131, pp. 276- 282.

87 Emmanuel Gaillard, *op. cit.*, p. 814.

88 Revue de l'Arbitrage, 1994, p. 196 and JDI 1992, No. 119, pp. 217-227.

89 ICSID Review 2001, No. 16, p. 168 and JDI 2002, No. 129, pp. 190-233.

90 ICC International Court of Arbitration Bulletin, Vol. 12 No. 2, Fall 2001, p. 111.

91 *Yearbook Commercial Arbitration*, Vol. XXIX, 2004, p. 46-65.

92 JDI 2003, No. 130, p. 162.

93 Revue de l'Arbitrage, 1994, p. 190.

94 See ICC Award 10346, op. cit.

95 Final Award of December 1996 rendered in Case 8769, ICC International Court of Arbitration Bulletin, Vol. 11 No. 2, Fall 2000, p. 70.

96 See ICC Award 10346, op. cit.

97 Op. cit.

98 ICC International Court of Arbitration Bulletin, Vol. 12 No. 1, Spring 2001, p. 127.

99 ICC International Court of Arbitration Bulletin, Vol. 12 No. 1, Spring 2001, p. 124.

100 ICC Case 10329 of 2000, *Yearbook Commercial Arbitration*, Vol. XXIX , 2004, pp. 108-132.

101 ICC Case 10274 of 1999, ICCA YB Awards.

102 Final Award of 1994 rendered in Case 7585, *ICC Arbitral Awards 1991–1995*, p. 606.

103 *Sylviana Technical Systems, Inc.* v. *Iran*, op. cit.

104 Final Award of December 1992 rendered in Case 7197, *ICC Arbitral Awards 1991–1995*, p. 500.

105 JDI, Vol. IV, 2001.

106 JDI, Vol. IV, No. 1, 2001, p. 165 et s.

107 W. Laurence Craig, William W. Park and Jan Paulsson, *International Chamber of Commerce*, Oceana Publications, 2000, p. 295.

108 ICC Award 5835 published in ICC Court of Arbitration Bulletin, Vol. 10 No. 2, 1999, p. 34, quoted by Yves Derains, *Le rôle des Principes d'UNIDROIT dans l'arbitrage commercial international : une vue européenne*, Bulletin de la Cour Internationale d'Arbitrage de la CCI, Supplément Spécial, 2002, p. 16 and seq. Likewise, the award given in ICC Case No. 7110 of 1995, published in the ICC International Court of Arbitration Bulletin, Vol. 10 No. 2, 1999, p. 40.

109 Articles 110 and 111 of Kuwaiti Code of Commerce.

110 Article 300, section 2 of Kuwaiti Civil Law No. 67, 1980

111 Article 300, section 3 and Article 304 of Kuwaiti Civil Law.

112 Yves Derains, op. cit. under 108, p. 15.

8

Means to be made whole:

Damages in the context of international investment arbitration

By ***Henry Weisburg***
Partner, Shearman & Sterling LLP, New York
and ***Christopher Ryan***
Associate, Shearman & Sterling LLP, Washington D.C.

INTRODUCTION

International investment law is one of the fastest growing fields of international law. As a result of the proliferation of bilateral investment treaties (BITS),[1] the evolution of hybrid trade/investment treaties – such as NAFTA, CAFTA and the Energy Charter Treaty – and the ever-growing demand for foreign investment by capital-importing states, legal developments with respect to the protection of foreign investment are accelerating.

Despite the wealth of precedent establishing the rights and responsibilities of foreign investors and host governments alike, the law of damages in this area is comparatively thin. Although it is well established that a state must fully compensate foreign investors for injuries caused by its actions,[2] there is surprisingly little precedent directing tribunals on how best to satisfy this obligation in a predictable manner. Historically, private investors had no direct recourse if their investments were harmed by a foreign government, but instead were forced to press their own governments to espouse their claims through some form of diplomatic protection.[3] Only since the emergence of the BIT era have foreign investors regularly had the ability to have an independent body adjudicate the actions of a foreign government.

Given the relatively short period in which investor-state arbitration has occurred, it is not surprising that there has been little development in the law of damages. What is surprising, however, is that claimants, respondents and tribunals frequently seem at a loss as to how damages should be computed in a particular case. In many cases, regardless of the nature of the claim, it appears that the parties simply default to methodologies that have traditionally been applied in cases of total expropriation. Perhaps such reliance on the default methodologies is to be expected. The prohibition against uncompensated expropriation may be the oldest protection afforded to international investment, and therefore there is substantial precedent to guide claimants and tribunals. However, in non-expropriation cases, such as those where a host government breaches its duty of "fair and equitable treatment", fails to provide "minimum protection and security" to a foreign investment, or breaches a contractual obligation, reliance on the default methodologies has occasionally led to strained or unexpected outcomes and has been the subject of criticism.

Nevertheless, the arbitral jurisprudence reveals some basic guidelines that should instruct future tribunals and claimants as they seek to resolve international investment disputes: (a) the quantum of damages must be sufficient to eliminate the injurious effect of the state's unlawful actions; and (b) the method of calculating damages should be dictated by the type of investment.

1. THE QUANTUM OF DAMAGES MUST ELIMINATE THE INJURIOUS EFFECTS OF A STATE'S UNLAWFUL ACTS

One of the earliest protections provided to foreign investors was the customary international law prohibition against uncompensated expropriation.[4] In the 1920s, it was recognized that customary international law required that states pay full compensation when expropriating the property of a foreign investor.[5] In the 1930s, the United States defined the notion of full compensation when, in response to a dispute over Mexico's nationalization of foreign-owned oil fields, US Secretary of State Cordell Hull announced that Mexico was internationally obligated to pay "prompt, adequate, and effective" compensation.[6] Known as the Hull Formula, this standard effectively became synonymous with the idea of full compensation.[7]

Beginning in the late 1950s and early 1960s, a number of newly independent and developing states began to question the propriety of the Hull Doctrine.[8] Indeed, in the view of many of these states, the international legal requirement that governments fully compensate foreign nationals for the expropriation of their property was an impermissible infringement on state sovereignty.[9] In response, the United Nations General Assembly passed Resolution 3171, which declared that a state expropriating foreign property "is entitled to determine the amount of possible compensation and the mode of payment, and [...] any disputes which might arise should be settled in accordance with the national legislation of [that] State".[10] This resolution appears to have been an effort to alter the existing norms of customary international law, invalidate the Hull Formula and sanction the payment of less than full compensation following the expropriation of property.

Despite the rhetorical value of General Assembly Resolution 3171, it had very little practical significance. International law continued to set the measure of compensation due in cases of expropriation. What changed, however, was the terminology used to describe the appropriate standard of compensation. As the sole arbitrator in the *LIAMCO* case noted, although "the classical formula of [prompt], adequate, and effective compensation remain[ed] as a maximum and a practical guide for assessment", it was not the sole standard of compensation permitted under international law.[11] Tribunals, therefore, spoke less frequently in terms of "prompt, adequate, and effective" compensation. Instead, they referred to "just",[12] "appropriate",[13] or "equitable"[14] compensation. For example, in *Shahin Shaine Ebrahimi* v. *Iran,* the tribunal held:

> "While international law undoubtedly sets forth an obligation to provide compensation for property taken, international law theory and practice do not support the conclusion that the 'prompt, adequate, and effective' standard represents the prevailing standard of compensation [...]. Rather, customary international law favours an 'appropriate' compensation standard."[15]

Similarly, in *Compañia del Desarrollo de Santa Elena* v. *Costa Rica*, the tribunal noted that:

> "The vocabulary describing the amount of compensation properly payable in respect of a lawful taking has varied considerably from time to time. It comprises such words as 'full,' 'adequate,' 'appropriate,' 'fair' and 'reasonable.' Sometimes, the descriptive adjective is elaborated by the additional mention of 'market value.'"[16]

Ultimately, the United Nations settled on a standard of "appropriate" compensation.[17]

Today, regardless of the terminology used, it is clear that the level of damages awarded in international investment arbitration is supposed to be sufficient to fully compensate the affected party and to eliminate the consequences of the government's actions.[18] As one tribunal recently noted:

> "The requirement of compensation to be 'just' and representative of the genuine value of the investment affected evokes the famous Hull Formula, which provides for the payment of prompt, adequate, and effective compensation for the taking of foreign owned property."[19]

A significant indicator that states now recognize their obligation to fully compensate injured investors is the fact that the full compensation standard has been codified repeatedly in the text of bilateral investment treaties. As the tribunal in *CME Czech Republic B.V. (The Netherlands)* v. *The Czech Republic* noted:

> "Today, these treaties are truly universal in their reach and essential provisions. They concordantly provide for payment of 'just compensation,' representing the 'genuine' or 'fair market' value of the property taken. Some treaties provide for prompt, adequate, and effective compensation amounting to the market value of the investment immediately before the expropriation or before the intention to embark thereon became public knowledge. Others provide that compensation shall represent the equivalent of the investment affected. These concordant provisions are variations on an agreed, essential theme, namely, that when a State takes foreign property, full compensation must be paid."[20]

Thus, for example, both the 1992 and 2004 US Model Bilateral Investment Treaties state that an expropriation may only be taken "upon payment of prompt, adequate, and effective compensation", which is further defined as the fair market value of the expropriated property immediately before the expropriation took place.[21]

In addition to ensuring that a foreign investor is made whole, at least one tribunal has found that the obligation to pay full compensation is essential to the very structure of international investment. The *AMINOIL* tribunal noted that it is a "fundamental precept" of international investment that damages "be calculated on a basis that such as to warrant the upkeep of a flow of investment in the future".[22]

Although it is clear that an award of damages must be sufficient to make a claimant whole, the arbitral jurisprudence reveals that tribunals occasionally have difficulty determining precisely how to satisfy this requirement. This difficulty is particularly apparent in cases involving claims other than the classic example of total expropriation. The proper level of damages in cases where a host-government breaches its obligation to provide "fair and equitable" treatment could be different than in cases where that same government expropriates a foreign investment. Indeed, the proper amount of damages necessary to fully compensate a claimant turns on whether the investment itself is totally destroyed or merely impaired. International law, however, has not produced a meaningful body of law dealing with cases where an investment is not completely destroyed. While both customary international law and the vast majority of investment treaties expressly deal with the measure of compensation required in cases of expropriation, they are silent about compensation in cases where a government breaches other forms of investment protection. As is discussed below, some tribunals have overcome the lack of precedent or clear standards by applying the rules governing expropriation to other types of injuries. Although seemingly reasonable, the reflexive application of the expropriation paradigm to all breaches of international investment law has the potential to distort awards.

2. THE METHOD OF CALCULATING DAMAGES WILL BE DICTATED BY THE NATURE OF THE INVESTMENT

The general principle of "full compensation" governs the calculation of damages in international investment arbitrations. This principle, however, is not expressed in formulaic terms. Tribunals exercise broad discretion in determining how best to provide full compensation in any given case.

A state's obligation to pay damages arises only when that state breaches one or more of the numerous protections afforded to foreign investments. As bilateral investment treaties evolve, so too do the types of commercial and financial ventures that constitute an "investment". Today, protected investments include such diverse items as intellectual property rights, debt, equity, leases and mortgages, as well as traditional commercial and industrial enterprises.[23] The amount of damages owed in cases involving intellectual property rights, however, is likely far different than the damages owed in cases involving the destruction or impairment of a commercial or industrial enterprise. Similarly, the measure of damages will almost certainly be different in cases involving a fully operational enterprise than in cases where a proposed enterprise is still in the planning or construction phase. Regardless of the type of investment, however, the sole objective of any international tribunal when calculating damages should be to make the claimant whole. This is true whether the property rights at issue are tangible or intangible assets, because in every case, "the object of damages is to place the party to whom they are awarded in the same pecuniary position that they would have been" if the injury had not occurred.[24]

As mentioned above, it does not appear that international investment law has developed to the point where claimants and tribunals can effectively determine how to accomplish this objective with predictability. The cases that deal with this issue, however, seem to fall into three categories.

First, there are cases where the tribunal does not expressly deal with the standard for determining damages. For example, in *Pope & Talbot* v. *Government of Canada*, the tribunal found that Canada breached NAFTA Article 1105's requirement to provide "fair and equitable" treatment. Although the investment was harmed by Canada's actions, it remained a viable enterprise. Consequently, the tribunal limited the claimant's damages to certain out of pocket expenses and rejected its claim for lost profits and various management expenses.[25] The tribunal, however, was virtually silent as to why these types of damages were appropriate for a breach of the fair and equitable treatment standard.

Second, there are cases where the tribunal has rejected the application of expropriation standards to non-expropriation claims. In *S.D. Meyers, Inc.* v. *Government of Canada*, the tribunal found that Canada had discriminated against the claimant (a US-owned company operating in Canada) and failed to provide an acceptable "minimum standard of treatment" to the claimant's investment when it enacted a regulation prohibiting companies from exporting PCB-contaminated waste to the United States for processing. In the tribunal's view, the regulation stripped the claimant of its competitive advantage –

the ability to process waste cheaply in the United States – so as to lessen direct competition with Canadian-owned waste processing plants.[26] After determining Canada's liability, the tribunal engaged in a lengthy analysis of why it was inappropriate to apply the expropriation-based standards outside of the expropriation arena:

> "Expropriations that take place in accordance with the framework of Article 1110 [...] are lawful under Chapter 11 {of NAFTA} provided that compensation is paid in accordance with the [...] fair market value of the asset [...] formula. Under other provisions of Chapter 11, the liability of the host party arises out of the fact that the government has done something that is contrary to NAFTA and is "unlawful" as between the disputing parties. The standard of compensation that an arbitral tribunal should apply may in some cases be influenced by the distinction between compensating for a lawful, as opposed to an unlawful act. Fixing the fair market value of an asset that is diminished in value may not fairly address the harm done to the investor."[27]

In the view of the tribunal, the lack of a clear standard in NAFTA for determining compensation in non-expropriation cases meant that tribunals were required to "determine a measure of compensation appropriate of the specific circumstances of the case, taking into account the principles of both international law and the provisions of NAFTA".[28] The tribunal felt that, in some cases, it would be appropriate to adopt the "fair market value" standard typically applied to expropriations, while in other cases tribunals would be forced to create new measures for valuing a claimant's damages.[29]

Finally, there are cases that have simply applied the expropriation-based standards to other breaches of international investment law. In *CMS Gas Transmission Co. v. Republic of Argentina*, an ICSID tribunal held that the Government of Argentina breached its obligation to provide "fair and equitable treatment" to a US investor when it enacted a series of measures in early 2001.[30] The tribunal, however, calculated damages using the same methodology that has traditionally been applied in cases of total expropriation. After recognizing that the bilateral investment treaty "offer[ed] no guidance as to the appropriate measure of damages or compensation relating to fair and equitable and other breaches of the standards laid down in [the BIT]", the tribunal found that the circumstances of the case warranted compensation equivalent to the fair market value of the investment.[31] Although the tribunal recognized that "this standard figures prominently in respect of expropriation", it concluded that the standard "might also be appropriate for other breaches different from expropriation if their effect results in important long-term losses".[32]

In *Metalclad Corp.* v. *United Mexican States*, the tribunal found that Mexico had breached its obligation to provide fair and equitable treatment under NAFTA Article 1105. The tribunal, nevertheless, calculated Metalclad's damages in accordance with the methodology set forth in NAFTA for calculating damages in expropriation cases. According to the tribunal, the use of the expropriation methodology was appropriate because Mexico's actions resulted in the complete destruction of the investment.[33]

In theory, the similarity in treatment between expropriation and non-expropriation cases is not surprising. International law requires that damages be sufficient to fully compensate a foreign investor for the harms caused by a host government, regardless of whether they are the result of expropriation or some other breach of law. Thus, in *S.D. Meyers*, the tribunal aptly noted that the measure of compensation in non-expropriation cases should "reflect the general principle of international law that compensation should undo the material harm inflicted by a breach of an international obligation".[34] In practice, however, the nature of the injury caused by breaches of the various protections accorded to foreign investments can differ greatly. For example, there likely will be a significant difference in the magnitude of harm caused in a case of total expropriation versus a case where a government has acted discriminatorily to a foreign investment, yet the investment continues as a going concern. Although in both cases a breach of international law has occurred, thus triggering the host-state's obligation to pay damages, the extent of the state's liability should be quite different. It is not clear, however, that the application of the methodologies traditionally applied in expropriation cases adequately compensates for this difference.

Going concerns

A "going concern" is generally understood to be a business enterprise with demonstrable future earning power.[35] In other words, it is a business that can show the likelihood of future profits. Where a going concern has been expropriated or its economic value has been impaired by state actions, its owner should be entitled to damages equal to the fair market value of the investment immediately before the injurious act occurred.[36]

What constitutes fair-market value and how best to calculate it have been the subject of much debate. Fair market value is a term of art that has generally meant the price that a willing buyer would pay a willing seller in an arms-length transaction. Traditionally, international law has required that the fair market value of a company be calculated by reference to two factors: *damnum emergens* – the value of the investment, including tangible and intangible assets, property rights, good will and contract rights; and *lucrum cessans* – lost profits.[37] Consequently, tribunals often struggle to capture these seemingly disparate elements in their awards.

Treating *damnum emergens* and *lucrum cessans* separately, however, is viewed as unnecessary in most modern cases. From an economic perspective, investments have little real value other than their ability to generate a stream of profits over their lifetimes. For example, imagine a scenario in which there are two identical enterprises, both of which have the same capacity to generate identical profits over time. Now, imagine that the owner of the first enterprise paid twice what the owner of the second enterprise paid to establish their facilities. If both owners tried to sell these enterprises, they would each be valued based on their abilities to generate revenues. The fact that one investor paid more for his investment would be irrelevant, since a rational buyer would not be willing to pay more simply because the original owner overpaid. The same should be true if both companies were expropriated. The fair market value of the companies would be tied directly to their abilities to produce revenues, without regard to the amount of money invested. Tribunals, therefore, are not likely to adopt any distinction between *damnum emergens* and *lucrum cessans* if the result is to value equally productive assets differently.

1. The discounted cash flow methodology

The discounted cash flow or "DCF" method is a tool that measures the value of a business by projecting the net cash flow for a fixed period of time into the future and then discounting it back to present value as of the date of the injury.[38] The discount rate should reflect the time value of money in the host country and the relative risk associated with the particular investment.[39] The principal benefit of the DCF method is that, unlike other methodologies, it does not depend solely on past costs or historical measures of performance. Rather, it recognizes that the true economic value of a going concern is the stream of revenue that it can generate over its operative life – i.e., the true value of a business is the profits it will generate.[40] Consequently, the benefit of the DCF method is that it should fully compensate foreign investors by allowing a tribunal to award an amount that reflects the net present value of both the physical assets that have been lost (*damnum emergens*) and the profits that have been deprived (*lucrum cessans*).[41]

Although the DCF method is the theoretically preferred method of calculating damages in cases involving going concerns, there are significant problems associated with its practical application. ***First,*** it can be extremely difficult to apply, and it can produce quite disparate results depending on who is performing the analysis. As a practical matter, the claimant and respondent almost always compute two vastly different damages amounts, both of which were derived from the DCF method.[42] This divergence is in many ways tied to the DCF's principal benefit – i.e., it requires tribunals to look forward and to project a company's future performance. There is no single means by which to determine the future cash flow and profits of a going concern. Rather, parties and tribunals must extrapolate future performance from a company's current financial position, past profitability, market trends and industry analysis. Doing so involves significant assumptions and frequently turns into a battle of multiple experts. Likewise, it is often extremely difficult to calculate an appropriate discount rate. As a general matter, the discount rate is based on factors such as inflation, lending rates and market volatility in the host country.[43] Where these factors are subject to extreme fluctuation or are simply viewed as unreliable (such as in cases involving non-market economies), it can be extremely difficult for a tribunal to determine a fair and reasonable discount rate. Finally, it is often difficult to obtain the objective data necessary to allow a tribunal to calculate a company's future revenue stream. In the absence of such data, some tribunals have been reluctant to award lost profits and, therefore, have declined to apply the DCF method.[44] For example, in *Autopista Concesionada de Venezuela C.A.* v. *Bolivarian Republic of Venezuela*, an ICSID tribunal refused to award the claimant lost profits, because in its estimation, the claimant was not able to provide sufficient evidence that its projected profits were reasonable.[45]

Second, many tribunals have concluded that the DCF method is only applicable when a tribunal is seeking to determine "the fair market value of a going concern which has a history of profitable operation."[46] Where an enterprise is new and thus lacking a performance record or where it has failed to make a profit, the DCF method may, in the view of some tribunals, be inappropriate to calculate the fair market value of an investment.[47] As a practical matter, however, the DCF method can be applied to value both new and established going concerns. The determinative issue in any case should be whether there is sufficient evidence on the record to permit a tribunal to reasonably calculate future revenues and to justify the award of lost profits.

Tribunals are split on what constitutes sufficient evidence. In *Metalclad Corp.* v. *United Mexican States*, for example, an ICSID tribunal refused to apply the DCF method because the investment at issue " was never operative and any award based on future profits would be wholly speculative".[48] Likewise, in *Wena Hotels* the tribunal rejected the DCF method because of the absence of an operating history that would provide a "solid base on which to found any profit" or to "predict [...] growth or expansion of the investment".[49] Similarly, in *Société Ouest Africaine des Bétons Industriels (SOABI)* v. *State of Senegal*, although the tribunal held that past and future losses are generally compensable if they are "ascertainable and direct", it declined to award the claimant damages for the loss of future profits, goodwill and commercial financing, because the claimant's inability to provide supporting documentation rendered such damages "wholly hypothetical".[50]

In *Southern Pacific Properties (Middle East) Limited v. Arab Republic of Egypt*, the tribunal declared the DCF method to be inappropriate for two reasons. ***First,*** because "the project was not in existence for a sufficient period of time to generate the data necessary for a meaningful DCF calculation", the tribunal feared that using the DCF method would lead to an award of "possible but contingent and indeterminate damage which, in accordance with the jurisprudence of arbitral tribunals, cannot be taken into account".[51] ***Second***, the tribunal feared that the DCF method would award the claimant future profits that could not have been earned if its investment had continued to operate. In this case, the claimant entered into a fifty-year renewable agreement with the Egyptian government to develop and sell various "tourist complexes".[52] The project was cancelled (i.e., expropriated) little more than four years after the initial agreement was concluded. The cancellation of the project occurred following a change in Egyptian law that created protective zones around many of Egypt's historical sites, land on which SPP had been given authority to build its resort complex. Shortly thereafter, the United Nations passed the UNESCO Convention for the Protection of World Culture and Natural Heritage, an international agreement to preserve and protect culturally significant property.[53] To value its losses, SPP calculated its projected revenue stream for a period of eighteen years. In the tribunal's view, this was inappropriate because SPP would have been legally precluded from selling property after the date that the UNESCO Convention became binding on its signatories.[54] According to the tribunal, any activities conducted by SPP in the protected area after the UNESCO Convention entered into force would be "in violation of international law", and therefore "any profits that might have resulted from such activities are non-compensable."[55] As such, the tribunal refused to award lost profits.

By contrast, in *Sapphire International Petroleum Ltd* v. *National Iranian Oil Co.,* the sole arbitrator awarded the claimant lost profits for the breach of an oil concession despite the fact that the land on which the concession was granted had yet to be explored.[56] The arbitrator accepted that it is a fundamental principal of international law that investors should be fully compensated for losses caused by government action and that such compensation includes both "the loss suffered (*damnum emergens*) [...] and the profit lost (*lucrum cessans*) [...] ."[57] Although the arbitrator acknowledged that the existence of lost profits was "uncertain", he held:

> "it is not necessary to prove the exact damage suffered in order to award damages. On the contrary, when such proof is impossible, particularly as a result of the behaviour of the author of the damage, it is enough for the judge to be able to admit with sufficient probability the existence and extent of the damage."[58]

Drawing on French and American case law, the arbitrator accepted the notion that investors should be compensated for the "loss of opportunity" – i.e., "when the victim had lost the opportunity of making a profit as a result of what someone else had done".[59] According to this notion, the fact that the existence of lost profits is uncertain is not determinative of whether they should be awarded.[60] Instead, the key issue is the claimant's position at the time that its opportunity was lost.[61] Tribunals should "accept that this opportunity itself has a value whose loss gives rise to compensation".[62] Of course, the arbitrator in *Sapphire* did not simply accept the claimant's assertion that it would have earned a profit had the concession been fully developed. As would be expected, the claimant was required to demonstrate "a sufficient probability of success" that the concession would have produced oil.[63] Ultimately, relying on expert reports and testimony, the arbitrator found that the claimant had met that burden.

2. The abuse of right doctrine as a constraint on damages in international investment arbitration

Recently, a new issue has arisen in the continuing controversy over whether to apply the DCF method to calculate the fair market value of a foreign investment: the abuse of right doctrine.[64] In two related cases, *Himpurna California Energy Ltd* v. *PT (Persero) Perusahaan Listruik Negara*[65] and *Patuha Ltd* v. *PT (Persero) Perusahaan Listruik Negara*,[66] the claimants entered into concession agreements with a foreign government to build power plants and to sell the power generated by those plants back to the government. A dispute arose and the government refused to purchase power as required by the agreement. The claimants ultimately submitted their disputes to arbitration, seeking billions of dollars in damages for both wasted costs (*damnum emergens*) and lost profits (*lucrum cessans*).

The *ad hoc* tribunals empanelled to arbitrate these disputes ultimately determined that the host government had, in fact, breached its agreements with Himpurna and Patuha. With respect to damages, the tribunals found that both Himpurna and Patuha were entitled to reimbursement of funds that they could prove had been spent in reliance on the contracts.[67] The tribunals, however, refused to accept either Himpurna's or Patuha's calculation of lost profits. Although acknowledging that investors are entitled to recoup lost profits, the tribunals refused to calculate the quantum of lost profits in a way that would economically harm the host government.[68] According to both tribunals, to do so would constitute an "abuse of right":

> "This is a case where the doctrine of abuse of right must be applied in favour of [the host government] to prevent the claimant's undoubtedly legitimate rights from being extended beyond tolerable norms, on the ground that it would be intolerable in the present case to uphold claims for lost profits from investment not yet incurred."[69]

In the tribunal's view, accepting Himpurna's and Patuha's calculations of lost profits would be tacit acknowledgment that they had "an unfettered right to create ever-increasing losses for the State of Indonesia (and its peoples) by generating energy without any regard to whether or not PLN had any use for it. Even if such right may be said to derive from explicit contractual terms [...] performance of the contract would be ruinous to the Respondent."[70] What troubled the tribunals most was the potentially crippling effect that awarding full compensation to the claimants would have on the host government.[71] Consequently, the tribunals awarded Himpurna and Patuha less than ten percent of their claimed lost profits.[72]

The application of the abuse of right doctrine in the *Himpurna* and *Patuha* has been controversial.[73] Simply stated, the abuse of right doctrine provides that situations may exist in which the exercise of a legally protected right by one party may result in unacceptable injury to an adverse party or to broader societal interests.[74] This doctrine has not typically been applied in the context of international investment disputes and has been accepted in only a small number of domestic jurisdictions.[75] Its emergence in the *Himpurna* and *Patuha* arbitrations creates a potentially awkward precedent. In neither case did the tribunals limit the award of lost profits because of any bad faith or malfeasance on the part of the claimants. Rather, the sole reason was the potential economic impact on the host government.

It remains to be seen whether the abuse of right doctrine is widely followed by subsequent tribunals, since its application would appear to be inconsistent with established international law. It should be noted that, as a practical matter, tribunals could achieve the same ends without relying on the abuse of right doctrine, given the substantial discretion inherent in the DCF methodology. For instance, if the circumstances so warranted, tribunals could limit the timeframe in which future revenues would be projected. Alternatively, the discount rate could be adjusted to account for the risk of harm to the host government associated with an award of future profits. In either case, the result would be to lessen the amount of damages by reducing the amount of future profits included in the final award.

Alternatives to the discounted cash flow methodology in calculating damages for enterprise-type investments

If a tribunal is reluctant to apply the DCF methodology, it must consider alternative means of calculating the fair market value of an investment. There are several generally accepted alternatives, including: "book value", the net value of an enterprise's assets; "investment value", the amount actually invested prior to the injurious act, "replacement value", the amount necessary to purchase the individual components of the investment at issue on the day immediately before the injurious act occurred; or "liquidation value", the amount a willing buyer would pay for an enterprise's assets in a liquidation process.[76]

None of these alternative methods is perfect and, indeed, each is appropriate only in limited circumstances. For instance, replacement value assumes that it is possible to reconstruct the value of the entire investment simply by replacing the physical assets. Lost in this methodology is the value that comes from, for example, existing customer relationships, a skilled work force and opportunities in established markets. Merely reconstructing the physical assets of a going concern cannot recreate these intangible assets, and therefore may not fully restore the value of the investment. The use of "book value" has different, but equally significant problems. The "book value" method calculates damages based on the difference between an investment's assets and liabilities as recorded in its financial statements, or the amount at which the investment appears on the investor's balance sheet after deducting accumulated depreciation in accordance with generally accepted accounting principles.[77] As a general matter, "the net book value of an asset has the advantage of being easily and objectively assessed".[78] In practice, however, this method of valuation is only recommended in cases where the book value of the investment has been recently assessed and can, therefore, be deemed to be a fair substitute for the replacement value.[79] As the *AMINOIL* tribunal stated, "the net book value method may be suitable when it is a case of a recent investment, the original cost of which is not far from that of the present replacement cost. But when that is not so, other methods are indicated."[80]

Despite the problems associated with these (and other non-DCF) methodologies, they occasionally represent the only means of valuing an investment. Tribunals must be free to calculate damages in a manner best suited to the facts of a particular case. This is especially true where the investment is comprised solely of intangible assets. In *Fedax N.V.* v. *The Republic of Venezuela*, the investment at issue consisted of six promissory notes issued by the Government of Venezuela.[81] After finding that ICSID properly had jurisdiction over the matter,[82] the parties ultimately reached a settlement on the merits but could not agree on the final amount of payment due from Venezuela. The tribunal, therefore, was forced to calculate damages just as it would if it had arbitrated the merits of the dispute. Rather than apply the DCF methodology or some other formula to determine the extent of damages, the tribunal looked to the precise terms of the promissory notes, determined the outstanding principal and calculated the interest due to compute the final award.[83]

In *Ceskoslovenska obchodni banka a.s. (CSOB)* v. *Slovak Republic*, a tribunal was again confronted with intangible assets – bank loans.[84] After finding that the Slovak Republic had breached its contractual obligations to CSOB, the tribunal employed a complicated hybrid methodology to calculate damages that considered whether to award lost profits, compound interest and the effect that fluctuating tax rates should have on the award. The tribunal's approach was governed by Czech law, which provided that compensation should consist of "actual damage" (*damnum emergem*) and "lost profits" (*lucrum cessans*).[85] Although Czech law required the tribunal to consider the two principal elements of the DCF method in calculating damages, the application of that method was clearly inappropriate given the nature of the asset involved. Thus, the tribunal calculated damages under domestic statutory provisions applicable to bank loans. This flexibility is essential in cases where established methodologies simply cannot be used to calculate appropriate levels of damages.

Awarding interest in international investment arbitration

One of the least developed and arguably most important aspects of calculating damages is the proper measure for the award of interest. International investment arbitration most often involves substantial sums of money. Moreover, a significant amount of time frequently elapses between the date on which a claimed injury occurs and the date on which an arbitral award is issued. Thus, interest may represent a significant portion of the final award and, in fact, it is not uncommon for the interest portion of an award to substantially exceed the actual damages.[86]

It is generally accepted that international tribunals may award interest to an injured claimant.[87] Indeed, as one scholar has noted, "the practice has become so widespread, it can be said that the liability to pay interest as part of an award of damages is an accepted international legal principal".[88] The type and amount of interest to be applied will largely be dictated by the applicable concession agreement, investment contract or bilateral investment treaty. If any one of these documents specifically addresses the issue of interest in awards, tribunals will generally award interest in accordance with its terms.[89] In the absence of an express contract or treaty provision, or if an existing provision is ambiguous, tribunals will look to law governing the dispute.[90] In cases involving breach of a concession agreement or other investment contract, this law will most likely be the law set forth in the contract. In treaty-based cases, or in contract cases lacking a choice-of-law provision, tribunals will almost always look to international law to determine the question of interest.[91]

The "tendency in international jurisprudence [is] to award only simple interest".[92] This tendency may stem from a belief that compound interest is prohibited in many domestic legal systems or by international law.[93] This belief, however, is questionable. Although compound interest may be disfavoured, many legal systems do permit courts and tribunals to award compound interest in specified circumstances.[94] It may also stem from a belief that compound interest is punitive in nature and could lead to an excess award.[95] Again, this belief is also questionable. As the *Santa Elena* tribunal noted, however, "It is not the purpose of compound interest to attribute blame to, or to punish, anybody for the delay in the payment made to the expropriated owner; it is a mechanism to ensure that the compensation awarded the Claimant is appropriate in the circumstances."[96]

Regardless of the reason why international tribunals have been reluctant to award compound interest, there is a growing perception that this reluctance runs counter to established legal principals and basic economic realities.[97] As the *Santa Elena* tribunal noted:

> "Where an owner of property has at some earlier time lost the value of his asset but has not received the monetary equivalent that then became due to him, the amount of compensation should reflect, at least in part, the additional sum that his money would have earned, had it, and the income generated by it, been reinvested each year at generally prevailing rates of interest."[98]

Drawing on the *Santa Elena* rationale, a number of tribunals have recently begun to express the view that compound interest should be generally available in international investment disputes. For example, in *Pope & Talbot* v. *Canada,* the tribunal stated, "applicable rules of international law [...] call for the award of appropriate interest, including compounding, as one of the elements of compensation."[99] Expanding on this view, the tribunal in *Wena Hotels* v. *Egypt* stated that it:

> "believes that an award of compound (as opposed to simple) interest is generally appropriate in most modern commercial arbitrations. As Professor Gotanda has observed, 'almost all financing and investment vehicles involve compound interest... If the claimant could have received compound interest merely by placing its money in a readily available and commonly used investment vehicle, it is neither logical nor equitable to award the claimant only simple interest'."[100]

Likewise, in *MTD Equity* v. *Republic of Chile*, an ICSID tribunal held that awarding compound interest "is more in accordance with the reality of financial transactions and a closer approximation to the actual value lost by an investor".[101] The common theme that runs through all of the decisions in which compound interest has been awarded is the desire to provide claimants with full compensation – i.e., to place the claimant in the position it would have been had it never been injured.[102]

Despite these precedents, there is no clear guidance as to when an award of compound interest should be made. Although international law does not require a tribunal to award compound interest,[103] there appears to be a growing recognition that compound interest may be necessary to fully and adequately compensate an injured investor.

CONCLUSION

Just as the substantive aspects of international investment law are continuing to expand, so too are the rules governing damages. Although there exist general principles to guide parties and tribunals in calculating "appropriate" damages in a particular case, there are no bright-line formulae that can be applied with regularity. Perhaps, at least for the moment, it is better this way. As the scope of protections accorded international investments evolves and the types of undertakings that qualify as "investment" expand, it is important that tribunals have the flexibility to respond adequately. Flexibility and adaptability, therefore, are crucial. However, the law should provide a measure of certainty and predictability. To date, the only two "certainties" appear to have developed are the dual guidelines set for the above: (a) the quantum of damages must be sufficient to eliminate the injurious effect of the state's unlawful actions; and (b) the method of calculating damages should be dictated by the type of investment. These guidelines should be sufficient to permit both the flexibility essential to the proper functioning of the international arbitral system and the stability needed to ensure its long-term viability.

END NOTE

1 Over 2,300 BITS are currently in force among approximately 180 countries. See Bishop, Crawford, Reisman, *Foreign Investment Disputes,* Kluwer 2005, 1.

2 See, e.g., *Restatement* (Third) *of the Foreign Relations Law of the United States*, § 712; International Law Commission Articles on State Responsibility, 53rd Sess., 2001, Article 31 ("The responsible State is under an obligation to make full repatriation of the injury caused by the internationally wrongful act."); Brice Clagett, 'Just Compensation in International Law: The Issues Before the Iran-United States Claims Tribunal', in *The Valuation of Nationalized Property in International Law*, Vol. IV, Lillich ed. 1987 ("One of the most hotly debated issues of public international law in recent years has been whether that law requires the payment of compensation when a nation expropriates the property of an alien investor and, if so, what the standard is for determining the amount of that compensation.").

3 See, e.g., Curtis A. Bradley, *Customary International Law and Private Rights of Action*, 1 Chicago Journal of International Law 421, 2000.

4 See, e.g., W. Michael Reisman & Robert D. Sloane, *Indirect Expropriation and its Valuation in the BIT Generation*, 2003 British Year Book of International Law 115, 116 (noting that "the prototypical FCN treaty did little more than impose upon the host state an obligation not to expropriate covered foreign investments without paying compensation for them.").

5 *Factory at Chorzow (Ger. v. Pol.)* (Indemnity), 1928 PCIJ (ser. A) No.17 (Judgment of Sept. 17) (holding "The essential principal contained in the actual notion of an illegal act – a principle which seems to be established by international practice and in particular by the decisions of arbitral tribunals – is that reparation must, as far as possible, wipe out all the consequences of the illegal act and reestablish the situation which would, in all probability, have existed if that act had not been committed. Restitution in kind, or, if this is not possible, payment of a sum corresponding to the value which a restitution in kind would bear [must be made] .... ").

6 See Hackworth, Digest of International Law, Vol. 3, 655-65 (1942).

7 See text, *infra* at note 18, citing, *CME Czech Republic B.V. (The Netherlands)* v. *The Czech Republic*, UNCITRAL Final Award of 14 March 2003, § 497.

8 See, e.g., Gloria Sandrino, *The NAFTA Investment Chapter and Foreign Direct Investment in Mexico: A Third World Perspective,* 27 Vanderbilt Journal of Transnational Law 259, 318, 1994 ("Most third world states oppose such high standards of valuation, and instead argue for 'appropriate compensation [...] taking into account [...] all circumstances that the State considers pertinent.'").

9 In response to the Hull Formula, many developing countries, particularly in Latin America, adopted the Calvo Doctrine, which provides that "there is in international law no rule universally accepted in theory nor carried out in practice, which makes obligatory the payment of immediate compensation nor even of deferred compensation, for expropriations of a general and impersonal character." See, e.g., L. Holzgrefe & Robert O. Keohane, *Humanitarian Intervention: Ethical, Legal, and Political Dilemmas,* 2003, pp. 26-27.

10 UN General Assembly Resolution 3171 (XXVII), Permanent Sovereignty Over Natural Resources, 28 UN GAOR Supp., No. 30, at 52, UN Doc. A/390, 1973, reprinted in 13 ILM 238, 1974.

11 *Libyan American Oil Co. (LIAMCO)* v. *Libyan Arab Republic*, 20 ILM 1, 86 (1981) (Mahmassani, sole arbitrator, 1977).

12 See id. at 79 (deeming the award to be "just and appropriate compensation").

13 See, e.g. *Shahin Shaine Ebrahimi* v. *Iran*, Iran-US Cl. Trib. Award 560-44/46/47-3 of 12 October 1994, § 88 (" .... The gradual emergence of this rule aims at ensuring that the amount of compensation is determined in a flexible manner, that is, taking into account the specific circumstances of each case. The prevalence of the 'appropriate' compensation standard does not imply, however, that the compensation quantum should be always 'less than full'."); *In the Matter of the Arbitration between Kuwait and American Independent Oil Co.,* (*AMINOIL*), Final Award, 24 March 1982, § 144, reprinted in 21 ILM 976, 1034, 1982 (finding that the claimant was entitled only to "appropriate" compensation following the lawful expropriation of its investment by the Kuwaiti government.).

14 See, e.g.,*LIAMCO* at 86 ("it would be reasonable and just to adopt the formula of 'equitable compensation' as a measure for the estimation of damages in the present dispute. This formulation is certainly in complete harmony with the general trend of international theory and practice on the concepts of sovereignty ...").

15 Iran-US Cl. Trib. Award 560-44/46/47-3 of 12 October 1994, § 88.

16 *Compañia del Desarrollo de Santa Elena v. Costa Rica* , Final Award, ARB/96/1, 17 February 2000, § 69, reprinted in 39 ILM 1319, 1329 (2000).

17 See United Nations General Assembly Resolution 1803. Notably, in debates surrounding General Assembly Resolution 1803, the United States maintained that the phrase "appropriate compensation" made "in accordance with international law" meant "prompt, adequate and effective" compensation as required under international law. See Andrew T. Guzman, *Why LDC's Sign Treaties That Hurt Them: Explaining the Popularity of Bilateral Investment Treaties*, 38 Virginia Journal of International Law 639, 649 (1998).

18 See, e.g., *CME Czech Republic B.V.* Final Award, 14 March 2003, § 501.

19 Ibid., § 497 (internal quotations omitted).

20 Ibid.

21 Treaty Between the Government of the United States of America and Government of [Country] Concerning the Encouragement and Reciprocal Protection of Investment, 2004, available at http://www.state.gov/documents/organization/38710.pdf.

22 *AMINOIL*, 21 ILM at 1033, § 147.

23 For example, the new US Model BIT defines the term investment as follows:
Every asset that an investor owns or controls, directly or indirectly, that has the characteristics of an investment [...]. Forms that an investment may take include: (a) an enterprise; (b) shares, stocks, and other forms of equity; (c) bonds, debentures, other debt instruments, and loans; (d) futures, options, and other derivatives; (e) turnkey, construction, management, production, concession, revenue-sharing, and other similar contracts, (f) intellectual property rights; (g) licenses, authorizations, permits, and similar rights conferred pursuant to domestic law; and (h) other tangible or intangible, movable, or immovable property, and related property rights, such as leases, mortgages, liens, and pledges.

24 *Sapphire International Petroleum Ltd* v. *National Iranian Oil Co.*, Arbitral Award, 15 March 1963, reprinted in 35 International Law Reports 136, 185-86 (applying this principle to breach of contract cases). See also Draft Convention on State Responsibility, 55 American Journal of International Law 545, 581, 1961, at Article 34.

25 *Pope & Talbot* v. *Government of Canada*, Award in Respect of Damages, NAFTA Chapter 11, 31 May 2002, § 81, 85.

26 *S.D. Meyers, Inc.* v. *Government of Canada* , UNCITRAL First Partial Award, 13 November 2000, § 251.

27 Ibid., § 308.

28 Ibid., § 309.

29 See ibid.

30 See generally *CMS Gas Transmission* v. *The Argentine Republic*, ICSID Case No. ARB/01/8, Award, 12 May 2005, *available at* http://www.cmsenergy.com/Invest/.

31 Ibid., § 409-10.

32 Ibid., § 410.

33 ICSID Case No. ARB(AF)/97/1, Award, 30 August 2000, § 113, reprinted in 40 ILM 36, 2001, (Finding the expropriation standard to be appropriate "since both situations involve the complete frustration of the operation of the landfill and negate the possibility of any meaningful return on Metalclad's investment.").

34 *S.D. Meyers, Inc.*, UNCITRAL Partial Award, 12 November 2000, § 315.

35 See, e.g., *World Bank: Report to the Development Committee and Guidelines for the Treatment of Foreign Direct Investment*, adopted 21 September 1992, reprinted in 31 ILM 1363, 1376, (1992) ("a 'going concern' means an enterprise consisting of income-producing assets which has been in operation for a sufficient period of time to generate the data required for the calculation of future income and which could have been expected with reasonable certainty, if the taking had not occurred, to continue producing legitimate income over the course of its economic life in the general circumstances following the taking by the State") ("World Bank Report").

36 See ibid ("Compensation will normally be 'appropriate' if it is 'adequate, effective and prompt'; 'adequate' compensation is fair market value immediately before public knowledge of the taking.").

37 See, e.g., Brice Clagett, "Just Compensation in International Law: The Issues Before the Iran-UN Claims Tribunal", III *The Valuation of Nationalized Property in International Law* 31, 61-62 n.86 ("International decisions rendered both before and after *Chorzow Factory* have declared as universally accepted rules of law that an investor cannot be fully compensated for the going-concern value of his expropriated interests unless he is awarded both the damage that has been sustained as a result of the taking and the reasonably ascertainable profit that has been missed.") (internal citations and quotations omitted).

38 See ibid ("'discounted cash flow value' means the cash receipts realistically expected from the enterprise in each future year of its economic life as reasonably projected minus that year's expected cash expenditure, after discounting this net cash flow for each year by a factor which reflects the time value of money, expected inflation, and the risk associated with such cash flow under realistic circumstances. Such discount rate may be measured by examining the rate of return available in the same market on alternative investments of comparable risk on the basis of their present value."). See also *Asian Agricultural Products Ltd (AAPL)* v. *Republic of Sri Lanka*, ICSID Case No. ARB/87/3, Award, 27 June 1990, § 102, reprinted in 30 ILM 577, 623 (1991) ("the projection of future profits in function of the 'Discounted Cash Flaw Method' (DCF) has to be envisaged simply as a tool to asses the level of Serendib's future profitability under all relevant circumstances.").

39 See Paul D. Freidland & Eleanor Wong, *Measuring Damages for the Deprivation of Income-Producing Assets: ICSID Case Studies*, 6 ICSID Review – Foreign Investment Law Journal 400, pp. 406-407.

40 It is a well-established accepted economic principle that the value of property is determined by its capacity to generate future income. See, e.g., J. Williams, *The Theory of Investment Value 1* (1938) ("in the end all prices depend on someone's estimate of future income."); I. Fisher, *The Theory of Interest* 12 (1954 ed.) ("The value of any property [...] is its value as a source of income [...]"); E. Solomon & J. Pringle, *An Introduction to Financial Management* 259 (1980 ed.) ("the age-old concept that the value of an asset depends not on its cost or its past usefulness but on its future usefulness [...] underlies the modern theory of value.").

41 See Brice Clagett, *Remarks at the American Society of International Law 92nd Annual Meeting* (1-4 April 1998), in 92 Proceedings of the American Society for International Law 303, 305 (1995).

42 See, e.g., *Tecnicas Medioambientales Tecmed, S.A.* v. *United Mexican States*, ICSID Case No. ARB (AF)/00/2, 29 May 2003, § 184-85, reprinted in 43 ILM 133, 183-83 (2004) (noting the remarkable disparity between the amount of damages calculated by the claimant ($52 million) and the respondent ($2.1 million) under the DCF method.).

43 See, e.g., *Amoco International Finance Co.* v. *Islamic Republic of Iran*, Iran-US Cl. Trib. Partial Award No. 310-56-3, 14 July 1987, § 213, reprinted in 27 ILM 1314, 1365 (1988) ("it will be necessary to determine the proper discount rate, taking into account the probable risks, inflation and the real rate of interest.").

44 See, e.g., *Tecnicas Medioambientales Tecmed, S.A.* 43 ILM 134, § 186, ("the difficulties in obtaining objective data allowing for application of the discounted cash flow method on the basis of estimates for a protracted future, not less than 15 years, together with the fact that such future cash flow also depends upon investments to be made ... building of seven additional cells [...] in the long term, lead the Arbitral Tribunal to disregard such methodology to determine the relief to be awarded to the Claimant.").

45 *Autopista Concesionada de Venezuela C.A.* v. *Bolivarian Republic of Venezuela*, ICSID Case No. ARB/00/5, Award, 23 September 2003, § 353-55.

46 *Wena Hotels* v. *Arab Republic of Egypt*, ICSID Case No. ARB/98/4, Award, 8 December 2000, § 123, reprinted in 41 ILM 896, 918 (2002).

47 See ibid. *See also Metalclad Corp.* § 119-20; *Southern Pacific Properties (Middle East) Limited v. Arab Republic of Egypt*, ICSID Case No. ARB/84/3, 20 May 1992, § 188, reprinted in 32 ILM 933, 973 (1993) ("In the Tribunal's view, the DCF method is not appropriate for determining the fair compensation in this case because the project was not in existence for a sufficient period of time to generate the data necessary for a meaningful DCF calculation.").

48 See ibid.

49 *Wena Hotels,* 41 ILM at 918, § 124. In *Wena*, the Claimant had operated one investment (a hotel) for less than eighteen months and was still in the process of renovating a second hotel. In addition, the tribunal found that there were some questions as to whether Wena had sufficient finances to fund the renovation and operation of its investments.

50 *Société Ouest Africaine des Bétons Industriels (SOABI)* v. *State of Senegal*, Award on the Merits, 25 February 1988, reprinted in 2 ICSID Reports 165, 171.

51 *Southern Pacific Properties,* 32 ILM 933, § 188-89 (noting that the project was in its infancy and, therefore, there was very little history on which to base projected revenues.).

52 Ibid., § 43-44.

53 Ibid., § 150.

54 Ibid., § 190 (finding that the "allowance of *lucrum cessans* may only involve those profits which are legitimate.").

55 Ibid., § 191.

56 *Sapphire International Petroleum Ltd* v. *National Iranian Oil Co.,* Arbitral Award, 15 March 1963, reprinted in 35 International Law Reports 136, 187.

57 See Ibid., at 186.

58 Ibid., at 187-88 (finding that "if the existence of damage is uncertain, it is nevertheless clear that the plaintiff had an opportunity to discover oil, an opportunity that both parties regarded as very favourable.").

59 Ibid.

60 See ibid.

61 See ibid.

62 Ibid.

63 Ibid., at 189.

64 In general, an action violates the abuse of rights doctrine if one of the following three factors is present: (1) the predominant motive for the action is to cause harm; (2) the action is totally unreasonable given the lack of any legitimate interest in the exercise of the right and its exercise harms another; and (3) the right is exercised for a purpose other than that for which it exists. See, e.g., Joseph M. Perillo, *Abuse of Rights: A Pervasive Legal Concept*, 27 Pacific Law Journal – *Yearbook Commercial Arbitration* 37, 47 (Fall 1995).

65 Final Award, reprinted in 25 *Yearbook Commercial Arbitration* 13 (2000) ("*Himpurna Final Award*").

66 Final Award, reprinted in 14 Mealey's International Arbitration Report B-1 (December 1999) ("*Patuha Final Award*").

67 *Himpurna Final Award* at 78-79.

68 The Patuha tribunal held that "damages for the loss of a bargain may in principle be granted even when the victim of a breach has not yet incurred significant costs." *Patuha Final Award* at B-42.

69 *Himpurna Final Award* at 93.

70 Ibid., at 90.

71 *Patuha Final Award* at B-42.

72 See ibid.

73 For a fuller discussion of these cases and the abuse of right doctrine, see, e.g., Irina Petrova, *"Stepping on the Shoulders of a Drowning Man" The Doctrine of Abuse of Right as a Tool for Reducing Damages for Lost Profits: Troubling Lessons from the Patuha and Himpurna Arbitrations*, 35 Georgetown Journal of International Law 455, 463 (2004); Louis T. Wells, *Double Dipping in Arbitration Awards? An Economist Questions Damages Awarded to Karaha Bodas Company in Indonesia*, 19 Arbitration International (No. 4) 471 (2003).

74 See Petrova at 463.

75 See *Karaha Bodas Co., LLC.* v. *Perusahaan Pertambangan Minyak Dan Gas Bumi Nega*, 364 F.3d 274, 306 (5th Cir. 2004) ("The abuse of rights doctrine is not established in American law.").

76 *World Bank Report*, 31 ILM at 1377.

77 Ibid.

78 *Amoco International Finance Corp.*, 27 ILM at 1374, § 249.

79 See *World Bank Report*, 31 ILM at 1377 (1992).

80 *AMINOIL*, 21 ILM at 1038-39, § 165.

81 *Fedax N.V.* v. *The Republic of Venezuela,* ICSID Case No. ARB/96/3, Award, 9 March 1998, § 1, reprinted in 37 ILM 1391, 1395 (1998).

82 See ibid, § 29, citing Decision on Jurisdiction of 11 July 1997.

83 See ibid, § 31-36.

84 *Ceskoslovenska obchodni banka a.s. ("CSOB")* v. *Slovak Republic* , ICSID Case No. ARB/97/4, Award, 29 December 2004.

85 Ibid., § 222

86 See e.g., *Santa Elena,* 39 ILM 1317, § 117 (awarding $4 million in damages and $12 million in compound interest.).

87 See, e.g., *Middle East Cement Shipping & Handling Co.* v. *Egypt*, ICSID Case No. ARB/ 99/6, Award, 12 April 2002, § 174 ("international jurisprudence and literature have recently, after detailed consideration, concluded that interest is an integral part of the compensation due after the award..."); Article 38(1) of the International Law Commission Articles on State Responsibility, 53rd Sess., 2001 ("Interest on any principal sum due under this chapter shall be payable when necessary in order to ensure full reparation."); UNIDROIT Principles on International Commercial Contracts, Article 7.4.9 ("If a party does not pay a sum of money when it falls due the aggrieved party is entitled to interest upon that sum from the time when payment is due to the time of payment whether or not the non-payment is excused.").

88 John Gotanda, *Supplemental Damages in Private International Law* (Kluwer 1998), § 2.1.

89 See John Gotanda, Compound Interest in International Disputes, 34 Law & Pol'y Int'l Bus. 393, 431 (2003), citing, *Anaconda-Iran* v. *Iran*, 18 Iran-US Cl. Trib. Rep. 199, 233, 238-39 (1988); *R.J. Reynolds Tobacco Co.* v. *Iran*, 7 Iran-US Cl. Trib. Rep. 191, 191-92 (1984).

90 See, e.g., *McCollough & Co., Inc.* v. *Ministry of Post*, Tel. & Tel., Award No. 225-89-3 (Chamber Three) of 22 April 1986, 11 Iran-US Cl. Trib. Rep. 3, § 90 ("Like any other decision of the Tribunal, a decision to award interest must be made on the basis of respect for law, and in this field as in any other, the applicable law is to be determined by the Tribunal in accordance with the guidelines contained in Article V of the Claims Settlement Determination."); LIAM CO, 20 ILM at 83 ("The arbitral tribunal takes into consideration the proper law of the contract ... ").

91 See, e.g., *Petrobart* v. *Kyrgyz Republic*, Stockholm Chamber Case No. 126/2003 (Energy Charter Treaty), Final Award, 29 March 2005 at 88 (finding that interest should be calculated on the basis of international rules rather than national rules because "the claim is based on a treaty and is therefore a claim under international law."); *Middle East Cement Shipping & Handling Co.* v. *Egypt*, ICSID Case No. ARB/99/6, Award, 12 April 2002 (awarding compound interest despite the fact that such an award conflicted with Egyptian law. According to the tribunal, Egyptian law did not apply to BIT-based claims. Instead, these claims were governed by international law. The tribunal further stated that "compound (as opposed to simple) interest is at present deemed appropriate as the standard of international law in such expropriation cases.").

92 *Santa Elena*, 39 ILM at 1332, § 97. See also, James Crawford, Special Rapporteur, Third Report on State Responsibility, International Law Commission, 52nd Sess., 22 UN Doc. A/CN.4/507 (2000), § 208 ("the general view of courts and tribunals has been against the award of compound interest, and this is true even of those tribunals which hold claimants to be normally entitled to compensatory interest."); *McCollough & Co., Inc.* 11 Iran-US Cl. Trib. Rep. 3, § 96-97 ("Most awards allocate only simply interest, but occasionally compound interest has been awarded and sometimes a percentage is added to the interest in consideration of the rate of inflation. It is difficult to draw any distinct conclusions from so diverse a practice. The Tribunal can conclude, however, that no uniform rule of law relating to interest has emerged from the practice in transnational arbitration ... ").

93 See Gotanda, *Compound Interest in International Disputes* at 394.

94 For a comparative analysis of laws relating to the awarding of compound interest, see ibid. generally.

95 See, e.g., Crawford, § 211 (" [...] allowing compound interest could result in an inflated and disproportionate award, with an amount of interest greatly exceeding the principal amount owed.").

96 *Santa Elena,* 39 ILM at 1333, § 104.

97 See ibid, § 103. See also Crawford, § 211 (noting that awarding compound interest is permissible when the facts are sufficient to justify "some element of compounding as an aspect of full compensation".).

98 *Santa Elena*, 39 ILM at 1333, § 104. See also *Maffezini* v. *Kingdom of Spain*, ICSID Case No. ARB/97/7, 13 November 2000, § 96 (holding that it was appropriate to award compound interest because the money at issue was withdrawn from a time-deposit account which paid interest on a compound basis).

99 *Pope & Talbot* v. *Government of Canada*, Award in Respect of Damages, NAFTA Chapter 11, 31 May 2002, § 89.

100 *Wena Hotels* v. *Egypt*, ICSID Case No. ARB 98/4, Award, 8 December 2000, reprinted in 41 ILM 896, 919 (2002) (awarding 9 percent interest compounded quarterly). See also, *Tecnicas Medioambientales Tecmed, S.A.*,§ 196 ("in the opinion of the Arbitral Tribunal, application of compound interest is justified as part of the integral compensation owed to the Claimant as a result of the loss of its investment.").

101 *MTD Equity* v. *Republic of Chile*, ICSID Case No. ARB/01/7, Award, 25 May 2004, § 251, reprinted in 44 ILM 91, 129 (2005).

102 The *Wena* Tribunal noted that that compounded interest will best "restore the Claimant to a reasonable approximation of the position in which it would have been if the wrongful act had not taken place", 41 ILM at 919, § 129.

103 See *Autopista Concesionada de Venezuela C.A*, § 393-97 ("there is no well established principle of international law requiring the award of compound interest ... "). See also N. Affolder, *Awarding Compound Interest in International Arbitration*, The 2001 American Review of International Arbitration, pp. 68-69.

9

Problems of delay and disruption damages in international construction arbitration

By ***Mr. Justice Vivian Ramsey***
High Court Judge, London[1]

INTRODUCTION

Given that the burden of proof in any claim for damages usually rests with the party making the claim, the problems of establishing delay and disruption damages in international construction arbitration are felt most acutely by the contractor or, in the case of a sub-contract, by the sub-contractor.[2] They may have suffered loss and expense, or may feel that they have, as a result of occurrences outside of their control or contractual responsibility. They may even consider that the employer[3] is responsible for the delay. Nevertheless unless they can satisfy the applicable requirements of procedural and substantive law, they cannot recover compensation. So far as this goes, this may seem like a statement of the obvious; unless the claim can be established, it cannot succeed. But making out a claim for delay and disruption damages under a construction contract can be problematic, and this paper considers the reasons why such problems arise.

Equally, delay and disruption claims cause problems for the party defending the claims. The complexity of the subject and of the issues means that the employer will often have to contend with significant difficulties in defending such claims, and to incur substantial expenditure in doing so.

The paper considers three particular aspects that lead to legal and factual problems: causation, concurrency and calculation. These cover the difficult areas with which tribunals most often have to contend.

1. CAUSATION

In many situations, the question of whether something has caused a particular effect can be simply answered. The law of causation, in its most basic form, is therefore both simple and obvious. As Lord Salmon remarked in the House of Lords[4], "what or who has caused a certain event to occur is essentially a practical question of fact which can best be answered by ordinary common sense rather than by abstract metaphysical theory." Recently, Lord Hoffman remarked in the annual Blackstone Lecture at Oxford University,[5] "There is nothing special or mysterious about the law of causation. One decides, as a matter of law, what causal connection the law requires and one then decides, as a question of fact, whether the claimant has satisfied the requirements of the law. There is, in my opinion, nothing more to be said."

However, in practice, particularly in construction disputes, the task of showing that the defendant has caused the loss may be much more difficult than this elegant simplicity would suggest. This can be illustrated by a recent decision widely reported in the specialist construction law reports in the UK, even though it is not a construction case. It raised the question of the degree of certainty required between a cause and an effect. In *Fairchild* v. *Glenhaven Funeral Services,*[6] a claim for compensation for asbestos-related cancer was brought against an employer. It could not be proved that the exposure to asbestos for which the employer was responsible had caused the cancer. The employee had been exposed to asbestos by other employers. After the initial court decision and two appeals, the Law Lords had great difficulty in holding that causation was established, since all that could be shown was a *substantial possibility* that the defendant employer had caused the harm suffered. Lord Hoffman described this in the Blackstone Lecture as a problem that "has puzzled lawyers since Roman times", the difficulty of proving the cause of loss, when more than one cause is possible. In a highly controversial ruling, the Law Lords in this case found that the *substantial possibility* was enough to establish causation.

Another aspect of this are the cases where a party has "lost a chance" of doing something. In those cases, the English Court of Appeal in *Allied Maples Group Ltd* v. *Simmons & Simmons* [1995] 1WLR 1602, a case involving professional negligence, held that where the loss depends on the hypothetical action of a third party, the claiming party only has to prove that there is a substantial chance that the third party would have acted so as to confer the benefit or avoid the risk, the evaluation of the substantial chance being a question of quantification of damages.

Tribunals in construction cases routinely have to deal with causation issues of similar or greater complexity. As is remarked in *Keating on Building Contracts*, "Contractors often have claims dependent on a number of separate causes each of which has contributed to delay and extra cost. In principle, the loss attributable to each cause should be separately identified and particularised but separation may be difficult."[7] These difficulties have led to a tension between the contractor's obligation to plead its case properly, including proof of causation of the loss allegedly suffered, and a recognition of the practical difficulties in doing so. The consequence of this tension has been the development of a phenomenon known variously as "global" "rolled-up", "composite" or "total cost claims", phrases which have acquired derogatory undertones.

Nearly 40 years ago, the English High Court[8] upheld the decision of an arbitrator to make a "global" award for claims arising under different terms of the contract, recognising that the loss incurred depended on an extremely complex interaction between different causes. The judge supported the arbitrator's pragmatism: "I can see no reason why (the arbitrator) should not recognise the realities of the situation and make individual awards in respect of those parts of the claim which can be dealt with in isolation and a supplementary award in respect of the remainder of these claims as a composite whole." An analysis of that case shows that the principle was being applied to a comparatively simple prolongation claim where the loss was being measured at a loss per week multiplied by the number of weeks.

The general approach was followed, and some 20 years later in *London Borough of Merton* v. *Stanley Hugh Leach*, the court held:[9] "If application is made ... for reimbursement of direct loss and expense attributable to more than one head of claim and at the time when the loss or expense comes to be ascertained, it is impractical to disentangle or disintegrate the part directly attributable to each head of claim then, provided of course that the contractor has not unreasonably delayed in making the claim and so has himself created the difficulty, the architect must ascertain the global loss attributable to the two causes ... ."

However, this kind of pragmatic approach has been attacked by lawyers, especially those representing employers. The criticism has usually focused on the difficulty of dealing with a case where a global sum is claimed for a multitude of events for which the employer is alleged to be responsible. As Ian Duncan Wallace QC[10] has observed, "claims on a total cost basis, *a fortiori* if in respect of a number of disparate claims, will, *prima facie*, be embarrassing and an abuse of the process of court, justifying their being struck out and the action dismissed at the interlocutory stage." Critics of the global approach to claims often refer to the decision of the Privy Council in the Hong Kong case of *Wharf Properties* v. *Eric Cumine Associates (No. 2)*[11] where actions against architects for negligent design and contract administration were struck out for being inadequately particularised and disclosing no reasonable cause of action. Lord Oliver observed that "the pleading is hopelessly embarrassing as it stands". While he was prepared to accept the difficulties of the complex interaction between the consequences of various events making difficult an accurate apportionment of the total extra costs: "This has, however, no bearing upon the obligation of a plaintiff to plead his case with such particularity as is sufficient to alert the opposite party to the case which is going to made against him at the trial."

In Australia, the courts had developed a more practical approach to the problems of global claims. Mr Justice Byrne in *John Holland Construction & Engineering Pty Ltd* v. *Kvaerner R J Brown Pty Ltd*[12] preferred to give the claimant the opportunity to amend the claim to provide the necessary particulars of causation rather than strike it out as incomplete. This approach was accepted in England by His Honour Judge Humphrey Lloyd QC[13] in *Bernhards Rugby Landscapes Ltd* v. *Stockley Park*[14], where he also allowed a global claim to be amended since "its current form is not so oppressive or abusive as to justify refusal of leave to amend [...] The deficiencies may [...] be cured by the provision of particulars or in some other way."

The *Stockley Park* case was characterised by a careful balance between the problems faced by the claimant in making out the claim and the difficulties that a global approach creates for defendants: A party "is entitled to present its case as it thinks fit", but "a defendant on the other hand is entitled to know the case it has to meet [...]. What is sufficient particularity is a matter of fact and degree in each case. A balance has to be struck between excessive particularity and basic information. The approach must also be cost effective."

Since *Stockley Park* there have been further important developments in the use of global claims to overcome causation problems.

The Society of Construction Law's Delay and Disruption Protocol, issued in October 2002,[15] is not of any statutory effect, nor is it a contractual document unless the parties choose to adopt any of its provisions as such. Nevertheless, it has been influential in promoting debate on how issues of delay and disruption should properly be handled by the parties. Its Guidance Note on Global Claims[16] is hostile to the practice, perhaps surprisingly so:

> "The not uncommon practice of contractors making composite or global claims without substantiating cause and effect is discouraged by the Protocol and rarely accepted by the courts.
>
> "1.14.2 If the Contractor has made and maintained accurate and complete records, the Contractor should be able to establish the causal link between the Employer Risk Event and the resultant loss and/or expense suffered, without the need to make a global claim. The failure to maintain such records does not justify the Contractor in making a global claim. The Protocol's guidance as to the keeping of records is set out in Guidance Section 2.
>
> "1.14.3 In what should only be rare cases where the financial consequences of the various causes of compensation are impossible to distinguish, so that an accurate apportionment of the compensation claimed cannot be made between the several causative events, then in this rare situation it is acceptable to quantify individually those items of the claim which can be dealt with in isolation and claim compensation for the remainder as a composite whole.
>
> "1.14.4 The Contractor will nevertheless need to set out the details of the Employer Risk Events relied on and the compensation claimed with sufficient particularity so that the Employer knows the case that is being made against it."

By contrast, in the Scottish courts there has been a decision which will have given some encouragement to contractors. John Doyle were employed as works contractors by management contractors, Laing, on the construction of a new corporate headquarters for a financial institution. John Doyle claimed a 22-week extension of time and nearly £5 million for loss and expense caused by delay and disruption. Laing argued that, since this was a global claim, if any of the loss and expense alleged was not caused by them, the whole claim must fail. The findings of the Inner House of the Court of Session[17] constitute an important reassessment of the modern law and have already been applied in England as well. They can be summarised as follows:

- Individual causal links must normally be proved between each breach/ claims event and each item of loss and expense.
- If this is impossible, the claims events can be pleaded as producing a cumulative effect, where it is not necessary to break down and isolate them.
- If, however, the employer is not liable for a significant cause of loss and expense, the claim fails.
- If there are only "some" events, not "significant" in this category, the claim need not fail. The tribunal may be able to apportion loss, although this will lead sometimes to rough and ready results.
- In pleading the claim, reasonable detail on events and heads of loss must be provided. Causation will be largely a matter of inference and based on experts' reports; consideration of these aspects should wait until all the evidence is before the tribunal.

It can be said that there are three main changes in emphasis in the law in *John Doyle* and each is, to a greater or lesser extent, encouraging of global claims.

- Whereas previously it was understood that *any* cause of loss shown to be not the responsibility of the defendant would be fatal to the global claim,[18] it now appears that this only applies if the cause of the loss is significant.
- The court seemed comfortable with the idea of apportionment of loss by the tribunal between causes for which the employer is and is not liable, even if this may be a rough and ready process. It is possible that arbitrators will often be better equipped than judges and more willing to make such apportionments.

- The issue of whether causation can be proved should normally wait until the trial when all the evidence is in and so, presumably, would not be decided at the interlocutory stage on an application to strike out. This would also, it is suggested, be more in line with the practice of arbitrators.

In a recent case, His Honour Judge Wilcox in the Technology and Construction Court in *Great Eastern Hotel Co. Ltd* v. *John Laing Construction Ltd*[19] found as follows:

> "I am satisfied that the Trade Contractor accounts are global claims, and if such a claim is to succeed, (Great Eastern) must eliminate from the causes of the loss and expense element all matters which are not the responsibility of Laing.[20] That requirement is mitigated in this case, because it is possible to identify a causal link between particular events for which Laing was responsible, and the individual items of loss. Such analysis was approved in the Court of Session Inner House in *John Doyle Construction* v. *Laing Management (Scotland) Ltd* I am satisfied on the basis of Mr Mitchell's[21] evidence that the *dominant cause* of Trade Contractor delay was in fact the delay to the project caused by Laing's proven breaches."

In summary, it may be said that causation represents one of the single greatest problems for a contractor in a delay and disruption claim. Changing attitudes to global claims reflect the balance between practical understanding of a contractor's difficulty in separating causes of loss and the requirement that a claim must be properly pleaded and proved, in fairness to the defending party.

2. CONCURRENCY

Whilst concurrency is related to the issue of causation, it is of sufficient importance to be treated in its own right. The word "concurrency" is used for a situation where a number of effective causes actually operate to create an effect. That effect is usually delay or disruption which gives rise to monetary claims. Causation is principally, although not exclusively, a problem for the claiming party, often the contractor, to overcome. Concurrency, on the other hand, creates major difficulties for all parties. It affects the employer whose liquidated damages entitlement may be challenged by a claim for extension of time, the contractor who seeks to base a claim for loss and expense for the period of delay which has led to late completion and the contract administrator, whether engineer or project manager, who must try to allocate responsibility for delay.

The principal problem with concurrency is that it leads to logical difficulties in applying simple concepts of causation. Very often, the underlying factual position will eliminate competing causes, but there will still be cases where there will be causative events of the same potency but with different parties being responsible for each one.

One particular problem is the absence of a consensus on the method of analysis. This applies both to the method of delay analysis and to the legal analysis of the consequences.

3. DELAY ANALYSIS

The Society of Construction Law Protocol deals[22] with the principal types of analysis available to show the effect of the different factors upon delay caused. It includes a table which indicates the suitability of the respective types of delay analysis according to the factual programming information available: as-planned programme without network, networked as-planned programme, updated as-planned networked programme or as-built records. It then sets out the types of analysis that can be used: as-planned versus as-built, impacted as-planned, collapsed as-built or time impact analysis.

It is certainly impossible in this paper to resolve the competing advantages and disadvantages of the different methods. Indeed, as the recent event held at King's College, University of London[23] has shown, it is still an area where experts on the subject disagree. At that event, an audience of nearly 300 construction professionals was given a set of hypothetical facts concerning an unhappy project in which work had come to a standstill in exceptionally bad weather when the contractor's water pumps broke down and the excavations collapsed. The employer meanwhile had asked for a re-design of waterproofing and instructed the use of a proprietary product, which was delivered late and took longer to apply than the contractor had allowed. A whole range of other mishaps occurred, from an alleged error in the setting out, resulting in a need for additional excavation and backfilling, to late release of the reinforcing bar-bending schedules. Despite weekend working by the contractors' reinforcement fabricators, work finished one week late.

The representative for the contractor argued for the "impacted as-planned" analysis of the events, which would not only free the contractor from liability for liquidated damages, but would give rise to a substantial delay and disruption claim and an acceleration claim. Opposing this, the person acting on behalf of the employer adopted the "as-planned versus as-built" method, which showed the contractor to be in serious trouble and obliged to accept full responsibility for the delay. The representative for the engineer proposed to resolve the dispute using the "as-built but-for" test. The adjudicator's advisor favoured the use of the "time impact" method of analysis, but the audience rejected the motion: "This house considers that the time impact method is the most appropriate for the analysis of delay in construction disputes."

The audience was asked in turn which of the four methods they favoured, and none commanded a clear majority. Rather, each had a committed band of supporters. It was clear that there was no majority in favour of "time impact" analysis. Further, nothing approaching consensus could be found on the correct methodology – rather the audience split into four significant minorities.

This clearly illustrates the major difficulty for both sides in any dispute that requires a delay analysis. Whilst a method can be found that will support a case either for the contractor or the employer, the difficulty will be in predicting, objectively, the likely outcome of the case, since there is no single approach that the tribunal will follow. Self-evidently, this represents a problem for the tribunal as well as a risk for the parties.[24]

4. LEGAL ANALYSIS

The delay analysts are not alone in disagreement over the correct approach to be followed in dealing with concurrent delay.

In an authoritative treatment of the subject to date, John Marrin QC[25] considered the "correct approach to contractors' claims arising out of concurrent delays in the execution of construction projects". The focus of the paper is a hypothetical project for the construction of a shopping centre. On a twelve-month contract, there is an overrun of one month; the causes of the delay being, on the one hand, extra work ordered by the architect and, on the other hand, the carrying out of the remedial work necessary to correct the contractor's defective workmanship, two causes to be assumed to be "of approximately equal causative potency".

The issue for discussion was whether, under the UK's widely used JCT Standard Form of Contract,[26] the following results would occur:

- The contractor would be granted a month's extension of time;
- The contractor would be entitled to a month's worth of prolongation costs;
- The employer would be entitled to a month's worth of liquidated damages.

The short response to these questions is that, in most legal systems, including England, there is no single authoritative right answer. This is so even though many standard forms of contract have been through many editions. In the case of the English JCT Standard Form, it is still estimated to be used on over three-quarters of UK construction projects.

John Marrin is obliged to consider five possible contenders. It is not possible to deal with them in detail here but they can be outlined.

First, he refers to *apportionment*: "a not unnatural response would be to suggest that the overrun and its consequences should be apportioned between the contractor and the employer [...] any such apportionment would be achieved by allocating financial consequences according to the tribunal's perception of the relative causative potency of the competing causes." His conclusion is that "in the context of contractor's claims under construction contracts, that approach has attracted only very limited support.[27] To some degree it is thought that this is because the courts of common law tend to apply the principles of causation in an 'all or nothing' way." Against this, Mr Marrin notes greater readiness to use apportionment in Canada and in New Zealand.

The second possible approach is described as *the American approach*. The US construction industry and the American courts recognise three distinct species of delay: excusable delay, compensable delay and inexcusable delay. Categorisation of a delay as one of these is a matter for the contract.

John Marrin notes that, "the American courts have arguably achieved the advantage of greater certainty. For example, delay not impacting on critical path activities is not even taken into account. Neither party is likely to be able to recover financial compensation unless a cause of delay can be clearly segregated from others. This latter point would conflict with the usual JCT position in the UK that an employer could recover liquidated damages even when it cannot show that contractor default is the sole cause of delay. For this reason 'it is thought that the courts in England would, if asked, decline to apply the American approach to a case governed by the JCT Standard Form'."

The third possible approach is the "but for" test. "On behalf of contractors, it is occasionally suggested that the correct approach in determining contractual delay claims is to apply the 'but for' test of causation. No doubt, this is because it is the test most favourable to the claimant. Thus, if a contractor worked well on the original specification and then incompetently and slowly on work ordered as a variation/change order, under the 'but for' test it could argue that the delay would not have occurred but for the variation/change order, making it the employer's responsibility. Not surprisingly, it is thought that the English courts are most unlikely to apply the 'but for' test of causation to a contractual claim unless the wording of the contract clearly demands it."

The construction law text Keating[28] has for a number of years, in successive editions, argued for the "dominant cause" approach. It was summarised in the 5th edition[29] as follows: "If there are two causes, one the contractual responsibility of the defendant and the other the contractual responsibility of the plaintiff, the plaintiff succeeds if he establishes that the cause for which the defendant is responsible is the effective, dominant cause. Which cause is dominant is a question of fact [...] to be decided by applying common sense standards."

This approach, when used by an arbitrator, was criticised by the English High Court in *H. Fairweather* v. *London Borough of Wandsworth*[30] in clear terms: "I do not consider that the dominant test is correct." As has been observed in a recent commentary,[31] "The problem with the dominant cause approach, as indicated by the *Fairweather* case, is that it necessarily requires a choice to be made between one cause or another [...]. The dominant cause approach will inevitably lead to injustice to one of the parties." Against this, it must be observed that the court in *Great Eastern Hotel* v. *John Laing* following *John Doyle* v. *Laing Management*[32] adopted precisely this wording.

The preferred option by John Marrin is the *Malmaison* approach. This gets its name from the English case of *Henry Boot Construction (UK) Ltd* v. *Malmaison Hotel (Manchester) Ltd*[33] in which Mr Justice Dyson[34] regarded the following statement as uncontroversial: "if there are two concurrent causes of delay, one of which is a relevant event, and the other is not, then the contractor is entitled to an extension of time for the period of delay caused by the relevant event notwithstanding the concurrent effect of the other event."

The case of *Royal Brompton Hospital NHS Trust* v. *Hammond (No 7)*[35] seemed to give further support to the *Malmaison* approach: "If Taylor Woodrow (the contractor) was delayed in completing the works both by matters for which it bore the contractual risk and by relevant events, within the meaning of that term in the standard form [...] it would be entitled to extensions of time by reason of the occurrence of the relevant events notwithstanding its own defaults."

As Burr and Palles-Clark note,[36] "*Malmaison* and *Brompton* do not appear to deal specifically with the entitlement to loss and expense, (only extension of time), although it would seem to follow that, where the contractor is in concurrent culpable delay, he will only be entitled to recover the specific additional costs incurred as a result of employer's delay, which because of the contractor's default will exclude his general time-related costs."

The Society of Construction Law Protocol's guidance on this last point[37] provides that, "If the Contractor incurs additional costs that were caused both by Employer Delay and Contractor Delay, then the Contractor should only recover compensation if it is able to separate the additional costs caused by the Employer Delay from those caused by the Contractor Delay."

While allocation of responsibility for the occurrence of events leading to delay is always to some extent a matter of contractual agreement, it must be regarded as highly unsatisfactory that there is no agreed methodology for delay analysis and no single legal approach to the concurrency issue, when these issues are commonly raised in construction claims. This in turn leads to uncertainty and unpredictability in the outcome of claims and unquestionably the encouragement of claims which might be non-starters on any mainstream analysis, could one be accepted as standard.

5. CALCULATION

It is not practical, in the context of this paper, to address all aspects of calculations of delay and disruption damages. The calculation of delay loss is, by comparison, much more straightforward than the calculation of loss caused by disruption. It has often been said that once a party has established a liability for delay or for disruption, the approach of the tribunal to the calculation of the quantum should be more flexible. This can be illustrated by two cases. In *Chaplin* v. *Hicks* [1911] 2 KB 786, the loss of an opportunity to appear in a "beauty contest" had to be assessed. The English Court of Appeal said this:

> "Then came the point that was more strenuously argued, that the damages were of such a nature as to be impossible of assessment. It was said that the plaintiff's chance of winning a prize turned on such a number of contingencies that it was impossible for any one, even after arriving at the conclusion that the plaintiff had lost her opportunity by the breach, to say that there was any assessable value of that loss. It is said that in a case which involves so many contingencies it is impossible to say what was the plaintiff's pecuniary loss. I am unable to agree with that contention. I agree that the presence of all the contingencies upon which the gaining of the prize might depend makes the calculation not only difficult but incapable of being carried out with certainty or precision. The proposition is that, whenever the contingencies on which the result depends are numerous and difficult to deal with, it is impossible to recover any damages for the loss of the chance or opportunity of winning the prize. [...]. I do not agree with the contention that, if certainty is impossible of attainment, the damages for a breach of contract are unassessable [...]. I only wish to deny with emphasis that, because precision cannot be arrived at, the jury has no function in the assessment of damages[...]. In such a case the jury must do the best they can, and it may be that the amount of their verdict will really be a matter of guesswork. But the fact that damages cannot be assessed with certainty does not relieve the wrongdoer of the necessity of paying damages for his breach of contract."

This is an approach also reflected in the Canadian case of *Wood* v. *Grand Valley Railway Company* (1915) 51 SCR 283 where the Court said at 289:

> "It is clearly impossible under the facts of that case to estimate with anything approaching to mathematical accuracy the damages sustained by the plaintiffs, but it seems to me to be clearly laid down there by the learned judges that such an impossibility cannot 'relieve the wrongdoer of the necessity of paying damages for his breach of contract' and that on the other hand for the tribunal to estimate them whether jury or judge must under such circumstances do 'the best it can' and its conclusion will not be set aside even if the amount of the verdict is a matter of guess work."

The suggestion of "guess work" may seem somewhat extreme, and tribunals usually adopt the more acceptable approach of "assessment". That assessment is generally based on the submissions of the parties. It is those submissions that put a value on the claim from the most optimistic view point of the particular party. Often, though, a defending party concentrates all its efforts on the liability aspects of the case rather than the detail of quantum. Whilst this may give the tribunal an unchallenged position, the process of assessment is still necessary to reflect only partial success on the issues.

One of the most difficult areas of proof of loss arising from delay is loss of profit. This claim can arise either as a claim by a contractor as a result of delay or disruption or as a claim by an employer resulting from delay where there is no enforceable liquidated damages regime.

Take the example of an oilfield where a defective piece of equipment causes a delay of a year to the start of production. What is the loss of profit? The oil is in the ground. Production is delayed at the commencement but can continue for a longer period at the end. What are the reserves? What will be the impact of earlier extraction from adjacent fields? There are therefore problems in assessing the quantity, the rate of extraction and the period over which the extraction takes place. Then comes the even more difficult question. What is the level of profit over, say, the 10- or 20-year period of production. In principle, if the level of profit is rising then the delay could be argued to be beneficial to the oil company. There is undoubtedly a loss of cash flow in the first year, but if the income stream, appropriately discounted, leads to an overall positive position for the oil producer, what is the loss?

Equally, supposing that a piece of equipment that is intended to have a maintenance cycle of 20 months in fact has a maintenance cycle of 16 months so that periodic disruptions are encountered, how is the loss of profit caused by that disruption to be evaluated? At what stage and to what extent should the damage be avoided by replacing the machinery?

Two further examples illustrate that, even where more simple aspects arise, calculation constitutes a problem in relation to delay and disruption claims. Take, for example, interest and head office overheads.

6. INTEREST

It might be supposed that a contractor's entitlement to interest in the event of late certification or non-certification or under-certification would be routine and long since settled in law. It is true that many of the principal standard form contractors purport to deal with this issue.[38]

However, the calculation of interest causes problems in most arbitrations.[39] First, the question is whether the claim for interest is a matter of substantive or procedural law. This, in turn, may be a circular argument. Secondly, whether a matter of substantive or procedural law, it may be a matter that a party has to consider in the context of enforcement. For instance, an award of interest may defeat enforcement in a number of Islamic countries. Thirdly, there is the question of pre-arbitration, post-arbitration and post-award interest, with different rules arising in each jurisdiction. The position in English law is still uncertain as to certain forms of interest, particularly interest as damages, and is uncertain where substantive English law applies and the seat of arbitration is outside England and Wales.

The Society of Construction Law Protocol[40] again sets out some of the background when it states that "There are often arguments as to the date on which interest on a Contractor's claim should start to run [...] the appropriate starting date will not be the same in all circumstances." English case law has taken different positions on whether interest is payable where an arbitrator or other tribunal holds that an engineer's decision on a contractor's claim was an under-certification. In *Morgan Grenfell* v. *Sunderland Borough Council*[41], the author as counsel successfully contended that the contractor was entitled to interest on the claim: "if the arbitrator revises (the engineer's) certificate so as to increase its amount, it follows that the engineer has failed to certify the right amount and the contractor becomes entitled to interest." However, in Scotland in *BP Chemicals Ltd* v. *Kingdom Engineering (Fife) Ltd*[42] and in England in *Royal Borough of Kingston upon Thames* v. *AMEC Civil Engineering*,[43] a quite different view was taken. The judge in the latter case made this clear:

> "If the engineer has done his contractual duty in issuing a certificate i.e. the amount that he certifies does indeed represent his opinion reached, in accordance with the terms of the contract, on the basis of the statement submitted by the contractor and is reasonable on that basis, he has not failed to issue a certificate, notwithstanding that an arbitrator may subsequently revise upwards the amount certified. That in such a case the contractor should not be entitled to interest on the ground of failure to certify is in my judgment consistent with the purpose of interim certification [...] the contractor is not entitled to interest merely because the arbitrator has revised the engineer's interim certificates upwards."

The ICE in its 1999 7th edition sought to deal with this point[44] with a "deeming" provision: "if in an arbitration pursuant to Clause 66 the arbitrator holds that any sum or additional sum should have been certified by a particular date in accordance with the aforementioned sub-clauses but was not so certified this shall be regarded for the purposes of this sub-clause as a failure to certify such sum or additional sum."

However, many contracts, both in the UK and in other jurisdictions, do not have an equivalent. As was recently pointed out,[45] "Those contracts, including standard forms and 'bespoke' contracts, still embody the possibility of a distinction between situations where the non-payment/under-payment is 'wrongful' or 'improper' and those where it is not, the interest provisions applying to the former but not the latter." This illustrates the problem that can occur in calculating what is often a substantial percentage of the overall recovery in these cases.

7. HEAD OFFICE OVERHEADS

In principle, if the contractor has suffered additional cost in its head office organisation as a result of delay for which it is not responsible, that ought to form a recoverable head of loss. An initial problem arises as, generally, it is difficult to establish that an element of loss is attributable to a particular delay or that there has been any additional cost as a result of the delay. Therefore, the basis of recovery is often this: the delay meant that head office resources were used for longer on the delayed project, and this meant, in turn, that the resources could not be used to obtain additional work which could otherwise have been obtained. Once the principal of recovery is established, then the mechanism for calculation is still far from straightforward. Whilst there is no agreed methodology, there are three principal formulae which are often applied: Hudson, Emden or Eichleay. The first two are taken from construction law text books; the third derives from a US case before the Armed Services Board of Contract Appeals.

These formulae are summarised in the SCL Protocol.[46] Hudson and Emden use an overhead and profit percentage which is applied to the contract sum and is pro-rated over the contract period. This gives a weekly sum which is multiplied by the number of weeks delay. The difference between the two formulae is that Hudson uses the tender percentage; Emden uses the actual percentage. The Eichelay formula is based on a percentage derived from the turnover from the delayed project compared to the overall turnover, and this is then applied to the overall overheads (not profit) of the company to give a contribution which it is assumed would be recovered on the delay project. Again that is divided by the contract period to give a weekly sum which is multiplied by the number of weeks delay.

There are, of course, divergent views about the merits of the respective options. The SCL Protocol[47] considers that, "The use of the Hudson's formula is not supported. This is because it is dependent on the adequacy or otherwise of the tender in question, and because the calculation is derived from a number which in itself contains an element of head office overheads and profit, so there is double counting." Kirsh[48] remarks that even Hudson itself (11th ed.) "accepts the greater precision of the Eichleay formula". However, while in Kirsh's view the Emden formula is "somewhat more realistic in its approach than the Hudson formula", because it takes the head office and profit percentage from reality rather than a tender figure, nevertheless it "should similarly be used with caution".[49]

Whilst there may be dispute as to the appropriate method, each method leads to a result which has a logical basis. The main problem often arises in the detail and can lead to disputes over what overheads or profit was included in the tender (such as the effect of buying margins); what was the level of overheads (such as whether financing should be included) or what is the appropriate accounting period for turnover or overheads and profit for delayed projects.

CONCLUSION

The single theme linking the components of this paper is the lack of certainty in the assessment of delay and disruption claims.

On causation, contractors face considerable difficulty in meeting the standard for proof of causation demanded to establish a claim. The task of separating individual causes of loss and linking them to quantifiable amounts of loss suffered will usually prove difficult if not impossible, at all stages from formulating to proving the claim. Tribunals have recognised this in permitting some use of "global" or "total cost" claims. However, these can prejudice the position of the party seeking to resist the claim. Consequently, they are treated with caution by tribunals.

The problems of concurrent delay relate to the difficulty of carrying out an underlying factual and legal analysis to achieve the risk sharing that underlies most contracts. This has led to an absence of an accepted methodology for analysis.

Against this background, it is very common for tribunals to be faced with conflicting approaches and different calculations from opposing parties in any dispute. The effect, then, is one of uncertainty: for contractors in formulating their claims; for employers in defending them and for arbitrators and other tribunals in deciding them. It is this uncertainty in delay and disruption claims which makes the role of assessment by the tribunal a necessary part of resolving complex construction disputes.

END NOTES

1 Until November 2005 Head of Keating Chambers, London. As a High Court Judge assigned to the Queen's Bench Division, he will spend substantial periods of his time dealing with cases in the Technology & Construction Court.

2 It will be convenient normally to refer to "the contractor", which is intended to include sub-contractors, where their position in a sub-contract would be similar to that of the contractor under the main contract.

3 The word "employer" is used synonymously with "owner" or "client" in this paper, meaning the party who is commissioning the construction of the building or facility.

4 *Alphacell* v. *Woodward* ,1972, AC 824, p.847.

5 The Blackstone Lecture by Lord Hoffman was delivered at Pembroke College, Oxford on 14 May 2005 and is published in the Law Quarterly Review, Vol. 121, October 2005, pp. 592-603.

6 2003, 1 AC 32.

7 *Keating on Building Contracts,* Stephen Furst and Justice Vivian Ramsey eds., 7th ed. 2001, Sweet and Maxwell, London, p.546.

8 *Crosby Ltd v Portland UDC,* 1967, 5 BLR 121.

9 1985, 32 BLR 31.

10 *Hudson's Building Contract* Ian Duncan Wallace, 11th ed. 1995 Sweet and Maxwell, London p.1092.

11 1991, 52 BLR 8.

12 1996, 82 BLR 81.

13 As he then was. His Honour Humphrey LLoyd QC is now an international arbitrator.

14 1997, 82 BLR 39.

15 The March 2003 reprint can be obtained from the Society of Construction Law: www.sc1.org.uk www.eotprotocol.com.

16 Guidance Note 1.14.

17 *John Doyle Construction Ltd* v. *Laing Management (Scotland) Ltd*

18 This was the argument put forward by Laing, the Management Contractor, in the position of the employer here.

19 2005, EWHC 181.

20 The employer was claiming against its Construction Manager in respect of loss and expenses claims by the Trade Contractors.

21 Expert witness on delay for the Employer.

22 Guidance Section 4.

23 The Great Delay Analysis Debate, King's College, London 18 October 2005, organised by the Society of Construction Law and the Centre for Construction Law and Management.

24 In *Skansta Construction UK Ltd* v. *Egger (Barony),* 2004, EWHC 1768 the English Technology and Construction Court chose to reject a time impact analysis put forward by one of the delay experts.

25 *Concurrent delay* by John Marrin QC, Society of Construction Law, London, 5 February 2002 (17 pages). Available from the Society of Construction Law at www.scl.org.uk.

26 Mr. Marrin was referring to the 1998 ed. The current edition is JCT 2005.

27 Although remarks in *John Doyle Construction* v. *Laing Management* (above) seem to be more receptive.

28 See note 7 above.

29 The editor was Anthony May QC, now Lord Justice May of the Court of Appeal, 1991.

30 39 BLR 106, 1987.

31 *The consideration of critical path analysis in English law* by Andrew Burr and Robert Palles-Clark Construction Law Journal, Vol. 21 No. 3, 2005, p.222.

32 See note 19 above.

33 0 Con LR 32, 1999.

34 Now in the Court of Appeal as Lord Justice Dyson.

35 76 Con LR 148, 2001.

36 op.cit at p.231.

37 Guidance Note 1.10.1.

38 See, for example, Clause 14.7 of the FIDIC Red Book.

39 See also *Recovery of damages for breach of an obligation of payment* by Nayla Comair-Obeid, p. 133 and *Means to be made whole: damages in the context of international investment arbitration* by Henry Weisburg and Christopher Ryan, p. 165.

40 Guidance Note 1.15.6.

41 21 Con LR 122, 1991.

42 38 Con LR 14, 1994.

43 35 Con LR 39, 1993.

44 Clause 60(7).

45 *The award of interest in the event of under-certification in construction and engineering contracts* by Ellis Baker and Anthony Lavers, Arbitration, Vol. 71, No. 2, pp 140-147.

46 In Appendix A.

47 Guidance Note 1.16.7.

48 *The Eichleay formula: computing and recovering unabsorbed head office overheads incurred by contractors as a result of employer-caused delay* by Harvey Kirsh Construction Law Journal, Vol. 11 No. 2, 1995, pp 90-94.

49 See also: *Assessment of prolongation claims: a contract administrator's perspective* by Bevis Mak, Construction Law Journal, Vol. 18 No. 3, 2002, pp. 181-204 on the position in Hong Kong and under English law.

10

The parties' costs of arbitration

By ***Bernard Hanotiau***
Member of the Brussels and Paris Bars; Hanotiau & van den Berg, Belgium; Professor at the University of Louvain

The costs of arbitration are increasingly a concern in many respects. What was in the beginning a relatively inexpensive method of dispute settlement has unfortunately become in some cases an extremely expensive way of deciding disputes, more often when the arbitration takes place in a common law procedural environment rather than in a civil law procedural context. Defence costs, which twenty years ago did not exceed a few hundred thousand dollars, sometimes amount nowadays to millions or tens of millions of dollars. Costs have therefore become a major concern. Some parties have reached the conclusion that arbitration has become too expensive, too burdensome, too lengthy and consequently wonder whether it is still the quick and cost-effective method of dispute settlement that their lawyers suggest.

The purpose of this paper is to present the issue of parties' costs as part of the overall compensation of the damages they are claiming. This is an important issue, considering the substantial amounts involved, which in some cases may even exceed the damages allocated, with the consequence that an improper allocation of costs would seriously affect the importance of the winning party's success.

In ICC arbitration, costs are dealt with in Articles 30 and 31 of the Rules. Article 30 provides for the payment of the costs of the arbitrators and the ICC advance, in several stages, while Article 31 is concerned with their final determination. Article 31 also requires the Arbitral Tribunal to decide how such costs should be borne by the parties, together with the fees and expenses of any experts appointed by the Arbitral Tribunal and the reasonable legal and other costs incurred by the parties for their defence in the arbitration.

I will not deal in this paper with the issue of the arbitrator's fees and expenses and the ICC administrative costs. It will be strictly limited to the parties' costs.[1]

1. THE PARTIES' COSTS

Article 31(1) of the Rules provides that the costs of the arbitration will also include "the reasonable legal and other costs incurred by the parties for the arbitration". What are these costs?

In the first place, the wording of Article 31(1) is intended to permit the Arbitral Tribunal the greatest possible discretion in fixing the costs of the arbitration pursuant to Article 31(3). Since there is no definition of these costs, their determination and the manner in which the relevant language of Article 31(1) should be construed is left to the discretion of the arbitrators. I will not deal in this section with the reasonableness of these costs but only with what is included therein.

The legal and other costs that form part of the costs of the arbitration include the fees and expenses of legal counsel, that is, those that are incurred during the arbitration procedure, but not necessarily all those that have been incurred before the start of the arbitration.[2] Among the latter, only expenses which were necessary for the preparation of the case and directly linked to the filing of the arbitration are considered as costs of the arbitration. Costs of a preliminary mediation or conciliation, for example, will not be considered costs of the arbitration.

On the other hand, should one consider as costs of the arbitration the fees and expenses that will have to be incurred after the issuance of the award until payment by the losing party? The answer is definitely negative.[3] Eventually, such costs could be considered and recovered as costs of the enforcement of the award.

The costs of the parties will also include the costs of experts and consultants who have been used in the instruction of the case. Article 31(1) refers to the expenses of experts appointed by the Arbitral Tribunal, pursuant to Article 20(4), and not experts designated by the parties. It is agreed, however, that by referring specifically only to tribunal appointed experts, Article 31(1) does not mean to exclude the costs of experts retained by the parties from the costs of the arbitration. These costs will not only include the fees and expenses of the experts and consultants, but also the costs associated to their testimony, costs of travel, accommodation and other ancillary costs.

The same rule applies to the costs of fact witnesses: costs for the preparation of their witness statements, costs of traveling to the place of hearing, accommodation and ancillary expenses, including telephone, telefax and photocopies.

Another type of parties' costs are the costs associated with the production of documents: not only the costs of searching, photocopying and dispatching, but also the costs of investigating into the archives of the other party if the latter authorizes its counterpart to have access to said archives and retrieval of any documents that it deems necessary or useful for the defence of the case.

It is not disputed that costs of interpreters and translators, whenever they are necessary, are to be included in the costs of the arbitration. Very often, the Arbitral Tribunal will determine in a procedural order that any document or testimony submitted in a language other than the language of the arbitration will have to be translated or interpreted in that language, that the costs of such translation or interpretation will be advanced by the party concerned and will be added to, and finally allocated with, the costs of the arbitration.

Another issue that is less easy to decide is whether the costs of ancillary proceedings may be added to the parties' costs. One will normally expect that the costs incurred in another arbitration proceeding cannot be claimed as costs of the arbitration. But what about court proceedings if a party to the arbitration had to go to court or to defend in court in relation to conservatory or provisional measures or other urgent (in the context of a référé or a request for a Mareva injunction) procedures directly connected with the arbitration? It seems that the allowability of these costs as costs of the arbitration is generally not accepted.[4] They should be claimed and allocated in the relevant procedures. Some of them might also be claimed as damages.[5]

In a few cases, the parties have claimed the payment of pre-award interest on the costs incurred in the course of the arbitration. In the cases which have been reported, this request has always been rejected[6] on the ground that "interests for costs awarded to claimant cannot be adjudged, these costs becoming due only at the date of service of the present award".[7]

Can a party claim the reimbursement of costs, such as defence costs, which have been, or will be, reimbursed by an insurer or other indemnifier not itself a party to the arbitration? The issue seems to have been addressed only in one case.[8] The Arbitral Tribunal concluded that such costs were properly recoverable in the arbitration, since counsel was retained, not by the insurer, but by respondents and that consequently the duty to pay counsel was incumbent on respondents; the counterpart being that respondents were obliged to reimburse the insurer all the corresponding costs paid by the losing party in performance of the award.

Another more important and much debated issue is whether the parties' costs include the costs of the time of the parties' personnel, including in particular in-house legal staff. Such costs are still not so often claimed in arbitration procedures. When they are, especially in large cases, they seem to be increasingly accepted, at least in respect of in-house counsel to the extent that the costs can be satisfactorily substantiated.[9]

In ICC case No. 6564 of 1993,[10] the Arbitral Tribunal decided that these costs were admissible in principle – but refused to grant them – on the following grounds:

> "In the Arbitral Tribunal's view in-house legal costs may well form part of a party's normal legal cost incurred in the conduct of a case. It is for each party to decide whether it wishes to retain outside counsel or prepare and argue the case by its own staff. There is no justification to privilege a party in terms of costs for the sole reason that it retained outside counsel.
>
> "A claim for a party's internal costs is admissible in principle also in those cases where outside counsel had been retained. A party must be free in allocating the work between its outside counsel and its own services. A party which decides to perform most of the preparatory work for the case by its own legal and technical departments should not be placed at a disadvantage compared to one which confers all work to outside counsel and experts.

> "There is, however, an important difference between the costs for outside counsel and those incurred in-house: the former are expenditures and can be clearly identified and evidenced; in the case of the latter this is not always the case. In view of this difference it appears justified to require some substantiation inter alia with respect to the nature of the cost, the personnel involved and type of work performed. In the present case, neither Party satisfied these requirements. Their claims are too general to permit an assessment of the justification and reasonableness of the costs claimed. Therefore, no allowance will be made for internal costs of the Parties."

On the other hand, in-house counsel's costs were fully rejected by the Arbitral Tribunal in ICC case No. 6293[11] on the following grounds:

> "Claimant has claimed compensation for the time of its personnel involved in the preparation of its case. This claim does not in my view form part of the costs of the arbitration, in the sense of being part of Claimant's 'normal legal costs', contemplated in Article 20(2) of the ICC Rules. It is really a separate head of damages claimed by Claimant and must be rejected together with its other damage claims. Assuming, however, that Claimant had proven that it was entitled to damages as a result of the breaches complained of in this arbitration, I do not consider that the twenty-three man-days claimed by it for its four employees involved in preparation of the case should be compensated. The per diem sum claimed for each employee, whether for salary alone or salary plus overhead, does not represent a special cost incurred by it for purposes of the arbitration but is part of its normal operating expenses. It is for the same reason that such amounts cannot in my opinion, form party of its legal costs."

2. MAY PARTIES' COSTS BE ALLOCATED BEFORE THE ISSUANCE OF THE FINAL AWARD?

Article 31(2) of the Rules provides that decisions on costs other than those fixed by the Court may be taken by the Arbitral Tribunal at any time during the proceeding. As determined in Article 31(3), the general rule in ICC arbitration is that the costs of the arbitration are fixed in the final award, unless the arbitration is terminated earlier. It is also the final award that includes the arbitrators' decision on the allocation of those costs between the parties.

It is not usual to have costs fixed and allocated before the final award, because the ICC Court is not in a position to fix the fees of the arbitrators and the ICC administrative costs earlier. Moreover, the costs of the arbitration will be dependent on the outcome of the case. However, there may be circumstances in which it might be appropriate for the Arbitral Tribunal to decide upon the allocation of the parties' legal and other costs before the final award, for example, in a partial award resolving certain of the issues in the arbitration; or if the Arbitral Tribunal decides in a partial award that it does not have jurisdiction over one of the parties to the arbitration and the party in question should therefore recover its costs from the party that improperly included it in the proceedings. This is why the last sentence of article 31 (2) has been included in the Rules.

3. THE FINAL DETERMINATION AND ALLOCATION OF THE PARTIES' COSTS

Fixing costs

Article 31(3) of the Rules provides that the final award shall fix the costs of the arbitration and decide which of the parties shall bear them or in what proportion they shall be borne by the parties.

The parties' costs, that is the determination of their amount, will be fixed in the final award. There is, however, no duty for the arbitrators to fix them if they decide that each of the parties shall bear its own costs, or if the arbitration clause provides so, which is not unusual. What is less usual is that even if it is so provided in the arbitration clause, it happens that the parties subsequently conclude in their submissions that the adverse party should bear the costs of the arbitration. The parties should then be questioned on their real intention. The tribunal might end up deciding that by their submission in the memorials, the parties have waived the provision included in the arbitration clause.

How will the Arbitral Tribunal determine what are the costs of the parties? The parties will generally make submissions on costs. In most arbitrations, they are even invited to do so after the final hearing or the post-hearing submissions. In large cases, each party will even be invited to comment on the costs submissions of the other party. These submissions should not only include the details of the costs, but also all relevant justifications such as invoices.

It happens sometimes, in relation to fees, that counsel does not tell the Arbitral Tribunal how much they have charged or will charge to their client. Instead they only report what their fees would normally be on the basis of a national fee schedule, or they fix their fees at a certain amount, without joining an invoice, having an understanding with their client that their honoraria will be fixed at the amount mentioned in their submission if they win the case and at a lower amount if they lose. In such cases, the Arbitral Tribunal will fix the fees at the amount it considers appropriate and will not necessarily allocate the full amount that is claimed.

It also happens from time to time that counsel claim, beyond their legal fees, a success fee. Such success fees are normally not included in the costs fixed by the Arbitral Tribunal. They are not properly defence costs, since they do not cover real costs exposed for the defence of the case. They are rather a reward granted in consideration of the success obtained in the defence of the case and should be fully supported by the party concerned.

How do Arbitral Tribunals deal with the requirement that the legal and other costs incurred by the parties for the arbitration have to be "reasonable"?[12] Do arbitrators refer to national law? They sometimes do so, but rarely. It is the exception rather than the rule.[13] Sometimes, they also refer to the general principles of international commercial arbitration, as in ICC case No. 8496 of 1996.[14] In most cases, they only refer to the discretionary power they are granted by Article 31 of the Rules. In one case,[15] the Arbitral Tribunal pointed out that acting as amiable compositeur, he enjoyed an even wider amount of discretion and decided that in view of the final result of the arbitration for each party, it was an equitable solution to decide that the costs of the arbitration were to be borne by the parties in the same proportion as their advances, namely one-third by claimant and two-thirds by respondent.

Whether the costs claimed by the parties and in particular their legal costs will be considered reasonable is a function of various factors, for example whether the submissions on costs have been disputed by the other party. But the fact that the submissions have not been disputed does not mean that the costs submitted will always be taken for granted by the Arbitral Tribunal. Arbitrators are auxiliaries of justice. They should make sure that the arbitration process is fair, including an award of costs. In one case, for example, the Arbitral Tribunal rejected part of the costs because the party concerned was represented by three law firms, which was found excessive by the members of the panel[16]. The arbitrators did the same in another case where invoices had been submitted in relation to the engagement of foreign counsel and where there was no evidence that the work of these lawyers was related to an alleged participation in the arbitration.[17] A similar decision has been reached when the amount claimed by a party is not supported by enough evidence;[18] or when the Arbitral Tribunal has determined that part of the submissions and witness statements was totally useless or dealt with issues which were not relevant to the arbitration.[19]

The allocation of costs

How are costs allocated by Arbitral Tribunals? The approaches of ICC arbitrators are diverse.[20] Sometimes awards contain just a few sentences relating to the question. In other cases, the matter of costs is dealt with in a more elaborate fashion. Still in other cases, it may be the subject of a separate, final award, after the merits have been dealt with in an earlier partial award.

According to Article 31(1) of the Rules, the arbitrators have complete discretion to allocate the costs as they see fit. Unlike some other arbitration rules, such as for example Article 40 of the UNCITRAL Rules,[21] the ICC Rules do not provide that the unsuccessful party will in principle bear the costs of the arbitration.

According to Yves Derains and Eric A. Schwartz,[22] the treatment of costs by Arbitral Tribunals is often influenced by their national backgrounds. These authors refer to three different approaches that are most commonly followed. One is to order that all the costs be borne by one of the parties, normally the losing party. This is often the case in England where it is said that "costs follow the event". Another approach, which seems to prevail in Germany, Switzerland and Austria in particular, is the allocation of costs in proportion to the outcome of the case, taking into consideration the relative success of the claims and defences. A further possibility is to require that the costs be shared equally by the parties or that they each bear their own costs. The arbitrators may also consider that administrative costs and arbitration fees and expenses, on the one hand, and legal and other possible expenses, on the other hand, should be treated differently.

In practice, the formulas adopted by Arbitral Tribunals are as diverse as the awards. In 1991, the ICC Secretariat undertook a study of the final awards rendered in ICC arbitrations between March 1989 and September 1991 in order to determine the manner in which the arbitrators had dealt with the allocation of arbitration costs in ICC cases. Reference is made to the conclusions of this study, which have been reprinted in the ICC Study,[23] as well as in the book of Yves Derains and Eric A. Schwartz.[24]

Many factors may enter into consideration in the determination of the final allocation of costs. The various approaches followed by ICC arbitrators are often influenced not only by their procedural backgrounds, but also by the substantive outcome of the arbitration and the behaviour of the parties. In some cases, the Arbitral Tribunal will conclude that although the claimant loses the whole case, the issues were extremely difficult to decide and one could easily understand why the case had been filed. Consequently, even though a respondent wins an arbitration, each party may have to bear its own costs. In other cases, the Arbitral Tribunal will penalize the bad faith or uncooperative behaviour of a party which has tried by all means to delay or to derail the arbitration.[25] But whatever the decision, the arbitrators are normally expected to provide reasons for their decisions, in accordance with Article 25 (2) of the Rules.[26]

One should also be candid and recognize that the final allocation of costs is in some cases an argument put forward by a member of the panel to have him accept a result that is different from the one he wanted to reach, with the consequence, for example, that the claimant wins the case in totality but is not awarded the totality of its costs.

Equitable concerns may also play a role in some decisions on the allocation of the parties' costs. In one such case, a claimant, originating from a developing country, lost the arbitration. The claimant was not condemned to bear the entire arbitration costs, given its good faith in bringing its claims and the fact that the defence of an arbitration claim in Paris – with several witnesses coming from that remote country – had already been a very expensive exercise.

CONCLUSION

Determining the costs of arbitration and how they should be allocated is an important issue. Arbitrators in ICC cases generally have no difficulty dealing with the issue and very wisely use the discretionary power that they are granted by Article 31 of the Rules. One area of greater concern is the continuous increase of these costs which, in some cases, have exceeded US$25 million on each side. If they are fully justified given the magnitude of the case, there is nothing to say about their amount. But this is not always the case. As was rightly pointed out by Professor Bruno Oppetit,[27] arbitration has become a business. Priority is consequently given by some lawyers to the generation of work and fees. Once again, it should not be overlooked that there is an increasing concern of parties that arbitration tends to become too expensive, too burdensome, too lengthy and is therefore drifting away from the traditional values of rapidity, efficacy and cost-effectiveness which have made its success. These parties wonder whether they should not go back to national courts. Let us make sure all together that they do not chose this alternative.

END NOTES

1 The most comprehensive coverage of this issue is to be found in Yves Derains and Eric A. Schwartz, *A Guide to the ICC Rules of Arbitration*, International Court of Arbitration, 2nd ed., Kluwer, 2005, Chapter 7, and the bibliography which is included. One will also refer to the article on the costs of ICC arbitration published by Eric A. Schwartz in the ICC Bulletin, Vol.IV, No. 1, 1993, p. 8, which is followed by the publication of extracts of ICC awards on costs, hereinafter referred to as the "ICC Study".

2 Award in case No. 5896 of 1992, ICC Study, p. 37, in which the arbitrators have decided that the costs of arbitration could not include those exposed before the filing of the arbitration, that is, the reception of the arbitration request by the ICC Secretariat. Some of these costs may be claimed as damages, for example if buyer, claimant in the arbitration, had to defend before criminal courts because of purchaser's (respondent's) fraudulent conduct before the acquisition.

3 Case No. 5759 of 1989, ICC Arbitral Awards, Vol. III, pp.175, 184, reprinted from the *Yearbook Commercial Arbitration*, 1993, 34.

4 See in this respect the references cited by Yves Derains and Eric A. Schwartz at footnote No. 95. The reasoning is that these costs should be claimed from the court which has to deal with these proceedings.

5 See above, the example cited at footnote 2.

6 ICC case No. 5896 published in ICC Study, p. 37 and ICC case No. 5759 of 1989, ICC Arbitral Awards, Vol. III, pp. 175, 184, reprinted from the *Yearbook Commercial Arbitration*, 1993, 34.

7 Idem.

8 ICC case No. 7006, reprinted in ICC Study, p. 49. See also Yves Derains and Eric A. Schwartz, footnote No. 98.

9 See Yves Derains and Eric A. Schwartz, footnote No. 96 and corresponding text.

10 ICC Study, pp. 45, 46.

11 ICC Study, p. 43.

12 Article 31 (1).

13 ICC final award in cases No. 6282 of 1992 and 6345 of 1991, ICC Study, pp. 42, 44.

14 ICC Arbitral Awards, Vol. IV, 321.

15 Final award of 28 March 1984 in case No. 3267, ICC Arbitral Awards, Vol. II, pp. 43, 52.

16 ICC final award in case No. 5726 of 1992, ICC Study, p. 35.

17 Final award in case No. 6564 of 1993, ICC Study, p. 45.

18 Final award in ICC case No. 8032 of 1995, ICC Arbitral Awards, Vol. IV, pp. 66, 74.

19 Final award in ICC case No. 5731 of 1989 and in ICC case No. 6959 of 1992, ICC Study, pp. 36, 48.

20 Yves Derains and Eric A. Schwartz, p. 370.

21 Article 40 (1) : "1. Except as provided in paragraph 2, the costs of arbitration shall in principle be borne by the unsuccessful party. However, the arbitral tribunal may apportion each of such costs between the parties if it determines that apportionment is reasonable, taking into account the circumstances of the case."

22 P. 371.

23 See *supra*, note 1.

24 Idem, pp. 371-373.

25 See for example final award in ICC case No. 7453 of 1994, ICC Awards, Vol. IV, pp. 94, 111: "The first defendant's conduct at the hearing was dilatory from the beginning until the end of the proceedings and that conduct was obstructive, and it was calculated to be obstructive, of the tribunal in carrying out its task. Much extra and unnecessary work was caused thereby for everyone concerned. The first defendant must bear and pay the entire costs of this arbitration [...] and also the entire legal costs of the claimant and out-of-pocket expenses of the counsel to the claimant [...]"; and final award in case No. 8486 of 1996, ICC Arbitral Awards, Vol. IV, 321, 331: "In the present case, the defendant loses its counterclaim, but the claimant's claim is granted only in part [...]. Nonetheless, the costs of the arbitration shall be borne totally by the defendant. According to the general principles of international arbitration law, the Arbitral Tribunal must take into account for its decision on costs not only the result of the proceedings but also the behaviour of the parties during the proceedings. According to good faith, the parties to an international arbitration must in particular facilitate the proceedings and abstain from all delaying tactics. The behaviour of the defendant during the entire proceedings did not comply with these requirements in any way [...]."

26 When the parties have spent substantial amounts of money for the defence of their case and have made detailed submissions on their costs to the Arbitral Tribunal, they even expect a very detailed decision and reasoning on costs.

27 *Théorie de l'Arbitrage*, PUF, 1998, p. 107.

Conclusions

By **Yves Derains**
Co-Editor
Partner, Derains & Associés, Paris;
Former Secretary General of the ICC International Court of Arbitration;
Council Member of the ICC Institute of World Business Law

The papers submitted at the 25th Annual Meeting of the ICC Institute of World Business Law, as well as the discussions which followed their presentation, reveal that the assessment of damages is at the crossroads of law and morals, sometimes even of law and religion. As far as arbitration is concerned, it is a special field where it is not always easy to distinguish the powers of the arbitrator deciding in law and the powers of the *amiable compositeur*, or of the arbitrator deciding *ex aequo et bono*. Moreover, principles generally strictly applied, such as the rules relating to the burden of proof or the right of the parties to be heard, are given, in this special context, very limited consideration.

It is generally agreed that when assessing damages, the basic principle is that of full compensation of the damages suffered by the victim of the breach of an obligation or, perhaps more accurately, of equivalence between the damages and the compensation. The victim should be put in the position it would have been in had the damaging event not occurred. This includes, according to the Roman law tradition, the damages actually suffered (*damnum emergens*) and the loss of profit (*lucrum cessans*). However, this basic principle is rarely applied to its full extent.

This is obvious as far as damages for the breach of an obligation of payment are concerned. A traditional distrust of interest, implicitly or expressly rooted in religious beliefs, limits their allocation: some national laws prohibit interest altogether; others cap the maximum amount of single interest; many exclude compound interest or, at least, restrict its application. All of these restrictions are at odds with the principle of full compensation and, at least during periods of inflation, may even be an incentive for the debtor not to fulfill his or her obligations of payment. But, on the other hand, this ignorance of the principle of full compensation with respect to the allocation of interest may turn to the advantage of the creditor, who does not have to prove a loss in order to obtain it.

Rules that introduce in the assessment of the damages an element of judgement concerning the behaviour of the debtor in breach of his or her obligations are other examples of a reaction to moral considerations, (albeit not contained in all national laws), which prevails over the principle of full compensation.

Punitive and exemplary damages, as accepted in several common law jurisdictions, are the more striking examples of the intervention of morals in the calculation of damages. Here, the basic idea is no longer to compensate the damages suffered by the victim of the breach, but to punish reprehensible behaviour. The power of arbitrators to award such damages, absent the parties' agreement, is, to say the least, doubtful. But it would be erroneous to believe that arbitrators always apply the principle of full compensation of damages and never sanction the behaviour of the author of a contractual breach when making their assessment of damages.

For instance, it was never suggested that arbitrators should hesitate to apply those national laws providing that only damages foreseeable at the time the contract was entered into may be compensated, unless in case of *dolus* or gross fault of the party responsible for the breach. Some authors explain that unforeseeable damages are not compensated by assimilating them into indirect damages, an assimilation hardly compatible with the refusal under some national laws to compensate indirect damages even in case of *dolus* of the debtor (i.e., Article 1151 of the French Civil Code). A more convincing explanation is that considerations of good faith and contractual justice do not allow the arbitrator to assume that the party responsible for the breach has taken the risk of covering damages it could not foresee, as if it could be accepted that a party can foresee not fulfilling its obligations. Whatever the correct explanation, and it may not be the same under each national law, the victim of the breach is not entitled to full compensation. However, when the debtor is guilty of *dolus* or gross fault, morals come to the rescue of the victim of the breach and resurrect its right to full compensation.

More generally, and without the express support of any national law, arbitral tribunals are often minded to take into consideration the respective behaviour of the parties when assessing damages, in particular when the victim of the contractual breach is not in a position to prove to the penny the damages it has suffered. Sometimes tribunals do it openly, as in the award rendered in

1994 in the ICC cases No. 6515 and No. 66516 (*Collection of ICC Arbitral Awards 1996-2000*, p. 241). More often, provided it is established that damages were actually suffered, they have recourse to equity or to formulas such as "all considered" to grant the victim of the contractual breach a lump sum on the basis of their *appreciation souveraine*.

Such approaches are not seen to be incompatible with the obligation to render their awards according to the law, and not as *amiable compositeur* or *ex aequo et bono*, probably because arbitrators do not replace a decision according to the law by another based on equitable considerations, but only use equity as one of several elements of fact, in light of which they fix a global amount. In reality, many national courts do more or less the same, and they are not suspected of acting as *amiable compositeurs*.

Yet, the law is not strictly applied. First, the principle *actor incumbit probatio*, which requires that a claim that is not proved fails, is distorted, since the victim does not always have to prove the precise amount of the damages it has suffered. Second, the various elements retained by the arbitrators to reach their global assessment are not disclosed to the parties, and even less submitted to their comments, in disregard of the right of the parties to be heard.

In reality, the works of the 25th Annual Meeting of the ICC Institute of World Business Law demonstrated that in the assessment of damages a cold and mathematical calculation of the compensation is frequently affected by a will to sanction the misconduct of the party responsible for a contractual breach. The law supports that tendency, but the role of the law remains limited. Indeed, as soon as the existence of damages is proved beyond any reasonable doubt, the assessment of their extent is not treated by the arbitrators so much as a legal problem, but as the mere exercise of their inherent power to assess any factual situation.

Selected bibliography

A

AFFOLDER (NATASHA)
Awarding Compound Interest in International Arbitration, The 2001 American Review of International Arbitration, p. 68

ALDRICH (GEORGE H.)
The Jurisprudence of the Iran-United States Tribunal, Oxford, 1996

ARNALDEZ (JEAN-JACQUES) & DERAINS (YVES) & HASCHER (DOMINIQUE)
Collection of ICC Arbitral Awards 1991-1995, 1997

B

BAKER (ELLIS) & LAVERS (ANTHONY)
The award of interest in the event of under-certification in engineering and construction contracts, Arbitration, Vol. 71 No. 2, 2005, p. 140

BAUDOUIN (JEAN-LOUIS)
Les Obligations, 4th ed., 1993

BEALE (HUGH) & HARTKAMP (ARTHUR), KOETZ (HEINZ) & TALLON (DENNIS), eds.
Cases, Materials and Text on Contract Law, 2002

BERGER (KLAUS PETER), ed.
The Practice of Transnational Law, The Hague, 2001

BISHOP (R. DOAK) & CRAWFORD (JAMES) & REISMAN (W. MICHAEL)
Foreign Investment Disputes, 2005

BLESSING (MARC)
Regulations in Arbitration Rules on Choice of Law, in: Planning Efficient Arbitration Proceedings – The Law Applicable in International Arbitration, Albert Jan Van den Berg ed., 1996, p. 391

BLESSING (MARC)
The New International Arbitration Law in Switzerland: A Significant Step Towards Liberalism, Journal of International Arbitration, Vol. 5 No. 2, 1988, p. 61

BÖCKSTIEGEL (KARL-HEINZ)
Arbitration and State Enterprises, 1984

BONELL (MICHAEL JOACHIM)
The UNIDROIT Principles of International Commercial Contracts, Special Supplement 2002, ICC International Court of Arbitration Bulletin, p.36

BONELL (MICHAEL JOACHIM)
The UNIDROIT Principles in Practice, New York, 2002

BRADLEY (CURTIS A.)
Customary International Law and Private Rights of Action, 1. Chicago Journal of International Law. 421 (2000)

BRIDGE (MICHAEL G.)
Mitigation of damages in contract and the meaning of avoidable loss, Law Quarterly Review, 1989, p. 398

BUFFELAN-LANORE (YVAINE)
Droit Civil, 9th ed., 2004

BURKE (TERENCE M.)
Delay under Australian Law, in: Selected Problems of Construction Law: International Approach, Peter Gauch and Justin Sweet ed., London, 1983

BURR (ANDREW) & PALLES-CLARK (ROBERT)
The consideration of critical path analysis in English law, Construction Law Journal, Vol. 21 No. 3, 2005, p. 222

C

CHENG (BIN)
General Principles of Law as applied by International Courts and Tribunals, 1953

CLAGETT (BRICE)
Just Compensation in International Law: The Issues before the Iran-United States Claims Tribunal, in: The Valuation of Nationalized Property in International Law, Lillich ed., 1987

CLAGETT (BRICE)
Remarks at the American Society of International Law 92nd Annual Meeting (April 1-4, 1998), in 92 Proceedings of the American Society for International Law 303 (1995)

COMAIR-OBEID (NAYLA)
Charging interest in the Arabian Peninsula, Middle East Commercial Law Review, Vol. 1 Issue 3, 1995, p. 92

COMAIR-OBEID (NAYLA)
The Law of Business Contracts in the Arab Middle East, 1996

CRAIG (W. LAURENCE) & PARK (WILLIAM W.) & PAULSSON (JAN)
International Chamber of Commerce Arbitration, 3rd ed., 2000

CRAWFORD (JAMES)
The International Law Commission's articles on state responsibility: introduction, text and commentaries, 2002, p. 218

CRAWFORD (JAMES)
Third Report on State Responsibility, International law Commission, 52nd Sess., 22 UN Doc A/CN/.4/507 (2000)

D

DERAINS (YVES)
Attente légitime des parties et droit applicable au fond en matière d'arbitrage commercial international, Travaux du Comité français de droit international privé, 1984-1985, Paris, 81

DERAINS (YVES)
Intérêts moratoires, dommages-intérêts compensatoires et dommages punitifs devant l'arbitre international, Etudes offertes à Pierre Bellet, Paris, 1991

DERAINS (YVES)
The Role of UNIDROIT Principles in the International Commercial Arbitration: A European view, ICC International Court of Arbitration Bulletin, 2002, p. 9

DERAINS (YVES)
Le rôle des Principes d'UNIDROIT dans L'arbitrage commercial: une vue européenne, Bulletin de la Cour Internationale d'Arbitrage de la CCI, Supplément Spécial 2002, p. 16

DERAINS (YVES) & SCHWARTZ (ERIC)
A Guide to the ICC Rules of Arbitration, 2nd ed., 2005

DRAHOZAL (CHRISTOPHER R.) & NAIMARK (RICHARD W.), eds.
Towards a Science of International Arbitration: Collected Empirical Research, 2005

F

FABRE-MAGNAN (MURIEL)
Les Obligations, Témis, 1st ed., 2004, No. 213, p. 575

FARNSWORTH (E. ALLEN)
Farnsworth on Contracts, 3rd ed., 2004

FISHER (IRVING)
The Theory of Interest, 3rd ed., 1954

FREIDLAND (PAUL D.) & WONG (ELEANOR)
Measuring Damages for Deprivation of Income-Producing Assets: ICSID Case Studies, 6 ICSID Review – Foreign Investment Law Journal 400, 1991

FRICK (JOACHIM G.)
Arbitration and Complex International Contracts – With Special Emphasis on the Determination of the Applicable Substantive Law and on the Adaptation of Contracts to Changed Circumstances, 2001, p.68

FURST (STEPHEN) & RAMSEY (VIVIAN), eds.
Keating on Building Contracts, 7th ed., 2001, London

G

GAILLARD (EMMANUEL)
La Jurisprudence du CIDRI, 2004

GAILLARD (EMMANUEL) & SAVAGE (JOHN)
Fouchard Gaillard Goldman on International Commercial Arbitration, 1999

GOEBEL (JOACHIM)
Rechtsgespräch und kreativer Dissens, zugleich ein Betrag zur Bedeutung der Sprache in der interpretativen Praxis des Zivilprozesses, 2001

GOLDMAN (BERHOLD)
La Lex Mercatoria dans les contrats et l'arbitrage internationaux: réalité et perspectives, Journal du Droit International 1987, p. 475

GOTANDA (JOHN Y.)
Recovering Lost Profits in International Disputes, 36 Georgetown Journal of International Law 61, 2004

GOTANDA (JOHN Y.)
Compound Interest in International Disputes, 34 Law & Pol'y Int'l Bus, 393 (2003)

GOTANDA (JOHN Y.)
Supplemental Damages in Private International Law, 1998

GUHL (THEO) & KOLLER (ALFRED) & DRUEY (JEAN NICOLAS)
Das schweizerische Obligationenrecht, 8th ed., Zurich, 1991

GUZMAN (ANDREW T.)
Why LDC's Sign Treaties That Hurt Them: Explaining the Popularity of Bilateral Investment Treaties, 38 Virginia Journal of International Law 639 (1998)

H

HAMMOUD (LARA) & SECOMB (MATTHEW)
Interest in ICC Arbitral Awards: Introduction and Commentary, ICC International Court of Arbitration Bulletin, Vol. 15 No. 1, Spring 2004, p. 2

HANOTIAU (BERNARD)
La détermination et l'évaluation du dommage réparable : principes généraux et principes en émergence, in Transnational Rules International Commercial Arbitration, Gaillard ed., 1993

HARRIS (DONALD) & CAMPELL (DAVID) & HALSON (ROGER)
Remedies in Contract & Tort, 2002

HOFFMANN, LORD (LEONHARD HUBERT)
Causation, Law Quarterly Review, Vol. 121, October 2005, p. 592

HOLZGREFE (J.L.) & KEOHANE (ROBERT O.), eds.
Humanitarian Intervention: Ethical, Legal, and Political Dilemmas, 2003

J

JARVIN (SIGVARD) & DERAINS (YVES) & ARNALDEZ (JEAN-JACQUES)
Collection of ICC Awards 1974-1985, Paris, 1990

JOLIVET (EMMANUEL)
The UNIDROIT Principles in ICC Arbitration, in UNIDROIT Principles: New Developments and Applications – 2005 Special Supplement, ICC International Court of Arbitration Bulletin, p. 65

JOLIVET (EMMANUEL)
Cour internationale d'arbitrage de la Chambre de commerce internationale, 2001, affaire numéro 10422, Journal de Droit International, Vol. 4, 2003, p. 1142

K

KIRSH (HARVEY)
The Eichleay formula: computing and recovering unabsorbed head office overheads incurred by contractors as a result of employer-caused delay, Construction Law Journal, Vol. 11 No. 2, 1995, p. 90

KOMAROV (ALEXANDER)
UNIDROIT Principles of International Commercial Contract, Special Supplement, ICC International Court of Arbitration Bulletin, p. 144

KÜHN (WOLFGANG)
Express and Implied Choice of the Substantive Law in the Practice of International Arbitration, in: Planning Efficient Arbitration Proceedings – The Law Applicable in International Arbitration, Albert Van den Berg ed., 1996, p. 380

KURKELA (MATTI S.) & SNELLMAN (HANNES)
Due Process in International Commercial Arbitration, 2005

L

LALIVE (PIERRE)
The UNIDROIT Principles as Lex Contractus, With or Without an Explicit or Tacit Choice of Law: An Arbitrator's Perspective, The UNIDROIT Principles of International Commercial Contracts – 2002 Special Supplement, ICC International Court of Arbitration Bulletin, p. 77

LANDO (OLE) & BEALE (HUGH)
Principles of European Contract Law Parts I and II, 2000

LAUMEN (HANS-WILLI)
Das Rechtsgespräch im Zivilprozeß, 1984

LAUTERPACHT (HERSCH)
Private Law Sources and Analogies of International Law, 1927, reprinted in 2002

LENZ (CHRISTIAN)
Amerikanische Punitive Damages vor dem Schweizer Richter, dissertation, Zurich, 1992

LITVINOFF (SAUL)
Damages, Mitigation and Good Faith, 73 Tulane Law Review, 1161 (1999)

LYNCH (KATHERINE)
The Forces of Economic Globalization: Challenges to the Regime of International Commercial Arbitration, 2003

M

MAK (BEVIS)
Assessment of prolongation claims: a contract administrator's perspective, Construction Law Journal, Vol. 18 No. 3, 2002, p. 181

MARELLA (FABRIZIO)
The UNIDROIT Principle of International Commercial Contracts in ICC Arbitration, ICC International Court of Arbitration Bulletin, Vol. 12 No. 2, Fall 2001, p. 49

MARELLA (FABRIZIO) & GÉLINAS (FABIEN)
The UNIDROIT Principles of International Commercial Contracts in ICC Arbitration, ICC International Court of Arbitration Bulletin, Vol. 10 No. 2, Fall 1999, p. 26

MARRIN (JOHN)
Concurrent delay, Society of Construction Law, London, 5 February 2002

McGREGOR (HARVEY)
McGregor on Damages, 17th ed., 2003

N

NAJJAR (NATHALIE)
L'arbitrage dans les pays arabes face aux exigences du commerce international, 2004

NICHOLAS (BARRY)
French Law of Contract, London, 2002

O

OPPETIT (BRUNO)
Théorie de l'Arbitrage, 1998

ORTSCHEID (JÉRÔME)
La réparation du dommage dans l'arbitrage commercial international, Prof. Gaillard, Coll. Nouvelle bibliothèque de thèse, Vol. 6, Dalloz, 2001

OSMAN (FILALI)
Les Principes Généraux de la Lex Mercatoria, 1992

P

PERILLO (JOSEPH M.)
Abuse of Rights: A Pervasive Legal Concept, 27 Pacific Law Journal – *Yearbook Commercial Arbitration* , Fall 1995.

PETROVA (IRINA)
"Stepping on the Shoulders of a Drowning Man". The Doctrine of Abuse of Rights as a Tool for Reducing Damages for Lost Profits: Troubling Lessons from the Patuha and Himpurna Arbitrations, 35 Georgetown Journal of International Law 455, 2004

PICOT (YVES)
Encyclopédie Dalloz, Répertoire de droit civil, Obligations, No. 39, 2003

R

REDFERN (ALAN) & HUNTER (MARTIN)
Law and Practice of International Commercial Arbitration, 1st ed., 1986 and 3rd ed., 1999

REISMAN (W. MICHAEL) & SLOANE (ROBERT D.)
Indirect Expropriation and its Valuation in the BIT Generation, 2003 British Year Book of International Law 115

RIBEIRO (ROBERT)
Damages and other remedies for breach of commercial contracts, London, 2002

RODNER (JAMES OTIS)
The Applicable Interest Rate in International Arbitration, International Court of Arbitration Bulletin, Vol. 15 No. 1, Spring 2004, p. 43

RUBINO-SAMMARANTO (MAURO)
International Arbitration Law and Practice, 2nd ed., The Hague, 2001

S

SANDIFER (DURWARD)
Evidence Before International Tribunals, Procedural Aspects of International Law Series, 1975

SANDRINO (GLORIA)
The NAFTA Investment Chapter and Foreign Direct Investment in Mexico: A Third World Perspective, 27 Vanderbilt Journal of Transnational Law 259, 1994

SCHMITTHOFF (CLIVE M.)
The Duty to Mitigate, Journal of Business Law, 1961, p. 362

SCHÖNLE (HERBERT)
Intérêts moratoires, intérêts compensatoires et dommages-intérêts de retard en arbitrage international, in: Etudes de Droit International en l´honneur de Pierre Lalive, 1993

SCHWARTZ (ERIC)
The ICC Arbitral Process – Part IV: The Costs of ICC Arbitration, ICC International Court of Arbitration Bulletin, Vol. 4 No. 1, 1993, p. 8

SCHWEBEL (STEPHEN M.)
International Arbitration: Three Salient Problems, 1987

SOLOMON (EZRA) & PRINGLE (JOHN J.)
An Introduction to Financial Management, 2nd ed., 1980

T

THIEFFRY (JEAN)
Arbitration and the New Rules Applicable to International Sales Contracts under the United Nations Convention, Arbitration International, Vol. 4 No. 1, 1998, p. 56

TREITEL (GUENTER H.)
Remedies for Breach of Contract – A Comparative Account, Oxford, 1988

TREITEL (GUENTER H.)
Remedies for Breach of Contract, (Courses of action open to the Party Aggrieved), in: International Encyclopedia of Comparative Law, Chapter 16, Vol. VII: Contracts in General, Arthur von Mehren ed., 1976, p. 16

TREITEL (GUENTER H.)
The Law of Contract, 11th ed., 2003

TRUONG (CAM QUYEN CORINNE)
Les différends liés à la rupture des contrats internationaux de distribution dans les sentences arbitrales CCI, 2002

W

WALLACE (IAN DUNCAN)
Hudson's Building Contract and Engeneering Contracts, 11th ed., 1995

WELLS (LOUIS T.)
Double Dipping in Arbitration Awards? An Economist Questions Damages Awarded to Karaha Bodas Company in Indonesia, 19 Arbitration Int'l No. 4, 471 (2003)

WERNER (JACQUES)
Making Investment Arbitration More Certain, a Modest Proposal, The Journal of World Investment, Vol. 4 No. 5, October 2003

WHITEMAN (MARJORIE M.)
Damages in International Law, 1943

WILKINSON (VANESSA L.D.)
The New Lex Mercatoria Reality or Fantasy? Journal of International Arbitration, Vol. 12 No. 2, 1995, p.110

WILLIAMS (JOHN BURR)
The Theory of Investment Value, 1938

Y

YOSHIDA (IKKO)
Comparison of awarding interest on damages in Scotland, England, Japan and Russia, Journal of International Arbitration, Vol. 17 No. 2, 2000, p. 41

Z

ZIEGEL (JACOB S.)
The Remedial Provisions in the Vienna Sales Convention: Some Common Law Perspectives, in: International Sales: The United Nations Convention on International Contracts for the International Sale of Goods, Galston & Smit ed., 1984

Case law index

A

B

C

J

K

L

M

N

O

P

R

S

T

W

Key-words index

With the kind help of Reinmar WOLFF
Rechtsanwalt, Shearman & Sterling LLP, Germany

A

C

D

E

M

P

Q

R

S

V

W

Contributors

NAYLA COMAIR-OBEID
is a Partner of Obeid Law Firm and Professor of Law at the Lebanese University in International Arbitration. She is a Council Member of the ICC Institute and Chartered Arbitrator. She is also Chairman of the Lebanese Branch of the Chartered Institute of Arbitrators.

YVES DERAINS
is a founding Partner of Derains & Associés, Paris, a law firm which specializes in international arbitration. A former Secretary General of the ICC International Court of Arbitration, he is also a Council Member of the ICC Institute and a Member of the International Council for Commercial Arbitration.

PAUL-A. GÉLINAS
is Member of the Montreal and Paris Bars. He is the former Chairman of the ICC Commission on International Arbitration (1994-2001) and a former member of the International Court of Arbitration (1974-1990). He acts mainly as arbitrator and mediator. He is a Council Member of the ICC Institute.

BERNARD HANOTIAU
is a Partner in the law firm Hanotiau & van den Berg, Brussels, admitted to practice in Brussels and Paris, and Professor at the Universities of Louvain and Namur, Belgium. He is Vice-President of the LCIA, CEPANI and the ITA (Dallas). He is also an Associate member of the ICC Institute and a member of the ICC Commission on International Arbitration.

ALEXANDER. S. KOMAROV
is Head of the Private Law Department of the Russian Academy of Foreign Trade, Moscow. He is an ICCA Council member and the Vice-President of International Federation of Commercial Arbitration Institutions (IFCAI). He is also a Russian Federation member of the UNIDROIT Administrative Council, Chairman of the Arbitration Commission of ICC Russia, and a Council Member of the ICC Institute.

RICHARD H. KREINDLER

is a Partner in the law firm Shearman & Sterling LLP, Frankfurt, admitted to practice in New York and Paris, and an Adjunct Professor at the Universities of Heidelberg, Münster and Mainz, Germany. He is a Council member of the ICC Institute and a Member of the ICC Commission on International Arbitration.

SERGE LAZAREFF

is Member of the Paris Bar, Chairman of the ICC Institute and Chairman of the French Arbitration Commission of ICC France. He was formerly General Counsel for International Operations and Vice-President Asia-Pacific of Pechiney, one of them leading French industrial groups.

JAN PAULSSON

is the head of the international arbitration and public international law groups of the law firm of Freshfields Bruckhaus Deringer. He is President of the London Court of International Arbitration and of the World Bank Administrative Tribunal, a co-author of the standard treatise, *International Chamber of Commerce Arbitration* (900 pages, 3rd edition 2000), and a Yorke Distinguished Visiting Fellow of the Faculty of Law of the University of Cambridge. His book *Denial of Justice in International Law* was published by Cambridge University Press in October. He is also a Council Member of the ICC Institute.

HUGO PEREZCANO DIAZ

is General Counsel for Trade Negotiations at Mexico's Secretariat of the Economy. He is also lead counsel for Mexico in State-State dispute settlement proceedings initiated under the WTO and NAFTA, as well as in disputes brought by investors under the NAFTA and bilateral investment agreements. Mr. Perezcano was formerly part of the Secretariat's legal team during the NAFTA and Uruguay Round Negotiations and was designated lead counsel for Mexico in trade negotiations with several Latin American countries.

MR. JUSTICE VIVIAN RAMSEY

is a High Court Judge in London and regularly sits in the Technology and Construction Court. He was previously Queen's Counsel and practised as a barrister, arbitrator and mediator and was Head of Keating Chambers in London. He is a Special Professor at the University of Nottingham and editor of Keating on Construction Contracts.

CHRISTOPHER M. RYAN

is a Senior Associate in Shearman & Sterling LLP's litigation group and is admitted to practice in New York and Washington, D.C. Mr Ryan's practice focuses on international arbitration and commercial litigation. In addition, Mr Ryan is an Adjunct Professor at the University of Virginia School of Law and the George Mason University School of Law, teaching courses on international investment law and dispute resolution.

YASUHEI TANIGUCHI

is Of Counsel at Matsuo & Kosugi, Tokyo, since 1998. He has been a Member of the Appellate Body of the WTO since 2000 and was its Chairman from 2004 to 2005; Mr Taniguchi is a Council Member of the ICC Institute of World Business Law and ICCA. He is also Vice-President of the International Association of Procedural Law and President of the Japan Association of Arbitrators. Mr Taniguchi is Professor of Law at Senshu University Law School, Tokyo.

HENRY WEISBURG

is a Partner in Shearman & Sterling's International Arbitration group in New York City. He generally handles matters involving cross-border investment disputes, sovereign defaults, joint-venture disputes, and disputes concerning highly structured financial products.

JACQUES WERNER

is Principal of Werner & Associés, Geneva, Switzerland. He is editor of *The Journal of World Investment and Trade* and Chairman of The Geneva Global Arbitration Forum. He is also Visiting Professor at the Hunan Normal University Law School, Changsha, China.

ICC at a glance

ICC is the world business organization, a representative body that speaks with authority on behalf of enterprises from all sectors in every part of the world.

The fundamental mission of ICC is to promote trade and investment across frontiers and help business corporations meet the challenges and opportunities of globalization. Its conviction that trade is a powerful force for peace and prosperity dates from the organization's origins early in the last century. The small group of far-sighted business leaders who founded ICC called themselves "the merchants of peace".

Because its member companies and associations are themselves engaged in international business, ICC has unrivalled authority in making rules that govern the conduct of business across borders. Although these rules are voluntary, they are observed in countless thousands of transactions every day and have become part of the fabric of international trade.

ICC also provides essential services, foremost among them the ICC International Court of Arbitration, the world's leading arbitral institution. Another service is the World Chambers Federation, ICC's worldwide network of chambers of commerce, fostering interaction and exchange of chamber best practice.

Within a year of the creation of the United Nations, ICC was granted consultative status at the highest level with the UN and its specialized agencies.

Business leaders and experts drawn from the ICC membership establish the business stance on broad issues of trade and investment policy as well as on vital technical and sectoral subjects. These include financial services, information technologies, telecommunications, marketing ethics, the environment, transportation, competition law and intellectual property, among others.

ICC was founded in 1919. Today it groups thousands of member companies and associations from over 130 countries. National committees work with their members to address the concerns of business in their countries and convey to their governments the business views formulated by ICC.

Some ICC specialized divisions

- ICC International Court of Arbitration (Paris)
- ICC International Centre for Expertise (Paris)
- ICC World Chambers Federation (Paris)
- ICC Centre for Maritime Co-operation (London)
- ICC Commercial Crime Services (London), grouping:
  - The ICC Counterfeiting Intelligence Bureau
  - The ICC Commercial Crime Bureau
  - The ICC International Maritime Bureau
- ICC Institute of World Business Law (Paris)
- ICC Services *(ICC affiliate*, Paris), grouping:
  - Publications Department

  ICC Publications, a Department of ICC Services, is the publishing arm of the International Chamber of Commerce.

  The content of our products is derived from the work of ICC commissions, institutions and individual international experts. Our specialized list covers topics ranging from international banking, including documentary credits and collections, international trade terms (Incoterms), law and arbitration, counterfeiting and fraud, model commercial contracts and environmental matters.

  The ICC Business Bookstore at **www.iccbooks.com** is designed to provide comprehensive information about each of our products. ICC Publications Department is committed to offering the best resources in global trade, with a staff dedicated to personal attention.

  - Events Department

  ICC's programme of conferences and seminars is the essential channel for passing on the world business organization's expertise to a wider audience.

  ICC Events, a Department of ICC Services, spotlights policy issues of direct concern to business such as banking techniques and practices, e-business, IT and telecoms, piracy and counterfeiting.

  ICC Events also runs training courses on international arbitration and negotiating international contracts for business-people, corporate counsel, lawyers and legal practitioners involved in international trade.

ICC Institute of World Business Law

Chaired by SERGE LAZAREFF and led by its Council, composed of 40 eminent authorities appointed by the ICC Chairman, the Institute constitutes a forum for lawyers, executives, academics and the legal world.

The main objectives of the ICC Institute of World Business Law are research, reflection on current international business problems, training and the dissemination of knowledge among practitioners and scholars in the field of international business law, particularly arbitration.

The Institute brings its know-how to ICC Events for the organization of training courses on these subject matters. It acts as a think-tank working closely with ICC policy commissions and ICC's International Court of Arbitration. Once a year, the Institute holds its Annual Meeting where some of the world's leading legal experts gather to share knowledge and expertise on a chosen topical issue. One of the aims of the conference is to create doctrine, the result of which is compiled in an annual publication, "Dossiers of the Institute".

DOSSIERS OF THE INSTITUTE

Parallel State and Arbitral Procedures in International Arbitration

In recent years, international arbitration procedures have made great strides to bring into line different traditions of law and practice. However, considerable problems remain. The aim of the new publication, *Parallel State and Arbitral Procedures in International Arbitration* prepared by the ICC Institute of World Business Law, is to give the reader a thorough picture of the practical issues raised by the conflicts arising when there is more than one arbitration on identical or very similar facts, and where only one party differs, and when arbitrations run in parallel with state legal proceedings.

No. 692 ISBN 92-842-1352-5

Arbitration and Oral Evidence

The issues divide counsel and arbitrators, and there is a need for a better understanding of what is right and wrong in the interaction between written and oral evidence. This book lays out the issues in a transparent and easy-to-understand way. It gives the reader a thorough picture of the practical issues raised by the oral presentation of evidence and presents a balanced series of solutions to the problems involved.

No. 689 ISBN 92-842-1344-4

Arbitration – Money Laundering, Corruption and Fraud

This book, containing the proceedings of a conference on arbitration and money laundering organized by the ICC Institute of World Business Law, focuses on both the nature of the problem and the response to it in legal and arbitration circles. Is the arbitrator's role in a case of fraud different from that in other disputes? Is the arbitrator bound to report a case of money laundering or fraud if he has a suspicion that something is wrong? Do counsel have an obligation to report someone who approaches them for advice on these matters? These are just some of the key issues considered in this timely publication.

No. 651 ISBN 92-842-1320-7

SELECTED ICC PUBLICATIONS ON ICC ARBITRATION

A Guide to the ICC Rules of Arbitration – Second Edition

By Yves Derains and Eric A. Schwartz

The ICC's International Court of Arbitration is the world's pre-eminent institution specializing in the arbitration of disputes arising under international contracts. Since its inception in 1923, thousands of cases have been submitted to the Court for review and decision.

A Guide to the New ICC Rules of Arbitration set out in detail the requirements for those wishing to submit a dispute to ICC arbitration or to one of the other conciliation services offered under ICC auspices.

The Second Edition of this classic text will appeal to a wide range of users:

- Laymen will appreciate the overview of ICC's arbitration-related services;
- Lawyers will benefit from the in-depth discussion of arbitral procedures;
- Business executives will profit from a broader understanding of the ICC system and its relevance to their company's activities.

No. 961 ISBN 90-411-2268-0

ICC International Court of Arbitration Bulletin

Since 1990, the ICC international Court of Arbitration Bulletin has been providing businesses and their lawyers with in-depth information on ICC dispute resolution services and arbitration law in general. Published twice yearly, the Bulletin contains commentaries, extracts from previously unpublished ICC arbitral awards, and ICC documents. Both procedural and substantive issues are covered, including those relevant to the construction sector.

For more information and for a full list of contents of back issues and special supplements, visit **www.storeiccwbo.org** or
contact Service Bulletin Tel : +33 1 49 53 29 52
Fax : +33 1 49 53 57 74 E-mail: bulletin@iccwbo.org